For
Tatiana

For Tatiana

When Love Triumphed over the Kremlin

Edward Lozansky

Henry Holt and Company • New York

Published in the United States by
Henry Holt and Company, Inc., 521 Fifth Avenue,
New York, New York 10175.
Published simultaneously in Canada.

Originally published in France under the title *Pour Tatiana*

Library of Congress Cataloging in Publication Data
Lozansky, Edward D. (Edward Dmitrievich), 1941–
For Tatiana: when love triumphed over the Kremlin.
1. Lozansky, Edward D. (Edward Dmitrievich),
1941–   . 2. Jews—Soviet Union—Biography.
3. Soviet Union—Emigration and immigration—Biography.
4. United States—Emigration and immigration—Biography.
I. Title.
DS135.R95A36   1986   947.085′092′4   [B]   85-30568
ISBN 0-03-005064-2

First American Edition

Designed by Jeffrey L. Ward
Printed in the United States of America
10 9 8 7 6 5 4 3 2 1

ISBN 0-03-005064-2

Those who love and are separated
may suffer but they do not despair;
they know that love exists.

—ALBERT CAMUS

Contents

Prologue   1

1. **Nationality: Jew**   13

2. **Tatiana**   75

3. **The Fight**   197

4. **Tatiana's Story**   253
      by Tatiana Lozansky

Eight pages of photographs follow page 166.

**For
Tatiana**

Prologue

The man was directly behind me. I hadn't heard him approach, had not even sensed his presence. He put his hand on my shoulder and said, "All right. Let's go."

The pressure of his fingers, and the flatness of his voice, chilled me to the core. I turned quickly to see a short, stocky man wearing the red-trimmed black uniform of the Soviet Customs Bureau. I could detect no animosity in his look; he seemed to be sizing me up with the same professional eye a horse trader might use in assessing a prize animal. After a quick glance at me and my coat—purchased, I might add, at one of the best furriers in Moscow—he added, "Follow me."

It was cold. Through the dirty, frost-covered windows of the customs section of the Brest-Litovsk train station, it was hard to see the gathering gloom of late afternoon. The room was drafty, the icy gusts carrying the smell of moldy wood mixed with the odor of burnt coal from thousands of steam locomotives. All the passengers had been forced to leave the Vienna-bound train while each car was inspected by the customs officials with a fine-toothed comb. Here in the customs shed, the shivering travelers watched their baggage turned upside down and the contents strewn unceremoniously onto the floor. Outside, the once-pristine snow was streaked with soot, worn down from the imprints of thousands of boots. It was a grim, oppressive, ugly late afternoon in winter.

"This way," the man said.

Glancing around desperately, I fell in behind him. *I knew it*, I kept thinking, *I knew this was bound to happen.* From the moment I had said good-by to my wife and friends at Moscow's Byelorusskaya Station and boarded the train for Vienna, I had lived with the fear that something like this was going to happen. During the first twenty-four hours on the train, I had been unable to sleep. I was too frightened. Alone in my compartment, I listened for the slightest suspicious sound. I was nervous and jumpy, expecting at any minute to see the door slide open and the men in black—all of whom look alike—to come in and grab me, twist my arms behind my back, handcuff me, and hustle me out of this train and onto another one heading in the opposite direction. In fact, I had left instructions with my friends in Moscow that if I had not telephoned them within three days of my departure, they should alert the Western press.

But despite my fears, *they* had left me alone. I had safely reached Brest-Litovsk, the border town that had once belonged to Poland, where the peace treaty between Kaiser Wilhelm II and the Russians had been signed on March 3, 1918, ending hostilities between the foes. For most of us international passengers who had been on the train for more than a day, Brest-Litovsk represented far more than a point of historical interest: It was our final stop before freedom. Unfortunately, it risked being a long one. The Soviet Union has wider-gauge tracks than the rest of Europe, so that at the border the train wheels have to be adjusted to the Western gauge. This delay gave the customs officials ample time to examine our baggage—and sometimes our bodies—with a zeal that often bordered on sadism. But I— and most of my fellow passengers, I'm sure—kept reassuring ourselves by saying over and over again, "Keep cool; this is the final humiliation. The last one." And then there had been that hand on my shoulder and the flat, terrifying voice saying, "All right. Let's go."

The customs official led me to a small room. Seated behind a wooden table was a man who looked utterly bored, as though he had been there from time immemorial. He raised his head, fixed his bloodshot eyes on me, and, summoning a bit of energy from some unexpected source, barked, "Strip! And be quick about it!"

I breathed a sigh of relief. I wasn't being taken back to Moscow. I took off my coat, my suit, my shirt. As I was bending down to take off my socks, I heard a strange noise: It sounded like a coin hitting the floor. I lifted my eyes and saw the man behind the table looking at me closely. I realized immediately that he was trying to trap me into thinking that the coin had fallen from my clothing. By my reaction of fear or panic, he could then discover where I had hidden the gold coins that presumably I was taking with me to the West.

Unable to restrain myself, I said, "Sorry. You're wasting your time."

"Maybe yes. Maybe no. Take off your shorts."

That last order left me speechless. For several seconds I stared at him with undisguised hatred. It was not the first such look he had seen. Or the last. His voice sounded bored and bureaucratic again as he intoned, "Hurry up. Otherwise the train may leave without you and you'll have to spend one more night with us before going over to join your American masters. God knows where we'd be able to put you up. We don't have any spare rooms in these parts for traitors."

"How about for Heroes of Labor?" I snapped.

"You'd better watch your tongue," he murmured, with just the trace of a smile. "Just remove your shorts. Unless, of course, you prefer that we perform this little chore after the train has left. . . ."

His words had their desired effect. If he was serious—and there was no reason to believe he wasn't—it meant that an hour from now I would have put the Soviet Union behind me forever. It meant that all my fears that the KGB staged all this—to make

my flight to freedom somehow end tragically—were groundless. I couldn't let this opportunity slip away. I took down my
shorts.

"Spread your cheeks."

He began to probe me with his finger. I bit my lips and
forced myself not to move.

"Nothing, eh?" the stocky customs man observed.

The other man shook his head.

"You can get dressed," he said.

While I was putting on my clothes, I glanced up anxiously
at the clock. Only one hour before the train was slated to
depart.

"You can leave," said the man behind the table.

I finished dressing and left without another word. I felt relieved, almost relaxed. But only for a few moments. When I
reentered the main customs area, I felt I had suddenly been
transported back in time, to an era I had been too young to have
lived through: Children were sobbing, women were screaming.
Here were scenes I had read about, and seen only in films of
World War II. A little girl, tightly clutching her mother's hand,
kept repeating over and over, "Mama, this is war, isn't it? Is it
war, Mama?"

It was not hard to understand her reaction. The customs
officials seemed to have gone berserk. They were flinging the
passengers' clothing and possessions across the room. Men,
women, and children were down on their knees, crawling about
and trying to pick up their things. They were crying, shouting,
hurling insults at the customs men, who simply laughed at their
victims' distress.

One short, chubby man, his chest crisscrossed with a pair
of cartridge belts, was screaming at his wife, who was clutching
a squalling one-year-old to her breast.

"You dumb woman! Take that bawling baby away from here!
Can't you see you're keeping the good comrades from doing
their job?"

At that point the woman burst into tears. She did her best
to soothe the baby, but his screaming only got worse. In fact,
the whole room was a madhouse.

A customs official standing beside my suitcase was going through my books. My clothes were strewn on the floor at his feet.

Lozansky, I said to myself, *keep your cool. Don't lose your temper. Just let them have their little fun this one last time.*

I walked over to the man. He jerked his chin in the direction of a pile of my books he had put aside.

"Seized," he said. "These books are not to leave the Soviet Union."

They were only college textbooks and manuals, but all were about atomic or nuclear physics. Sacred words. Taboo words that in the eyes of the customs men meant "top secret." In fact, a fair number of the books in the pile had been translated from English. He had also seized a copy of my doctoral dissertation, which had been published a few months earlier. Doubtless the name of the publisher—Atomizdat—had struck him as suspicious.

As I was trying to figure out what photographs and illustrations he had ripped out of the other books, I heard someone cry out, " 'Board! All aboard!"

Those words set off an even greater panic among the passengers, who immediately began cramming their scattered belongings into their suitcases and hand luggage.

The customs man who had just seized my books burst out laughing. I realized that he and his colleagues were having one last laugh at our expense. The train was not scheduled to leave for another forty-five minutes.

The laughter of the customs officials failed to drown out the screams and shouts of the passengers, who, leaving behind anything they had not been able to scoop up, raced toward the exit, holding their children in their arms.

There they ran straight into the barrier of the border guards, who issued the exit permits. Then, like a maddened herd, the passengers disappeared into the train.

Even though I knew it was a false alarm, I couldn't resist grabbing my things, stuffing them in my bag, and racing toward the train. After all, maybe it wasn't a game. Maybe the authorities had decided to move up the departure time. I was taking no chance. In the confusion, I managed to retrieve some of the books from the "confiscated" pile. The customs official was laughing so hard he didn't notice.

The train conductor, an elderly man with gray eyes, had witnessed this scene many times. He had seen the chaos in the customs buildings, just as he had seen so many times the tearful farewells on the platform of the station in Moscow, where those leaving embraced their families and loved ones, knowing they probably would never see them again. For these emigrants, most of them Jews, it was an emotional voyage, their last chance for freedom. For the conductor, it was just another trip.

Not that he had anything to complain about: Few Soviet citizens had jobs that permitted them to cross the Russian border. I was sure he took advantage of these trips to dabble in the black market, buying in Vienna the kinds of things he could sell in Moscow at a nice profit. Perhaps, too, he was working for the KGB. It was not an unfamiliar role for train conductors in the Soviet Union. As he worked his way through the train, he kept a close eye on the passengers. As usual, the "regular" passengers, the nonemigrants—mostly diplomats and businessmen—carefully refrained from having anything to do with the likes of us. They read their papers or stared at the ceiling rather than lower themselves to talk with us. Whether this reaction arose from fear or revulsion, I cannot say.

The conductor watched them all, both emigrants and nonemigrants, but he was more interested in the "traitors," the "kikes," than in the others. I strongly suspect he was thinking to himself: In a few hours they'll be free. And as for me, I'll have to take this stinking train back to Moscow. At one point, I saw him pause in the doorway of a compartment and mutter, loud enough for the occupants to hear, "If you want my opinion, Hitler didn't go far enough!"

One man inside the compartment jumped to his feet and lashed at the conductor, who screamed and retreated, while the man's wife and daughter grabbed him and held him back.

Exactly on schedule, the train lurched away from the Brest-Litovsk station. The passengers breathed a communal sigh of relief and rushed to the windows, to be sure to witness the border crossing. As though prolonging our agony, the train inched forward for a good ten minutes. Then someone shouted, "The border. We're at the border!"

We had just crossed the Russian-Polish border, a frontier fraught with both symbolic and historic implications.

There was still daylight. In the distance, against the gray sky, we saw a black control tower, with the silhouette of an armed soldier outlined at the highest point. The border guard turned on his floodlights, and suddenly a whole no-man's-land, filled with barbed wire, sprang into view. A little farther on, in another control tower, the border guard wore a slightly different uniform.

Some people jumped to their feet and embraced one another. Others remained seated, apparently lost in their thoughts. We were only in Poland. Another long night still lay between us and freedom.

We were scheduled to have a short stopover in Warsaw, a city I had always dreamed of visiting. Several years earlier, some Polish friends had invited me to visit them, but I had been unable to obtain authorization to leave Russia, even to visit another Communist country. Since it was unlikely, once I had become a resident of the United States, that I would ever be able to visit any of the Eastern bloc countries, I had decided to make a quick visit to Warsaw during my ride to freedom. In fact, that was the main reason why I had chosen to leave by train rather than plane. Although we had only an hour and a half, I left the train station by cab and asked the driver to let me see as much as possible of the city in the time available. But it was so dark, and I was so afraid of missing the train, that I kept the itinerary short and saw very little, except for some monuments and the shimmer of some street lights reflected in the Vistula River.

The taxi driver spoke Russian. In the course of our trip I told him my story. As he returned me to the train station, he said, "Maybe one day you will come back. To a free Poland."

"Maybe," I replied. But I must confess that I didn't believe my own words.

The train left Warsaw right on time. Again I spent a sleepless night. Several times, customs people came in and searched the compartment: first Polish, then Czech, then, as dawn was breaking, Austrian. At that point, even a hardened pessimist like me had to admit there was no longer any doubt: We were free.

Standing in the corridor, watching the neatly painted houses, the orderly fields and gardens, and the strange-looking automobiles, I tried to put some order into my thoughts.

It had really happened. Here was this free world for which I had battled so long, for which I had given up so much, turning my back on the country where I was born. I had a feeling of elation tempered with a deep sadness. My country, the land where I had grown up, gone to school and college, where I had fallen in love, married, had a child, worked, and taught—all that was part of my past. I had left behind not only dear friends, but also my wife and daughter. I had reached the point where I could no longer breathe in that land.

To obtain that freedom, I had already paid a steep price: a mock divorce without which I could not have left, plus the unhappy prospect of having to wait for a year before my wife and daughter would be allowed to join me in the West. *They* had promised me. But could I trust those promises? Can one believe men who had used lies as a cornerstone of their whole system of government?

As these weighty thoughts ran through my mind, I felt a hand on my shoulder. Again I gave a start, as I had back in Brest-Litovsk. But it was only the little man with the cartridge belt who had so roundly scolded his wife in the customs room at the station. He smiled pleasantly at me and said, "Won't you join us for breakfast?"

"Thank you," I said, "but I'm really not hungry."

"I'm sure you are. Please come."

His wife emerged from the compartment and insisted. "You look sad," she said. "I know you left your loved ones behind in Moscow, that you're alone. So I insist you join us."

I didn't have the strength to refuse. The man quickly pulled the compartment door closed and began to talk rapidly in a high-pitched voice: "We did it. We really did it! Fooled them, I mean. You heard me shouting at my wife? I did that on purpose, to distract them. Look what we had hidden in our baby's diapers."

He opened a small box and took out two stunning strings of pearls.

"They've been in our family for generations," he said. "There's no one back in Moscow we could entrust them to, so we decided to take them with us."

His wife gazed at him tenderly.

"I was so scared," she said, shaking her head. "You have no idea. If ever they'd found them, I hate to think what might have happened to us. . . ."

"It wasn't that great a risk," her husband replied. "All they would have done is confiscate the pearls. Friends of mine told me what to do if customs ever finds jewelry on you. You tell them the jewels are fake, that they have only sentimental value. 'Here,' you say to them, 'keep them as a souvenir.' Nine times out of ten, the customs guy will stuff the jewels in his pocket and let you go. Sometimes you have to offer a bribe as well. A set price. It's a lot of money. More than we had with us. Anyway, nothing happened, so we don't have to worry about it." He smiled and repeated, "We did it! We really did it!"

His good humor had a positive effect on me.

"Come on, now," he said, "let's celebrate."

About half an hour later, the conductor stuck his head in the compartment door and said, "Vienna. Next stop Vienna."

Everyone scrambled to gather belongings. Now there was no question: We were at freedom's border.

The Vienna train station looked like an armed camp, swarming with Austrian soldiers. Later I learned that a few weeks earlier some Palestinian terrorists had attacked a trainload of Jewish refugees arriving from Russia.

An Austrian immigration official shouted, in pidgin Russian, over and over again, "Those going to Israel, to the right. Those going to the United States, to the left."

Slightly intimidated, we clambered from the train and lined

up as directed. The travelers headed for Israel were surrounded
by soldiers armed with submachine guns and herded onto buses.
They were driven to a castle on the outskirts of the city, where
they remained for several hours before boarding a plane for Tel
Aviv. Those of us who were destined for the United States were
taken to different hotels, where we were told that the formalities
of American immigration would take three days. As I was leaving
the station, I felt a hostile presence behind me. Turning, I saw
the train conductor staring at me. I stared back.

"Never again," I muttered under my breath, "never again
will I have to deal with the likes of you."

I was mistaken. Badly mistaken. And even as I walked toward
my bus, saying to myself, *You're free, you're free*, I had a sinking
feeling in the pit of my stomach.

My wife and daughter had planned to stay with my sister in
Kiev. I had promised to call them as soon as I arrived in Vienna.
After checking in at the hotel, I dialed my sister's number. She
answered, sobbing uncontrollably, and I could not understand
what she was saying.

I tried to calm her down.

"They're not here," I finally heard. "They're back in Moscow.
They've kept them in Moscow. They'll never let them out. Tatiana's mother called me and said that if we tried to interfere,
they'd pay for it."

By this time she was screaming into the phone. I replaced
the receiver, my fingers trembling with rage. So *they* had be-
trayed me, gone back on their word. I was furious with myself
for ever having believed them.

I stumbled out of the phone booth, so distraught that I must
have frightened the man waiting in line. My heart was pounding
so loudly I was sure he could hear it. Vienna was bathed in
sunlight, a brilliant winter's day. I stood there on the sidewalk,
blinded by the morning light, dumbly watching the people walk
by. It was December 4, 1976. Tania's fifth birthday. Tania. Tatiana. Tania. Tatiana. I kept hearing my sister's voice saying,
"They'll never let them out. Never!" I remembered the train
conductor's hostile stare, eyes filled with hate. And I caught

myself saying, as I walked through the streets, "I'll get them out. We *will* see each other again. I swear we will."

I didn't realize when I uttered those words that I would be taking on the whole Soviet regime. Or that the process would take six long years.

1
Nationality: Jew

My story begins a long way from Vienna, a long way from either Europe or America, light years from this free world of which I had dreamed so long and to which I now belong. And yet my forebears came from Western Europe. Lozansky is a Jewish name, and so far as we can tell, it means "a native of Lausanne, Switzerland." No one knows precisely when or for what reason my ancestors decided to emigrate eastward, finally settling in the Ukraine, on the banks of the Dnieper. Neither my parents nor my grandparents, nor even my great-grandparents, could shed any light on the family mystery. They were all so poor, and so uneducated, that the subject of genealogy had little meaning for them. All they knew was that they were Jews and that they came from a long line of serfs. They had tilled the soil for generations, helping, like millions of others, to make the Ukraine what it is today—a fertile land producing more wheat than all of France, one of the richest regions in the Soviet Union.

My father was the first Lozansky to rise above the peasant status. Having served in the Red Army during World War II, he settled in Kiev, determined to offer his children an education that would enable them to shake the clay off their feet and claim an "honorable" profession.

My parents dreamed of having their only son become a musician. For years they scrimped and saved from my father's miserable salary to help me achieve their ambition. They sent me to a music school to study piano and cello. I did as I was told. And even though I liked music, I did not have a passion for it; it was not something to which I wanted to dedicate my life. Gradually, I felt more and more drawn to science, no doubt in part because of the climate of the time. These were the 1950s, and in Russia, as elsewhere, the profession of nuclear physicist was extremely prestigious. After reading the Russian edition of Robert Jungk's *Brighter Than a Thousand Suns*, I became even more convinced that I had found my chosen calling. My two boyhood heroes at the time were Robert Oppenheimer and Edward Teller, and my only frustration came from not being able to pin posters of them over my bed.

I was fourteen, which probably explained in large part why my parents did not take me seriously when I told them of my intentions. What was more, I kept up with my musical studies, and my teachers indicated that I was making good progress. But after a few months, my parents had to face the truth: Science had become an obsession with me.

My family began to apply pressure, telling me to stop having pipedreams and return to reality.

"Professor Sukalsky, your cello teacher, tells me that you have a bright future as a musician," my father would say. "So forget physics, forget the university." And then he would cite the names of two famous child prodigies, both Jewish, who had won all the top music prizes a few years before. He would end his lecture by reminding me, "They never went to the university. They couldn't have gone, because they were Jewish. Don't fool yourself, Edward, or you'll ruin your whole life."

He was speaking from firsthand knowledge. Despite having escaped their ancestors' peasant status, my parents still lived in near-poverty, with the constant fear of what tomorrow would bring. We lived in the heart of Kiev, in the old quarter that had not been destroyed during the war. We shared a five-room apartment with four other families. One family per room; twenty people in the apartment. At the time, those kinds of conditions were the lot of most Soviet citizens.

We were six in our room: my father and mother, my grandmother, my two sisters, and me. Thanks to my father's skill as a handyman, he was able to divide the room into three tiny compartments, so that for years we had a semblance of privacy. I was never able to figure out how he managed it, but he had also squeezed in an upright piano, which he had bought for almost nothing at the end of World War II. I practiced my scales on it every day, driving everyone crazy.

Everyone included the neighbors. Living in such close quarters meant that we were all constantly on edge. Tempers were frayed and humors foul, with good reason. There was only one bathroom for all five families, and a communal kitchen with one three-burner stove. In the morning, the waiting line for the bathroom rivaled the queue in Moscow outside Lenin's tomb. Even today, roughly half of the city dwellers in the Soviet Union live a similar kind of *kommunalka*.

My father was the only member of the family to work. My mother, whose life was dedicated to educating her three children, decided that that was a full-time job in itself. To this day, I do not understand how my father was able to support the six of us on the meager salary he earned as an office clerk. Once in a while my sisters had a new pair of shoes or item of clothing, but during my seventeen years in Kiev, I don't believe I ever did. My clothes were all hand-me-downs, often in shreds; my shoes were of canvas.

To make ends meet, and to help pay for my musical studies, my father took a second job. When he left the office in the afternoon, he went directly to the shop of his cousin, who was a shoemaker, and helped him. From that point on, I rarely saw my father: He left at dawn and came home late at night. Despite his two jobs, however, our situation seemed to get worse rather than better. I suspect that what kept my parents going was the hope that my musical career would one day raise them out of their endless, wearisome poverty. But I was too young to understand that; all I knew was that I wanted to become a physicist. Period.

For a year my family did everything in its power to dissuade me from that mad course. My father was especially stubborn. More than once, he and I almost came to blows. And he was not alone in trying to talk sense into me. At various times, my mother, my grandmother, and my sisters took me aside and urged me not to abandon my music. But I stood firm. Maybe I had inherited some of my father's stubborn streak. Eventually his patience gave out. I didn't want to become a musician? I continued to dream about going to the university? All right. In that case, I would have to enter a technical school and learn a trade.

I had no choice but to obey. But after a few months at the trade school, I knew that wasn't working either. I was hopeless at mechanical drawing and my building materials course put me right to sleep. I decided I needed to get a job and go to night school. Besides, if I were serious about going to the university, I would need a secondary-school diploma. Without asking anyone's advice, I quit trade school. That was my first real declaration of independence.

The tension in our apartment was almost unbearable. My father was furious and stopped talking to me. For two years, he acted as though I no longer existed. Fortunately, his brother took pity on me and helped me get a job as an apprentice in a small factory that produced medical equipment not far from the Kiev Drama Theater. I worked there full time during the day and enrolled in night school. That full schedule precluded even a semblance of keeping up my musical studies, but I still played in a symphony orchestra every Sunday.

After a year at the factory, I was promoted from apprentice to full-fledged worker. Though my salary was modest, it gave me a feeling of independence and the opportunity to help alleviate slightly my parents' financial worries.

I had always thought that after obtaining my secondary-school diploma, I would enter the physics program at Kiev University.

But as time went on, I came up with a better and even more grandiose idea: I would apply to Moscow University.

Moscow was the dream of every Soviet student. It was not only the most famous and prestigious Russian university but also by far the hardest to enter. The entrance exams were ten times more difficult than those for other universities, and often there were ten or fifteen candidates for every opening. I knew all that. But I wanted the best. I also wanted to get away. Going to Moscow would be an adventure. It would also relieve me from the prospect of enduring the impossibly close quarters of our Kiev apartment. I would say good-by to adolescence, to a city and milieu that seemed stifling.

I had few real roots in Kiev. As a Ukrainian Jew, from childhood I had suffered all the humiliations that are the lot of Jewish children in the Soviet Union—insults about my race, gibes about my nose, the usual problems. Yet I did not feel particularly Jewish. My parents were not at all religious, and they had never conveyed the notion that we were different from other Russian citizens. Nor had my sisters and I ever been made particularly aware of Jewish traditions or history. Despite the fact that we were constantly the victims of what I might term latent anti-Semitism—which sometimes became overt and aggressive—we led the life of an ordinary Soviet family. Like many Soviet Jews, my parents still believed that the "country of socialism" was unique in fostering the notion of "many races, one equal country."

If I did not feel especially Jewish, I also did not feel deeply committed to the section of the country where I had been brought up. True, I loved the beauty of its landscapes, the splendor of Kiev. And I was not indifferent to the history of the Ukraine. I knew that the Ukrainian people had once been proud and independent—and to some extent they still are. As rich and populous as France, the Ukraine has its own customs and culture. Its people are intelligent and courageous. Whatever they set their minds to, they seem to accomplish. The great success of the Ukrainian farmers who settled in Canada is proof enough.

Unfortunately, as so often happens after a country is defeated and oppressed, the Ukraine sank into a kind of resigned lethargy.

Although they have remained fiercely nationalistic, with a strong sense of their traditions and identity, the Ukrainians have for the most part given up any notion of ever regaining independence. Soviet power is just too overwhelming. All the Ukrainian political leaders known to oppose Soviet domination—men the Soviet regime feared far more than it did the dissidents, because these political leaders enjoyed the support of the people—were identified, tracked down, arrested, and either deported or executed. In contrast to Poland, which has never resigned itself to outside domination, the Ukraine has, at least for the moment, yielded its soul to the Russian system. A Soviet republic since 1922, the Ukraine today is the USSR's granary; its language is simply a local dialect. In the cities of the Ukraine, as in all cities of the Soviet Union, Russian is spoken. At home our family spoke Russian. Even though I still understand Ukrainian, my mother tongue is Russian.

For me, as for millions of other Russians of my age, the City of Light, the Center of the World, was Moscow. I wanted to live in Moscow. I was young, naive, and full of illusions. For me, in 1958, being free meant living in a student dormitory, mingling with students from all over the world, and studying, studying, studying.

In the Kiev library I found books that covered the entrance-exam questions for Moscow University. To my horror, I soon realized that most were way over my head. Clearly, night school was not going to be sufficient—I had only one more year there. During that time, I read far into the night, desperately trying to fill the vast gaps in my knowledge. My friends did their best to dissuade me. "You're aiming too high," they would say. "Moscow University's not for the likes of you and us. We provincials don't stand a chance of getting into that temple of science. Be reasonable, Edward."

At the time, I had a girlfriend, Galya, who used the same arguments, but she was even more aggressive than my friends. Her sharp tongue soon began to chill our ardent relationship. I had the feeling she was trying consciously to hurt me. I argued back, trying to persuade her to follow me to Moscow. She refused. The idea of leaving her parents, of moving 700 kilometers away to live in a dormitory, was more than her imagination could encompass. It was hard enough getting into Kiev University; Moscow was out of the question. Our differences led straight to the breakup of our relationship. I was devastated. I was sure that I was madly in love with Galya.

To my great surprise, my father and mother raised no further objection to my applying to Moscow University. I was momentarily elated, until I heard the reason why. "After all," my father said, "you're free to choose whatever university you want. What difference does it make whether Kiev, Moscow, or Vladivostok turns you down?" And they laughed, the way people laugh at the slightly demented bum who announces himself as the Czar. I found it hard to laugh with them. Anyway, what did it matter? It would take more than their mockery to dissuade me.

The fact is, there was always that question of "nationality" that I preferred to ignore, but others were sure it was an insurmountable obstacle. I knew that in the Soviet Union it was best to be Russian—that is, preferably blue-eyed and blond, or at least to have the word *Russian* inside your passport under the column headed *Nationality*—since the Russians, and the Russians alone, rule the Soviet Empire. But I also knew, being young and naive, that I had been taught, and still believed, the slogans that proclaimed ours as a classless society, a society where everyone had equal rights, a society where power was vested in the workers. I felt the equal of any of the other 270 million Soviet citizens: Russians, Ukrainians, Georgians, Armenians, Lithuanians. We were all members, like every one of the 130 "nationalities" in the Soviet Union, citizens of the country of socialism. Everyone, even those who like me carried a passport that bore, after the word *Nationality*, the description *Jew*. I believed. "All I hear about anti-Semitism is grossly exaggerated," I would say whenever the subject was raised. "True, some universities refuse to take Jews. But they also refuse non-Jews. What counts is being up to snuff, being the best, more qualified than the others."

It was in this frame of mind that I boarded the train for Moscow. I will remember forever that all-night train journey, and especially my arrival, the following morning, in that storied

city, the capital of all Russians. The majesty of the Moskva flow-
ing by, the almost oppressive beauty of the Kremlin, the churches
of Saint Basil and of the Virgin of Georgia, their domes glittering
in the autumn sunlight, the broad avenues, the massive university buildings, surrounded by the Lenin Hills—all struck me
as grandiose. By contrast, I felt small and unworthy as I trod
the thoroughfares of Ivan the Terrible and of the October Revolution, the streets where most of Russia's great heroes had once
strolled. Even the overwhelming banality of the university's
architecture, built under Stalin in the early 1950s, had a grav-
ity to it that emphasized the inaccessibility of this "temple
of science." And yet I had a feeling of immense deliverance.
Moscow, here I come, I said to myself. Nothing could stop
me now.

Like all the other entrance-exam candidates who did not
have a place to stay in Moscow, I was admitted to the university
dormitory. It was an eye-opener. From the first day I rubbed
shoulders with the top students in the Soviet Union—brilliant
scholars testing their mettle, competing with their fellow students, stimulating one another. There was tension in the air,
but also a kind of serenity, for no meanness or pettiness was
manifested anywhere. After the years of isolation I had endured
in Kiev, alone with my own hopes and ambition, I could at last
hobnob with people who shared my goals and dreams. I struck
up a friendship with one student in particular, Sasha Polyakov.
He was the embodiment of the handsome young Russian de-
picted on the official posters: blond hair, gray eyes, prominent
cheekbones, and sharply defined features. He was warm and
open, and our instant friendship proved, in coming years, to be
strong and enduring as well.

His family belonged to what is known in Russia as the *nomenklatura*, the Soviet elite. His father was a deputy mayor of
Moscow, and Sasha had been brought up with the Soviet Union's
"golden youth," who, like their counterparts around the world,
seemed bent on proving their superiority over their less blessed
compatriots. The degree of their disdain apparently was in in-
verse proportion to the length of time since their parents had
attained positions of power. In Moscow this privileged caste

drowned its boredom in alcohol, spending endless afternoons at the National Hotel on Karl Marx Avenue ostentatiously smoking American filter-tipped cigarettes and guzzling beer imported from Western Europe. Sasha, on the other hand, had no intention of taking advantage of his father's position to advance his own career. He preferred to make his own mark. So, even though he did not stay in the dormitory with us, he spent all day with us cramming for the examinations. The only noticeable difference was the black, chauffeur-driven limousine that dropped him off each morning and picked him up at night.

The Soviet Union has a five-point grading system for each exam, ranging from a top grade of five to an unacceptable one. In the entrance exams, a candidate needed a total of eighteen points from the four parts to qualify. Receipt of two points in any one examination was also tantamount to disqualification. By the end of the first three examinations, I had garnered fifteen points, which meant that in physics, my strongest subject, I would need only three points to pass. I was sure I was in.

The night before the final exam, a number of us (including Sasha), who had done well in the first three rounds, were feeling in a celebratory mood and prowled the streets of Moscow till three in the morning. I had almost forgotten Kiev, my family's cramped quarters, my night classes, my doubts and anxieties. I was euphoric at the idea of attaining the "mad" goal I had set myself. I fell asleep in a happy mood, dreaming of my brilliant future.

When I awoke the following morning, I had a splitting headache, a fever, and a sore throat. I had caught a terrible cold the night before. I could have reported to the university doctor and asked for a medical certificate allowing me to take the examination at a later date, but I was so certain of my success that I decided to take the exam anyway. At worst, I could still get those three points, all I needed.

In the Soviet Union, some of the entrance exams are oral, and this was the case for physics. The student arrives and picks up at random a slip of paper on which is written a problem to be solved and a series of theoretical questions. He has half an hour to organize his thoughts before being called before the examiners. I picked up a slip from the pile, sat down at a table, and tried to concentrate. Happily, the problem was easy. Forgetting my fever, I worked out the solution before making some mental notes about the theoretical portion of the exam. When it was my turn, I got to my feet and walked unsteadily toward the examiners.

"What's the matter?" one of the professors asked, glaring at me with eyes of steel. "You look terrible. Get hold of yourself. Is the question too hard for you?"

"The question has nothing to do with it," I said. "I have a bad cold, that's all. I'm ready."

"Who are you trying to fool?" another examiner went on. "I know all the tricks. I've even seen some students pretending to have heart attacks. Don't try to play any such games with us. We only have so much time. Answer the question and then go home and take care of yourself."

"I seem to remember having told you I was ready," I said icily.

As soon as I'd said that, I knew I'd made a terrible mistake. I should have learned to hold my tongue. The examiner who had been lecturing me took my retort personally, and throughout my interrogation he kept interrupting me to ask extraneous questions that had nothing to do with the problem at hand. But I managed to get through it. The least partial of the examiners finally nodded and said that I had answered all the questions.

Immensely relieved, I was preparing to leave the room when my tormentor stopped me. "I agree that you did solve the problem and answer the theoretical questions correctly," he said, "but you had an easy problem and the questions were so elementary that we have decided to test you again."

He handed me another slip. Now I was feeling ten times worse. My teeth were chattering and chills ran up and down my spine. As I tried to figure out the new problem, I could barely make out the writing on the paper. The words were dancing before my eyes. After the examiners observed me for a few minutes, I heard my chief executioner's voice saying, "I think it's clear he can't handle the question. You all agree?" He glanced around at his colleagues, none of whom objected.

"That will be all," one of them said. "Wait out in the hall-way."

As I left the examination room, I was surrounded by my fellow students, all hurling questions at me.

"They're tough, eh?"

"How did you do?"

"Did they ask you any extra questions?"

"Was your problem difficult?"

"What grade did you get?"

I waved them off and slumped to the floor, burying my head in my hands in an effort to conceal my despair.

Suddenly the door to the examination room opened and the examiner who had been the most friendly to me called in the next student. Seeing me, he walked over, and, without a word, handed me a piece of paper. I opened the folded sheet and read my results—Physics: 2. An ugly, humpbacked 2 that looked for all the world like a bishop's crosier. I lifted my head. For some reason the examiner was still standing there. I struggled to my feet.

"Why only a two?" I asked. "You said I had answered every-thing correctly."

"You didn't answer the supplementary question," he said.

He turned and walked back toward the examination room, then pivoted, came back to me, and put his hand on my fore-head.

"Why didn't you go see a doctor this morning?"

"I thought of it, but I was so sure I would get a three or a four that I didn't think it was worth it."

"You were wrong. Anyway, go to the infirmary now. Maybe it's not too late."

He patted me on the shoulder and returned to the exami-nation room. I appreciated his advice and hurried off to the infirmary. The doctor on duty, a peevish woman, prescribed all sorts of medicines for me but steadfastly refused to sign a medical certificate.

"You should have come first thing this morning," she said. "Now it's too late."

I left the infirmary and ran straight into Sasha, who was also on his way to see the doctor. In a few words, I told him my story.

"Wait here. I'll be right back."

I dropped onto a waiting-room chair, my mind filled with nothing but dark thoughts. I felt like crying. *How could I come that close and miss? How could I have done it? Good old over-confident Edward!*

Sasha emerged from the infirmary and shook my shoulder gently.

"Don't worry, my friend. I also got a two. Let's go out and have a drink to celebrate. Everything's going to be all right."

"What do you mean, all right?"

"Just what I said. Our results have been annulled. You and I are going to take the examinations again."

"Listen, Sasha, I'm not in a mood to joke."

"I'm not joking," he said. "I just spoke to my father on the phone and he's arranged everything."

He looked serious. And I remembered that his father was an important man. In Russia, the big wheels don't stand on ceremony. When he learned that Sasha received a two in physics, his father had telephoned the university rector and arranged for his son—and me in the bargain—to take the exam a second time. Using the pretext of illness—which was at least partially true—the rector had issued instructions allowing us to retake the physics portion of the exams. I found it hard to believe. But, a few minutes later, when we each received written authorization in the rector's office, I knew it was true.

"Why did you help me?" I questioned Sasha.

"Aren't we friends?" he asked.

I gave him a bear hug. It's not every day that life comes up with this kind of gift.

The following day we took the test again and both passed, Sasha with a four, I with a five. Sasha was overjoyed. I doubt that I had ever been happier in my life.

That evening, Sasha's parents gave a party to celebrate the happy occasion. I was invited but said that I couldn't go. I had no decent clothes to wear, and I didn't want to admit that to Sasha. But he wouldn't take no for an answer. When the black

limousine pulled up, he pushed me in ahead of him. The party
was at the Polyakovs' dacha outside Moscow, but the chauffeur
drove us first to their city apartment. It was huge, with four or
five bedrooms, furnished in the old style—gold-framed paintings
on the walls, a library where a Steinway grand piano reigned. I
had never seen such luxury. Sasha outfitted me in one of his
suits, down to a pair of glistening shoes. As I was getting dressed,
I could not help but think of our Kiev apartment, where, I was
sure, the five families were still getting on one another's nerves
from morning till night. I reassured myself that I was taking a
first step toward helping my family out of their cesspool.

I began to marvel that all this was really happening to me.
I fingered the sharp crease in my borrowed trousers, which fitted
me perfectly and felt silken against my skin. The sight of the
rich rugs and period furniture, the smell of old wood, excited
my imagination, as did the smell of the leather seats in the
limousine. I was intoxicated by it all.

The limousine left Moscow behind, and we journeyed through
the countryside for quite a while until we entered the "residen-
tial village" of Abramtsevo, the weekend refuge of the Moscow
gentry. There, in sumptuous villas tucked among the pine trees,
waited on by swarms of servants and domestics paid for by the
government, the elite of the Soviet Union left behind their worries and rivalries. In this oasis of calm, they enjoyed moments
of comfort and pleasure while they could. For in the Soviet
Union, nothing ever lasts. Those who share in the pie of privilege
know that at any moment it all might be removed. Even those
at the pinnacle of power—the members of the Politburo and
the military chiefs, who have several dachas, huge apartments,
stretch limousines, and every appliance and gadget that can be
imported from the West—even they live in dread that everything is not really theirs, that it could be taken away from them
at any time. In Russia, good living goes with the job. For those
who lose their jobs, the material manifestations of power can
disappear in a flash.

Obviously, Sasha's father was still very much in favor. Their
dacha was a generous two-story house, and the way in which
the host received his guests was in no way "socialist." In the

shade of the tall pine trees, some young men were playing table tennis, while slender girls in party dresses strolled through the alleyways, chattering and sipping fruit juice or cocktails. Servants passed among them, offering a wide variety of delicious snacks. At nightfall, there was dancing.

The next day, without waiting for the official results of the exams, I boarded the train for Kiev. I wanted to spend the week before the school year began with my family and friends. It was a triumphant week. My parents still had trouble believing what had happened. They telephoned everyone they knew, and the conversations were always the same. "Can you believe it? Moscow University! Who would have thought it possible?"

My father asked me to forgive him for ever doubting my abilities, and, magnanimously, I forgave him immediately.

My countless cousins all came to see with their own eyes this Eighth Wonder of the World, whose name was Edward Lozansky. Almost without exception, they asked my father how much he had had to shell out to the authorities in bribes, and when he said he had not paid a ruble to anyone, they refused to believe him. Some were even upset and angry that he adamantly refused to share this key bit of inside information with them.

As for my Kiev friends, there was a decided mixture of opinions. Some seemed genuinely pleased by my success, others less so. Their sour smiles or shrugged shoulders said a lot about their jealousy. I decided to call Galya and make one last effort to see her. She was unresponsive at first, but when I suggested she leave Kiev University and come with me to Moscow, she replied, "Your Moscow doesn't interest me in the least!"

And that was the end of Galya. I was sad, but also amazed at how quickly my sadness dissipated. I suppose my happiness at the prospect of enrolling in Moscow University left no place for sadness in my heart.

My parents pooled all their savings and bought me a new suit, some shirts, and a pair of shoes. I made a vow that as soon as possible I would not only repay them but help them enjoy a better life.

The day of my departure arrived. The train was scheduled

to leave at 9 P.M. My parents had invited all our relatives to dinner that evening, after which the whole contingent planned to make a triumphal journey with me to the station.

About two hours before the guests were slated to arrive, the doorbell rang. I was alone in the room; all the other members of the family were busy in the kitchen, even my little sister. I opened the door and the postman handed me a letter. I opened it and began to read:

Dear Comrade Lozansky:
After due consideration, the Admissions Committee has decided not to accept your candidacy for study at Moscow University for the coming academic year. It has been determined that the decision to allow you to take the physics examination a second time was an error.
> *Signed*
> *Inspector of the Admissions Committee*

At that moment my mother entered the room to get some spices. She saw the envelope in my hand and the look on my face.

"What's the matter?" she asked.

I handed her the note, and, without even waiting for her to read it, ran from the house.

My whole world had crumbled. Even today, when I think of that evening, I can feel the pain. How can I describe the feeling of shame I experienced that night—the horror, humiliation, and despair? In a few seconds, my dream had died. Moscow, the temple of science, my new friends, my brilliant future—all gone. How could I have harbored such fantasies?

For days I wandered the streets of Kiev alone. Not only was I dishonored in my own eyes, I had also dishonored my parents. Even worse, I had made them look ridiculous. The words that had sentenced me to this awful fate kept ringing in my ears: "The decision to allow you to take the physics examination a second time was an error."

Since then, I have experienced rebuffs, disappointments,

and countless humiliations, but none has left me so much at a loss, so miserable, as did that one.

For weeks I spoke to no one. I would get up early in the morning, leave the house, and wander the streets of Kiev, seeking out distant roads and nooks where I was sure I would run into no one I knew. I even refused to speak to my family. Several times I descended the sandy banks of the Dnieper and walked endlessly through the woods that surrounded the city.

It was autumn, and the foliage of the chestnut and maple trees was bursting with beauty. But it had no effect on me. I was alone, miserable, depressed.

But those whom life wounds she also restores. Since that time, I have always hated pessimists and those who blame all their problems on others, or on the world they live in. Lying, cowardice, spite, and stupidity are anathema to me. When I am down, I am at my best. I attribute that quality in large measure to the long hours I spent during the autumn of 1958 in the Kiev woods, alone with my shame and anger, before I finally came to my senses.

I had touched bottom; the whole world was allied against me. My only recourse was to recognize the facts and face up to them. It was my only chance for survival.

It turned out that although I had seen no one during my solitary walks through Kiev, a number of my friends had spotted me and reported my whereabouts to my family. They had also reported their concern, for they were worried about where such a state of mind might lead. My parents kept their own counsel, which was just as well. They counted on time's healing balm. "He'll come around," they told each other. "Then he can put his fantasies about a scientific career behind him and resume his music, or something else realistic that will enable him to earn a decent living."

I had no intention of giving up. I had proved that I had the ability to get into Moscow University. No "technical error" was going to keep me out. I decided that I would apply for the exams the following year, but meanwhile, I had to find a job.

I wanted no help from anyone. I set out on my own to look for work. And for the first time I began to understand the true

nature of anti-Semitism in the Soviet Union. I would respond
to an announcement for a specific job, and when I arrived at the
personnel office, I was always asked first to show my internal
passport, a kind of national identity card. I could see their eyes
moving down to *Nationality*, then pausing on the word following:
Jew. Then they would inform me that "the job has been filled."
Or, "You don't have sufficient qualifications." The fact was, those
posts were still open, but it was clear they did not want them
filled by Jews. What could I do? I swallowed my anger and kept
on looking.

Finally I found a job as an unskilled worker in a small factory
that manufactured electronic equipment. They were also involved in construction, and I was assigned to work on a new
building. The salary was pitiful, and for months my job consisted
of carrying hods full of bricks and mixing cement with a shovel.
The work was exhausting, and I was happy to leave it for another
job in the paint shop . . . which proved even worse. My job
there was to lift heavy metal frames while another worker coated
them first with a primer, then with a top coat. The fumes made
me dizzy and gave me constant headaches. Next I had to cart
the frames to another part of the factory, where they were dried
at a high temperature. I tried several times to get a new assignment, but to no avail. In all, I worked there for nine months.

Later I learned that it was against the law to use workers
under eighteen for such jobs. They had simply forgotten to
tell me.

It was June 1959. Once again, I began to think of leaving for
Moscow. As I had done the year before, throughout the winter
I had buried myself in my books, month after month, solving
thousands of problems. I knew the textbooks virtually by heart.
This time I was completely ready. This time I felt sure I would
pass, no matter what.

But it was not going to be easy. While I was still in Kiev,
my problems began. For those applicants who had not gone
directly from secondary school to the university, the authorities
required a certificate from an employer attesting to one's merits
and character. My factory director stubbornly refused to give

me a certificate, on the basis that I had not participated actively in the factory's "volunteer activities," and therefore had not earned the right to enter the university. Several of my fellow workers filed a petition on my behalf. Even the union boss spoke up in my favor. At his request, I had formed a jazz group that had played at factory parties. Wasn't that "volunteer" work? But the factory director remained adamant. No one understood why, especially since these certificates usually were a mere formality. Only later did I learn the real reason. The Central Committee of the Communist party had issued instructions for a strict quota system regarding the future enrollment of minorities in the university system. Since I was a member of a minority, the factory director, good Communist that he was, was only obeying instructions. To the letter.

I had almost given up hope when the union boss, who felt he owed me a favor, came up with a possible solution. He introduced me to the director of another small factory. The man, in return for a modest fee, would employ a person for a few days and then furnish him with the necessary certificate. There was also a small gratuity due to the local party secretary and the union boss of that factory, both of whose signatures were required on the form. Those three "modest" gratuities added up to more than my whole year's salary!

To come up with the money, I worked double shifts throughout the summer, unloading freight cars after work, from 5 P.M. until midnight. I also sold my watch and a number of my books. Somehow my father came up with the difference, and I was able to pay off the three men and board the train for Moscow.

At first, the exams were a repeat performance of the previous year. But the total number of points required for admission had been reduced from eighteen to seventeen. At the end of the first three tests, I again had amassed fifteen points. I could not imagine what pretext the examiners might use to reject me this time.

The night before the physics test, I went to bed early and woke up fresh and ready. I responded to the main and supplementary questions without a hitch. As the examiners were about to let me go, a new man walked in. Short and bald, with a perpetual sneer on his lips, he asked me an entirely new question, one that was far more difficult than any of the ones for which I had studied. Nonetheless, I managed to solve it by using integral calculus, which I had taught myself during the course of the summer.

The little man pored over my notes, lifted his head, and said, "You have the right answer . . ."

I breathed a sigh of relief.

". . . but I can't give you credit, because you used the wrong method. You should have used plain math, which apparently remains beyond your abilities."

"All right," I said, "I'll solve it another way."

"We have other candidates to examine. You had your chance. Your time is up."

Even the other examiners seemed to be shocked by his tone and his insulting manner.

I paused for a moment to collect myself and then said, quietly and evenly, "Why are you treating me this way? What have I done wrong?"

"Don't try to tell me how to do my job," he barked. "Get out!"

There was a moment of heavy silence. It was almost as though everyone knew what was going to happen next. As I walked past the raised platform on which the examiners were sitting, I grabbed the back of the bald man's chair and pulled it back, so that he fell over, spilling his papers onto the floor. The clock he used to time the exams also fell with a clatter. I refrained from looking back to savor the sight.

As I left the room, someone rushed up and hugged me. It was Sasha Polyakov, who had just learned that I was again in Moscow for the entrance exams and had come looking for me. He was so sure I had passed this time that he didn't even ask about my scores, attributing the strange look on my face to my surprise at running into him.

"Let's go have a drink," he said.

I nodded and we left the university. We couldn't find any place open, so we ended up buying a bottle of wine and sitting on a park bench. Sasha talked and talked, but I was delighted at the endless flow of words. His presence was a godsend. I don't know what I might have done otherwise. His news was mostly positive. The only negative note was his announcement that his father was no longer deputy mayor of Moscow.

"Anonymous letters accused him of corruption," Sasha said, "said he took bribes. But who doesn't take bribes in Russia? My father swears the people who accused him take bribes themselves. But how can you prove it? Anyway, that accusation is only an excuse so that Khrushchev can move some of his cronies into the job. But enough of all that. This year I know you'll pass."

"I'm not so sure," I said, and I told him what had just happened. He stood up and began to pace back and forth in front of the bench.

"You must be angry with me. I mean, I'm in the university, which I really don't deserve, and you're not. They should have let you take the exam again. You really were sick, and I wasn't. Anyway, I want you to know that my father fought for you as hard as he did for me—not only with the rector, but with some members of the Central Committee. But it's clear from what happened today that they provoked you deliberately. I'm afraid your nationality is working against you, whatever the official line. There must be something we can do."

"Nothing I can think of," I said, "except to try again next year. I swear that next year they can roast me over an open fire and I won't respond. I'll play their little game in their own way."

I was overcome with rage, and for several seconds I uttered the longest string of swearwords I had ever heard emerge from my mouth. I took another swig of wine.

Nothing Sasha said could calm me.

"Let's go see my father," Sasha said. "He still has a few connections, even if they aren't what they used to be. I'll bet he will come up with a good idea."

Polyakov greeted us warmly in the office to which he had been relegated following his demotion. He was not overly optimistic about my chances.

"I'll be happy to call the chancellor," he said, "though I doubt it will do much good. Anyway, it's worth a try. In exchange for a few little favors he did me last year, I helped him find an apartment for several of his friends. Let's see how good his memory is."

So that's what it cost to get Sasha into the university, I thought.

Sasha's father dialed the chancellor's number. A secretary answered, and, after she asked who was calling, there was a long silence, following which she announced that "the chancellor is in a meeting." Polyakov put in a call to another important person, and, after an extended conversation, hung up and shrugged his shoulders helplessly.

"It's even worse than I thought," he said. "I've just learned that they had a hard time discouraging the bastard whose chair you tipped over from pressing charges against you. He finally agreed not to, but only on the condition that you not be admitted." He paused. "It could have been worse. They could have jailed you for hooliganism."

"I'm not sure that's what you would have called him a year ago," I murmured, so low that no one heard.

But what difference did it make?

Despair, bitterness, frustration. Over the years to come, these feelings would sometimes push me to dangerous extremes. My mind was filled with nothing but negative thoughts. It was clear that I was destined to be a pariah, a stranger in my own country. Me become a physicist? Why? Why persist? It was just flailing against the wind. My friends had been right: Such dreams were not meant for the likes of me. The only solution was to vanish from the scene, disappear into the anonymous poverty that was the fate of most of my compatriots. Accept my fate. That's what they wanted from me. Well, that's what they would get.

Without a ruble to my name, without a ticket, I boarded the train for Murmansk, a city of ice and wind and ultimate despair.

The trip was a nightmare. An endless journey of sleepless nights and wary days, trying to keep one jump ahead of the conductor; of hopping off the train to keep from being apprehended, and shivering for hours on an empty platform waiting for the next train to arrive.

Not only was I determined to make myself anonymous, I also had decided to take up the most difficult profession I could imagine: working on a fishing trawler in the icy northwest waters of Russia.

Murmansk was everything I expected—and less. I arrived at dawn and wandered along empty wooden streets that were so slippery it was almost impossible to walk without falling, past rundown wooden houses that reeked of salt, alcohol, and dead fish. The port itself was peopled with drunks staggering about, begging for work. I was hungry, so I sold my jacket for a handful of rubles.

At the employment office I was told that no work was available to me, since my passport was not in order.

"What's wrong with it?"

"It says you live in Kiev."

"I do."

"So you have no right to be here."

What did it matter? Here. There. . . .

I finally ran into a sympathetic man, the captain of a dilapidated fishing trawler who said he would take me in for a few days on the condition that I clean his boat from stem to stern. When I finished the backbreaking job, he sent me packing.

One afternoon I went into a bar, more to get warm than in the hope I would find something to eat or drink. There was a piano in the bar, and, after a while, I sat down and began to play. Before long I was surrounded by a dozen drunken sailors, singing at the tops of their lungs. They kept offering me drinks, which, because of my empty stomach, went straight to my head. By nightfall I was as drunk as the rest. We all left the bar but had no place to sleep.

"Let's try the employment office," they said. "It has a pot-bellied stove."

The place was already filled with other homeless men, of all sizes and shapes, stretched out on the floor trying to find comfortable positions. They told us there was no more room, and when they insisted, we began to shout back. They tried to kick us out, and our shouts and protests soon degenerated into a brawl. They called the police. I wanted no part of the police, so I stumbled out onto the street, intent merely on getting away. Instinctively, I headed for the train station.

In the waiting room I could smell food cooking, so I headed for the steam-filled diner, where they served borscht and meat pies. Carrying a few rubles left from my stint on the trawler, I took a seat, planning to kill some time before the westbound train was due to leave. I had had enough of Murmansk, of the bitter cold and utter loneliness. At least in Kiev I would not be so completely alone.

I heard a chair scrape; someone was sitting down beside me. Then a voice asked, in a thick accent, "Mind if I join you?"

I shook my head and looked up to see a young man with brilliant blue eyes looking at me.

"Lithuanian," he said, as though he figured I was trying to place his accent. "That's where I'm from. In my village no one spoke Russian." He fell silent for several minutes, then said, "What are you doing in Murmansk? You don't look like a sailor to me."

I told him my story. He nodded, wiped his forehead, then rubbed his chin several times, as though trying to make up his mind about something. I knew he was going to reveal some deep, dark secret. Finally, he blurted out, "You should leave this country. I can help. I have a plan all worked out to get to Sweden. I need someone to go with me. It's dangerous, but my plan ought to work."

I looked at him wide-eyed, in obvious disbelief, then burst out laughing. He got to his feet, his face reddening. Clearly I had insulted him by my reaction. I tried to make amends, to explain that I wasn't laughing at him or his plans— which in fact sounded as though they might work—but that I had no desire to leave. Why would I want to leave my family and friends? Despite all my problems, Russia was still my country.

The man looked crestfallen. "If that's the way you feel. . . . I'm sure you'll look back one day and wish you had taken me up on my offer. You may never get another chance."

He was right. Over the years, I thought back to that incident many times, and to his words, and wished I had accepted.

He made one last effort to persuade me, then desisted with a fatalistic shrug.

"What made you pick me?" I asked.

"Actually, I was supposed to go with somebody else," he said, "another Lithuanian. But at the last minute, he backed out. You looked like you might be right for it. I'm positive your kind could make a go of it in the West. . . . Sure you won't change your mind?"

I shook my head. "Sorry. I was pretty far down, but I still think I can make something of myself here."

"In that case. . . ."

We shook hands. I wished him good luck, and he turned and disappeared through the steam into the icy night.

Several hours later, I boarded the train and headed back to Kiev.

My mother almost fainted when I walked in the door. Her first thought was to telephone everyone she knew. Good news: The prodigal son has returned home. Her joy was a soothing balm to my broken spirits. Yes, there were still some people in the world who did love me. My father was almost as happy to see me as my mother was. He told me he wanted to let bygones be bygones and that he would do his best to help me find a job. He didn't have the connections of a Polyakov, but one of his wartime comrades was highly placed in the local government and had agreed to help him.

There ensued a highly complex series of heavy negotiations involving a number of important people and several different organizations. The upshot was that one of my father's friends moved into a larger, more comfortable apartment; another, after waiting in vain for several years, had a telephone installed unexpectedly; still another received a huge jar of caviar and a pair of new shoes. As for me, much to my surprise, I was taken on by a factory working for the military. I had thought that my escapade in Murmansk might have closed all doors to me. Ap-

parently the KGB there took little or no interest in the talk—
or brawls—of the town drunks.

After all my tribulations, this was a godsend. My job was to
check the parameters on semiconductor diodes and triodes that
went into military aircraft and space satellites. Nice, clean work
in a nice, warm room. When my shift was over, I often stayed
on and studied late into the night.

In the spring of 1960, as I was preparing to take the Moscow
University entrance exams for the third time, I received an army
induction notice. It was a terrible blow, for it meant pushing
back my university enrollment for at least another three years.

I went to the local recruiting office and filled out all the
forms. Then I asked the recruiting officer if there was any chance
I might get a deferment until autumn.

The major gave me a knowing look and opened my file. I
could see his eyes scanning it, and I knew exactly what he was
looking for in it.

"Who are you trying to con, Lozansky?" he asked, looking
up from the file. "You people are always trying to work some
con. Let Ivan do the dirty work, eh?"

There was a long silence. The major must have seen by the
expression on my face that he had gone too far, for his tone
suddenly changed.

"I'll see what I can do," he said. "You don't seem to have
any special qualifications, and normally we take on your kind of
recruit in the autumn. . . . We'll see."

I left the office in a somewhat better frame of mind. There
was still a ray of hope that I might be deferred until fall, but I
knew that sooner or later they would get me. This meant I would
have to study all the harder. This time I had to pass, since it
could well be my last chance.

That same evening, a military messenger came to our door
and handed me an order to report for a physical the following
morning. I was surprised by the speed of things, but assumed
that the date had been set before the major's promise, so I
thought little of it.

The physical was thorough and rigorous. For three hours, a

battery of doctors checked me out in exquisite detail. When it was finished, they told me to get dressed and wait in the hallway. While I was waiting, the major strode by without saying a word. *Bad sign*, I thought. Then I rationalized that he probably hadn't recognized me.

Minutes later, the major emerged from his office and handed me a sheet of paper. "Lozansky, Edward. Follow me."

I followed him into his office, where he informed me that I had been assigned to the Construction Corps. He handed me a form letter.

> *By order of the draft board of the City of Kiev, you are hereby ordered to appear with your personal belongings at the appointed place indicated below at 0900 on April 9, 1960. Failure to appear is punishable by law.*

The major confiscated my passport and issued me a receipt.

Back out on the street, I had the feeling that my head was going to explode. I sat down on the steps and tried to think. What was I going to do? All my pipedreams, all my plans to run away were deterred by the simple words *punishable by law*, which meant *sent to jail*.

If I had been able to continue my studies in the army, the way draftees can do in the armies of Western Europe or the United States, I would have felt less desperate. But in the Red Army, soldiers do not study. In the Red Army you do not progress; you regress.

The Red Army. A nightmare. That mighty machine that strikes fear into the hearts of the entire world is a school of a very different kind, one filled with lies, corruption, drunkenness, racism, and misery. In this so-called revolutionary army, the hatred between the Russians and the non-Russians is so strong that it is difficult to say how many countless "impure" soldiers have been killed by their blue-eyed comrades during fights. The ignorance of Soviet soldiers, and their manifest contempt for their superiors, is legendary. The army is so distrustful of its troops that arms and ammunition are issued only in cases of "extreme necessity." Many soldiers do not speak a word of Rus-

sian, the language in which they receive their orders. They are
expected to obey those orders blindly, without trying to understand them. They are lied to on all levels, even regarding the
purpose and place of their missions. The Soviet troops who
invaded Czechoslovakia and Afghanistan, for example, were told
they were going off to fight German, Chinese, and American
"aggressors."

Malnutrition is rampant, with all its attendant consequences:
infections, ulcers, eye trouble. Alcoholism is also a major problem, even among the officer corps, with one man in three affected—a fact that raises serious problems about the Red Army's
ability to defend the homeland. The soldiers drink anything they
can lay their hands on: rubbing alcohol, antifreeze, even wax-
based alcohols.

In the context of that army, the Construction Corps to which
I had been assigned occupied a very special place. It was made
up primarily of Asians, whom the Russians called *chuchmeki*
("niggers"), and was assigned the most difficult and menial jobs,
both civilian and military. They built roads and highways, landing strips, military housing, even entire cities, and at night they
slept in barracks that were as unsanitary as they were over-
crowded.

Over the years, I had seen these soldiers working on the
roads or in the fields, and I had always wondered why most of
them seemed to have been Asian. Many years later, one of my
colleagues at the prestigious Military Tank Academy in Moscow,
where I was then teaching physics, explained why. When I
pointed out to him that there were surprisingly few Muslim,
Estonian, Baltic, Armenian, and Tatar officers at the school, and
an overwhelming percentage of Russians and Ukrainians, this
colleague—who was a general—laughed and took me affection-
ately by the arm.

"You act as though you were born yesterday," he said. "How
could you think for a moment that we could put Estonians or
Latvians in positions of command? Let alone Armenians. The
first thing they'd do would be to turn their guns against us. And
you can carry that over to the Hungarians, Czechs, and Poles.
In all the satellite countries, the only people we can count on

are the militia, who are fanatically devoted to us. And even there . . . I suspect some of them would love to stab us in the back if they ever got the chance."

He leaned over and whispered:

"To tell the truth, we really don't trust your Ukrainian compatriots, either. But there are 40 million of you, and that we can't ignore. But I'll tell you this: Any time we bestow a position of authority on a Ukrainian, you can be sure there are several Russians assigned to keep an eye on him. We trust Russians, and only Russians, that's something you'd better remember. All those high-blown slogans about ethnic equality you hear day in and day out are a bunch of crap. This country hasn't fallen apart only because all the key posts are in the hands of Russians. Come on, Edward, I'm not telling you anything you didn't know. The truth is, nobody in Russia really believes in communism anymore, except maybe a handful of crazies, most of whom are in the loony bin. That fairy tale ended in 1937. One thing keeps this country going, my boy, and that is Russian nationalism. Of course, that's not something we can shout from the rooftops, but it's the truth. The reason this country's leaders keep spouting all that nonsense about communism is that it seems to have an effect on the Western intellectuals. They're the only ones who still believe it. The only dinosaurs who still really believe live not in Russia but on the other side of the iron curtain."

Later I learned from other sources that the same ethnic factors played a major role not only in the armed services but also and especially in the nuclear establishment. To get a job in this area, it was essential that after the word *Nationality* in your passport, the word *Russian* follow. But even that was not enough. A special commission examined not only the candidate but also his family, for several generations back. It is highly recommended that any candidates for posts in the nuclear defense section have blond hair, blue eyes, and an aquiline nose.

I have blond hair and blue eyes, but the shape of my nose betrays my origins. Thus my assignment to the Construction Corps.

Sitting there on the steps of the recruiting station, my head in my hands, I couldn't help but remember the words of the sailor in Murmansk: "I'm sure you'll look back one day and wish you had taken me up on my offer." If he had materialized that day, I would have followed him to the ends of the earth, without hesitation.

About a week before I was due to report to the army, two young men knocked on our apartment door. They flashed identification cards, showing them to be from the secret police, and asked me to follow them. "A simple formality," they said.

Somehow I was not overly concerned, maybe for the simple reason that I was so depressed anyway that I couldn't imagine anything worse happening to me.

At the local KGB headquarters where they took me, they began by asking all sorts of innocuous questions. Where did I work? What were my interests in life? Who were my friends? Then they moved on to more serious matters, and their tone became more urgent.

"At Moscow University," they said, "there are certain unsavory elements who go around dabbling in the black market— selling icons, buying clothes from tourists, sometimes drug-dealing. You know how it goes: They approach some foreign tourists and ask to buy Western clothes, or maybe books or magazines. Nothing very serious. But people who break the law in a minor way often move on to more serious crimes. You begin with a pair of blue jeans and end up spying for the West."

I put on my most innocent expression, but finally I couldn't help asking what all this had to do with me.

"I'm sure you've heard of this kind of thing," one of them said. "Think back."

I surmised that the agents knew that I, like virtually all Soviet youngsters, did upon occasion hang out at the Intourist Hotel in Kiev, in the hope of meeting some foreigner and picking up some news about the outside world. I figured it would be silly to lie to them, so I told them just that.

"You have nothing to be afraid of," the man said, his voice dripping with honey. "We know that you haven't been involved in any of this. What we need is for you to help us find and punish

the real criminals. Give us the names of those you know have
been involved. We'll keep anything you tell us confidential."

"I've told you everything I know. Besides, I hardly know
anyone in Moscow."

"How about Kiev? Maybe you know some people like that
here in Kiev? No? I'm sorry to hear that. We thought you were
one of us. Anyway, there's no hurry. Go home and think about
it. If you have second thoughts, or if your memory improves,
give us a call at this number. Oh, by the way, I wouldn't plan
to take any trips in the near future. We might need to call on
you again."

"But I'm leaving next week for the army," I said, in a tone
I hoped sounded joyful.

They exchanged looks, then one of them wrote something
in his notebook.

The next day I was summoned to the recruiting station,
where my passport was returned to me. "The major has pushed
back your date of induction," I was told.

I wasn't sure whether to be pleased or worried. I said nothing
to my parents about my visit to the KGB, since I knew it would
upset them. I hoped that things would take care of themselves
in the long run, and I tried not to worry.

Three weeks later, I was called to KGB headquarters again.
This time I was questioned by several agents, all of whom used
several tactics, including intimidation, in an effort to have me
collaborate, or reveal information. Eventually they came to the
conclusion that I knew nothing, and let me go.

I finally decided to try my luck not at Moscow University but
at the Moscow Physical Engineering Institute. The institute had
the highest reputation, having trained some of the most famous
physicists in the country. The entrance exams were held in July,
a full month earlier than those for Moscow University. I applied
for experimental and theoretical physics, and passed with flying
colors, earning three points more than required. But that did
not mean I was admitted. The final word had to come from a
secret commission charged with verifying the political purity of
the candidates. My fear was that recent events would work against

me and I would once again be turned down. But either the KGB had closed its file on me, or the lack of computers in those days kept the agency from transmitting any negative data about me. In any event, I was accepted. My long battle was over. This also meant that the impending threat of military service was over, too.

Looking back, I felt it was outrageous that I had had to wait so long, and expend so much energy and emotion, simply to get into a university. But I also realized that those two years had taught me a great deal and put an end to many of the ingenuous notions I had previously accepted as gospel. I had learned much about the world I lived in, about the Soviet system, and, above all, about myself.

The next five years of my life, which I can only characterize as "study-crammed," flew by faster than I had ever thought possible.

The institute was situated right in the center of Moscow, opposite the main post office. The course load was such, however, that we students had little time for leisure pursuits. In addition to our regular science and engineering courses, we had endless hours of ideological courses. History of the Communist Party, Marxist Economics and Philosophy, Scientific Communism, and Atheism were but a few of them.

As for the scientific part of the program, it was rigorous but marred by the complete absence of electives. It was as if the Soviet educators were totally disinterested in giving the students a broad cultural base. In the Soviet Union, students are not allowed to participate in any religious or unauthorized political or social activities. Any student who tries to voice his opinion is expelled immediately, and expulsion means that he will receive an army induction notice a few days later. One student in my group was thrown out for having drawn a moustache on the portrait of a high-ranking party official; he was in the army within a week. What might be considered a mere prank in other countries is treated as ideological subversion and dealt with accordingly.

This repression produced the desired results. Any student

who had overcome all the obstacles and finally gained admission to an institution of higher learning was little inclined to challenge the conventions or contest the restrictions. As a result, student life was the poorer for it. For relaxation, all we could do was drink vodka, play cards, and sing songs.

The tight controls over the development of free thought in the Soviet Union were dealt a severe blow in the 1950s with the introduction of the tape recorder. This little machine was capable of capturing Western music and transmitting it in multiple copies throughout the country. Thousands of tapes of a record or a song heard on the radio were made and distributed. This gave rise to a whole network of free enterprise, as budding Soviet entrepreneurs recognized these tapes as a potential source of considerable revenue. Subsequently, Soviet singers and poets took advantage of the same mechanism to transmit their songs and verse, which Nikita Khrushchev's censors until then had been able to squelch.

The first songwriter to become famous via the tape recorder was Bulat Okudzhava. His songs were so radically different from the patriotic pap we heard on the radio, his message was so sincere and human, that he quickly became the most popular lyricist in the country. Everyone—students, workers, even soldiers—was singing his songs.

Encouraged by his success, a number of other poets and singers followed suit and inundated the country with "clandestine" songs. The tape recorder became essential for everyone, so that you could listen in the relative privacy of your home to the latest recordings of Vladimir Vysotsky, Alexander Galich, Novella Matveeva, or Yuli Kim, to mention only the best known.

Anyone capable of playing a guitar, however poorly, also got into the act, and singing became an integral part of our lives. At parties, after the usual banter and pleasantries, the evening would inevitably end with someone strumming a guitar while everyone else chimed in, singing the forbidden lyrics.

The authorities were quick to react, seeing this new vogue as a dire threat to the regime. Soviet citizens were supposed to sing only those songs that glorified Lenin, the Communist party, and the Soviet State. If youngsters began singing songs that not only failed to fulfill that basic mission but, far worse, made fun of the Soviet system and its leaders, sedition could not be far behind.

The newspapers ran a series of articles attacking these unauthorized "bards" and "minstrels," accusing them of a whole host of wrongdoings, including serving the forces of imperialism.

But it was too late. Millions of people already knew the songs by heart. Despite all its power and efficiency, the Soviet police had not found a way to stamp out people's memories. These "free songs" of the 1960s played a major role in developing among Russian youth something that a totalitarian regime fears more than anything else—a critical mind.

A friend of mine at the institute, Sergei Potapov, knew most of these poets, some of whom even composed songs especially for him. Sergei quickly amassed a large repertoire of these songs and soon became one of their leading performers. I used to tape Sergei, then memorize the songs myself, since I had learned to play the guitar. Thus, on evenings when Sergei wasn't there, I could stand in for him.

Many of these songs seem dated today, but none of us who learned them will ever forget them. Whenever we émigrés get together in Paris or London, New York or Washington or Boston, we inevitably end our evenings with nostalgic renditions of the most popular songs of the 1960s.

During my student years at the institute, I left Moscow every summer in search of odd jobs in which I could earn enough money to support myself during the following school year. I was always short of cash, and even during the winter months, I often helped replenish my meager savings by unloading freight cars early in the morning or in the afternoon after classes.

At the start of my final year at the institute, someone broke into my room and stole almost everything I owned: clothes, books, my camera, my savings from the previous summer. I had to find a part-time job. The director of the institute was understanding, and he authorized me to both work and continue my studies full time.

When I started job-hunting, for once luck was with me.

Before Khrushchev's fall from power in 1964, he had modified the Soviet system of primary and secondary education, lengthening it from ten to eleven years. As a result, there was an immediate shortage of teachers. To cope with the situation, the authorities sometimes allowed schools to hire fourth- and fifth-year students from the universities.

So I went to the Moscow Bureau of Education to look through their list of job openings. I hoped to find some tutoring work, but my eye almost immediately caught one announcement: "Secondary school seeks math teacher. Ten hours teaching per week. Applicants must first pass school-administered exam."

Intrigued, I dialed the number indicated in the announcement. A woman's voice answered, and when I identified myself, she said, "Please come over right away."

A few minutes later, I rang the doorbell of an apartment, which turned out to be quite comfortable. An older woman ushered me into a room, sat me down at a table, and handed me a sheet of paper covered with math problems.

"You have two hours," she said in a rather pompous voice. She left the room, closing the door firmly behind her.

All my efforts to get into Moscow University stood me in good stead. At the end of an hour, I had finished the test, and I opened the door to let the woman know. No one was anywhere about. I coughed discreetly once or twice, then opened the door across the hall. It was a bedroom, and in the bed was a sallow-faced man, who I judged to be in his sixties, propped up on two pillows reading a magazine. Raising his eyes, he murmured in a barely audible voice, "Exam too hard for you?"

Without answering, I walked over to the bed and handed him my papers. While he went through them, I looked around the sparsely furnished room. Prominently displayed on the wall was a photograph of an old man with a teenage boy.

Glancing up, the man asked, "You recognize him?"

"No."

"That's Arnold."

I had heard of Arnold, who was the youngest lecturer at Moscow University and one of the most talented mathematicians in the Soviet Union.

"Is he your son?"

The old man smiled. "Spiritual son," he said. "I was his teacher at School 59. Do you know about that school?"

I shook my head. "I have spent most of my life in Kiev," I said.

"In any case, you have answered all the test questions correctly. Let me introduce myself. I am Ivan Vasylievich Morozkin, a teacher at School 59. Now, tell me a little about yourself."

I began a rambling account of my life, which he listened to patiently for a few minutes.

"Fine. Fine. I'm afraid I can't hear any more, because my doctor is due any minute. I want you to go right over to School 59. Here's the address. I'll call to say you are coming. Don't worry about a thing. You'll be teaching two classes of top students. They're all very bright. And also very nice. You'll enjoy them."

He was telling me I'd been hired. In a slight daze, I backed out of the room, as Ivan Vasylievich picked up his magazine and resumed reading.

Morozkin turned out to be the top mathematics teacher at School 59, a man who enjoyed the highest reputation in educational circles. At the start of the school year, he had become ill, and it became clear he could not go on teaching. Most of his students had been assigned to other teachers, but no one had wanted to take over his two senior honors classes. Two weeks into the school year, the honor students still were without a teacher, which was becoming embarrassing. The director of the school was growing increasingly uneasy, especially since a number of the students were from prominent Russian families. Even the school's geography added to the director's growing concern. The school was next door to a building owned by the Central Committee, which housed, among other luminaries, Politburo member Pyotr Demichev; one of the party's top ideologues, Pyotr Fedoseyev; ex-Premier Nikita Khrushchev; and Stalin's daughter, Svetlana Alilluyeva and her two children, Osya and Katya, who attended School 59.

I was unaware of all these facts as I headed for the school, which was located in central Moscow, on Starokoniushenny Lane, just across from the Canadian Embassy. I was greeted at the door by one of the teachers, who led me to the office of the director, a short, stooped man who struck me immediately as unpleasant. Obviously he was not overjoyed at seeing me.

"Ivan Vasylievich told me a young man was coming, but I must say I never expected. . . ." He gestured vaguely in my direction. "You look more like one of our students than you do a teacher. *Are* you a student?"

I nodded. He looked me over once again, as though searching for some good reason to send me away. "Can I see your passport?"

Here we go again, I thought. The more things change, the more they stay the same, even after four years.

"I'm sorry, I don't have it with me. I only learned about this job opening this morning and didn't expect things would move this fast. Anyway," I said after a pause, "I don't have it. It was stolen."

The director shook his head mournfully, probably cursing Morozkin for sending him someone who not only had no passport but looked more like a derelict than a future teacher.

"What can I do?" he said, more to himself than to me. "Those two honors classes . . . two weeks without a teacher. It can't go on. Can you begin tomorrow? You really must. This whole situation is driving me crazy. . . . By the way, have you ever taught before?"

"Of course," I lied with a straight face. But there was, in fact, a grain of truth in my reply: I had tutored several students for the math competition sponsored by the institute.

"As for your outfit," he said, throwing up his hands, "I trust that tomorrow you will be wearing a suit and tie, and not these. . . ."

Rags was the word he could not bring himself to say.

He was right. When my room had been robbed, I had been taking a shower down the corridor. When I returned, all I found was my briefcase and a few books. I had spent the entire evening going from room to room, trying to beg a pair of trousers and a shirt from other students. Finally, someone had taken pity on me and loaned me some threadbare clothes.

I promised I would show up in a suit, although I didn't have the faintest notion of where I would find one. The director handed me a class schedule.

"Proper dress is a must," he said. "The seventeen-year-old girls in the class are harsh judges. If they don't like the looks of you, you'll be in deep trouble. Now, let's take you down to meet the principal, who will work out the details with you."

He led me down the hall to a smaller office, where he introduced me to his second-in-command, a plump, jovial-looking man who smiled and shook my hand. The span of wrinkles at the corner of his eyes suggested that he was a man who enjoyed a good laugh.

"I'll leave you two," the director said mournfully, as if trying to make his colleague understand that he was taking me on only because his back was to the wall. "And don't forget the suit," he said as he closed the door.

The principal looked me over carefully. "I'll bet you don't have one, do you?"

"You're right." Then, screwing up my courage, I said, "Give me an advance against my salary and I'll have one by tomorrow morning."

"Out of the question. First of all, it will take two weeks to get your paperwork processed. I might be able to lend you a few rubles. How much do you need?"

"A hundred rubles. For a decent suit, that's the least I'd need. Counting the shirt and tie."

"Are you joking? Where do you think I could ever find that kind of money? And even if I could, it would take you two months to pay it back."

That was how I learned what my salary would be.

"But what about the girls in my class? How do you think they will react to these rags?"

He looked at me for a second, then burst out laughing. He took out his address book and made several calls. Finally, he wrote an address on a slip of paper and handed it to me, together with three ten-ruble notes.

"You'll get the balance at this address," he said. "You can pay me back in two months."

The man he sent me to was not a moneylender, but obviously a friend of his. He asked me no questions, not even my name. Clearly it was not the first time he had loaned money in this way. If the principal vouched for me, that was good enough for him. In the Soviet Union, where salaries are low and credit nonexistent, this personalized lending network is commonplace. Everyone borrows according to his needs, and lends to friends in like manner, knowing that one day the good deed will be reciprocated. It makes daily life a little more bearable.

I went to a store and bought myself a suit, shirt, and tie. The clerk had to teach me how to tie the tie, for I had never worn one before.

Next morning, I studied my image in the mirror and gave myself a passing grade. My roommates all whistled when they saw me decked out.

Feeling slightly strangled and very nervous, I set out for my first day at School 59.

It went better than I had expected. The girls were hard-working and pretty, the boys bright and unpretentious. To check the level of their ability, I gave them a test of tough and tricky problems, which they attacked like a pack of hungry animals. I was delighted, but the ease with which they solved the "tough" problems gave me fair warning that I had my work cut out for me.

Teaching these young men and women, who were only a few years younger than I, was sheer pleasure. I tried to vary the courses for them and come up with new and original exercises every day, and that often led to lively discussions on a broader scientific level.

We quickly became close friends and spent a great deal of time together outside the classroom. One day they invited me to join them on a hike in the country outside Moscow, and soon our weekend excursions became regular affairs. We would hike for ten or fifteen miles through the fields and forests, then pitch our tents, build a fire, cook supper, and end our evening with a rousing songfest.

In winter we skied, both downhill and cross country, spending the night in a peasant hut in some village. One of these weekend excursions brought us even closer together. It was a cold but sunny day in midwinter. After a full day of skiing, we were getting ready to return to Moscow when somebody said, "What say we stay over an extra day?"

"Yes," came the chorus, "let's stay!"

I found the whole class looking at me intently, waiting for an answer. I knew I shouldn't say yes, that it would spell trouble, but who could resist the silent entreaties of those bright faces? I agreed.

We spent most of the evening trying to concoct a credible story. The best we could come up with was that two of the students had been lost in the woods and we had spent the better part of the night searching for them. It sounded like a good story at the time.

After we had supper and sang a round of songs, the students walked down to the village post office to call their parents.

The next day was magnificent. After a full day of skiing, we boarded the train for Moscow in a state of blissful exhaustion.

The next morning, as soon as I arrived at school, I was told to report to the director's office. I had been prepared for trouble, but the force of his wrath took me aback.

"And you call yourself a teacher? Where is your sense of responsibility? Your sense of discipline? Don't stand there like a *muzhik*. What's your excuse?"

I blurted out the story we had made up.

"And you expect me to believe that? You're the worst liar I have ever heard!"

Over the next several days, the director summoned all my students one by one to grill them about our weekend escapade. All the stories jibed with mine—until one day a girl named Irene broke down and told the truth.

Poor Irene. She was incapable of lying. But she paid dearly for her honesty. The whole class gave her the cold shoulder for several months. Tears streaming down her cheeks, she came to see me, and I told her not to worry, that it wasn't the end of the world.

"I've never lied in my life," she sobbed. "I just don't know how. And I never will."

Years later, during a reunion to which my former students at School 59 had invited me, someone jokingly reminded Irene of the incident.

Irene's face suddenly became very serious.

"Listen," she said, "I have something very important to tell you all. I want to admit that I was wrong. That was a wonderful experience we all shared that day. I remember it as something very special, very beautiful. That day we felt ourselves in contact with nature, and with one another. What is more beautiful than beauty and friendship? Isn't the joy we all felt that day extraordinarily rare? What we felt and experienced was nobody's business. And look who was accusing us of lying. The guy who forced us to lie every day by repeating senseless slogans of the Communist party. Isn't it true that in a country like ours, we have to lie to protect ourselves?"

Her declaration was greeted by a long silence, after which it seemed that everybody wanted to talk at once. Irene had put her finger on one of the horrors of the Soviet system: the vital need to dissimulate. One by one, they all came to the same conclusion that Irene had just voiced. I was impressed by their lucidity and maturity. The point of departure—the little white lie that hurts no one—may seem puerile, but it is in just such circumstances as these that many young Soviet citizens are made aware of the malaise in which they live. They discover how much they would prefer to live in a free and open society founded on respect for the individual.

Our free and open discussion, it turned out, was taped by one of those present and turned over to the KGB the next day. That, too, is part of the mores of the Soviet Union.

After Irene's confession about our escapade, the director of the school summoned me to his office.

"I regret to inform you that your services at this institution are hereby terminated," he declared solemnly.

From his viewpoint, I couldn't fault him, but my students would not hear of it. They sent a delegation to Morozkin to plead my cause. Morozkin called several influential parents, who in turn exerted pressure on the director to keep me. Much against his better judgment, he finally relented. But also they pressed him for a further concession: They wanted my contract renewed for another year.

My unorthodox methods were in large part responsible for my success: Virtually all my students had been admitted to Moscow University or other prestigious institutions of higher learning. Their parents were interested less in methods than in results. And as far as I was concerned, I had "produced" for their children.

With great reluctance, the director called me in once again, and, in a pained voice, he offered me the post for the following year.

"I frankly don't see what these people see in you," he lamented. "Your pedagogical methods are, how shall I say, unorthodox at best. Nonetheless, I am formally making you the offer. May I assume you accept?"

"I'm terribly sorry, but I can't."

"You can't? Why in the world not?"

"My thesis director, Professor Oleg Tigrov, has asked me to become a teaching assistant and researcher at the Kurchatov Institute of Atomic Energy."

"The Kurchatov Institute?"

"The Kurchatov Institute," I echoed, savoring both the repetition of the hallowed name and the look of surprise and disbelief on the director's face.

The Kurchatov Institute, which was originally called the Experimental Laboratory of the Academy of Sciences, was created at the end of World War II at the instigation of Joseph Stalin.

Stalin, the story goes, was as close to a heart attack as any time in his life on the day he learned about the Manhattan Project, whereby the Americans were on the verge of exploding an atom bomb.

After he had vented his rage on his colleagues and collaborators, who had never given him the slightest idea that this superweapon was even a remote possibility, he decided that the only recourse was to catch up to the Americans as quickly as possible. He called a meeting of the nation's top scientists and asked them for the name of the Soviet scientist most likely to produce a Soviet A-bomb. One of those present, Abram Ioffe, a highly respected physicist, suggested Igor Kurchatov.

"He's an innovator," Ioffe said, "but also highly practical. And he's also a very capable administrator. I think he's the man for the job."

"All right," said Stalin, "let him get started."

Stalin summoned Kurchatov to the Kremlin and told him that he would have unlimited funds and whatever manpower he needed to do the job. He was free to "steal" any scientists he needed from any laboratory in the country. Thousands of German prisoners of war were sent to help build the institute itself. Foreign Soviet spies channeled whatever information they had on the subject directly to the institute, especially from the United States and Great Britain. But not only spies contributed: Western scientists devoted to the cause of communism also provided key information on Western nuclear research. People with names that became historic, or notorious—or both—such as Julius and Ethel Rosenberg, Klaus Fuchs, and Bruno Pontecorvo.

As of 1986, Fuchs, after serving a prison term in Great Britain, was working in East Germany. Pontecorvo, who defected to the Soviet Union in 1950 with his entire family, is at the Joint Institute for Nuclear Research in Dubna, not far from Moscow. He is a member of the Academy of Sciences and a recipient of the Lenin Prize. I met him a number of times when I was working with his son in Dubna, and was very impressed with him. Sometimes when we were talking openly and freely about subjects other than science, I was tempted to ask him what had made him defect. He had been fully aware of the mass purges, the executions, the political prisoners in the Soviet Union, the subjugation of Eastern European countries. But who was I to open old wounds, especially when I knew what his answer would be? He would have told me that all those things were figments of the imperialist imagination. Besides, he would have added, how could he, believing firmly in the ideals of socialism, have managed to live with himself if he had refrained from serving its lofty cause?

Whether or not he has changed his mind today, I cannot

say. Perhaps if he ventures back to Italy, which he is now free to visit since the statute of limitations has run out, someone will question him and perhaps get an honest response. But in a country where lies and dissimulation are standard procedure, one must judge a person not on his actions but on what he refuses to do. And Pontecorvo, to his credit, has always resisted the pressures of his new masters: He has, for example, steadfastly refused to sign petitions against his former colleague Andrei Sakharov, and that cannot have been easy for him.

Stalin was in a frenzy about the American bomb, which hung over him like a sword of Damocles. It was a situation he abhorred, and he made sure the Soviet project progressed as quickly as possible.

One of Kurchatov's close collaborators told me that Stalin had once admitted to the head of the institute that President Harry Truman's nuclear threat was all that had stood between him and settling accounts with "that piece of filth, Marshal Tito."

This same collaborator told me another fascinating story.

Sometime after Kurchatov had given Stalin the list of scientists he wanted for the project, asking the dictator to authorize their departure from the laboratories where they were working, Stalin summoned him to the Kremlin.

"I've gone through this list," he said, "and I have to say that I recognize many of the names on it. I want you to let these people know that had it not been for me, they would never have made your list. Many were on the list of suspects the KGB gave me in 1937. I struck them off. So tell them that for me, and tell them to work doubly hard."

What Stalin had failed to tell Kurchatov was that without any hesitation, he had signed execution orders for many scientists, but his intuition told him to save prominent physicists and chemists. They had been kept out of combat, and, on Stalin's personal orders, spent the war behind the lines in the eastern part of Russia.

Stalin had made the right choice. Kurchatov soon became one of his fair-haired boys. Unlimited funds and manpower were poured into the effort, and not only did the Russians build an

A-bomb, but they also made a hydrogen bomb before the Americans did. The directors of that H-bomb project were named Andrei Sakharov and Igor Tamm.

The idea of working in the shadow of these illustrious elders filled me with elation. I had the feeling that I had at long last entered the mainstream of Russian science.

After Professor Tigrov's invitation, my entrance into the Kurchatov Institute should have been a mere formality. All I was required to do was to pass a physics exam, show proof of my ability to read and write a foreign language, and, of course, give clear indication of my knowledge of the history of the Soviet Communist party.

In order to take these exams, I needed recommendations from the Moscow Physical Engineering Institute, where I had studied. In addition to a recommendation from my science professors, I also needed one from the institute's president, one from the secretary of the party's Marxist-Leninist section, and another from the Komsomol, the organization of Communist youth. The political recommendations were refused. Professor Silantiev of the Marxist-Leninist section checked his records and found that I had missed ninety percent of his lectures. He declared with crushing logic that students like me had no business in the Kurchatov Institute. (In all fairness, I should note that I had found the Marxist-Leninist lectures so boring that I had indeed cut most of the classes.) In any event, with this damning evidence, the chairman of the State Examination Commission who made the final decision on such matters—and who, it goes without saying, was a member of the KGB—decided that he would make up for past errors: He found me an "excellent" post in a laboratory specializing in sewage disposal.

Feeling that I had strong legal grounds to contest that decision, I refused the post. Strong legal grounds because even in the Soviet Union it is forbidden to assign a person with a master's degree in theoretical nuclear physics to a job having nothing to do with his area of specialization.

"You refuse?" said the chairman of the commission. "Then

I have no choice but to turn this over to the public prosecutor. He'll have to decide whether you should be put in prison or given forced labor."

He wasn't joking, but I was not unduly alarmed. Even though the law did provide for such sanctions, they were rarely applied. And I also knew that the chairman was on shaky legal ground. Besides, I had already crossed swords with bureaucrats of his ilk and was less frightened than a neophyte might have been.

I was determined to get those recommendations.

On advice from more experienced hands, I decided to attack the Komsomol first—or, more accurately, the local delegate, of whom it was said that he would sell all of Russia for a bottle of vodka. Several of us took him to a restaurant, got him drunk quickly, and obtained his signature on the recommendations we had written ourselves.

Our next attack was on the bastions of the Marxist-Leninist section. It was decided that I would make the first reconnaissance, and if I were successful, the others in my predicament would follow. One of the section's teachers was named Murzin, a man as innocuous as he was stupid. He delivered his lectures in a whiny voice that all of us mimicked unmercifully. His mind was as threadbare as his clothes, and at times I found him so pathetic I almost felt sorry for him. At the end of each lecture, after he had finished reading his yellow pages of class notes, he would raise his eyes, blink them as if adjusting to the light, sniff the air, and in a whisper ask, his voice poised somewhere between boredom and despair, "Are there any questions?"

It was the signal for bedlam.

"Sir?"

"Yes?"

"What is the Marxist-Leninist doctrine on premarital sex?"

"Well . . . er. . . ."

"Sir? Sir?"

"Lenin termed Trotsky a 'prostitute,' did he not?"

"Well, yes, that is. . . ."

"Are there any other prostitutes on the Central Committee? Or was Trotsky the only whore in the whole lot?"

At each question, Murzin would wipe his eyes (which always ran), cough, and open his mouth to answer—just as another question would zero in on him from the floor.

One day, when he had gone on at great length about how the State would wither away with the advent of true socialism—all of which, it goes without saying, was predicated at some remote and undetermined point in the future—I raised my hand.

"Sir?"

"Yes?"

"Will we live long enough to witness the disappearance of the Communist party from the Soviet Union?"

A sinister hush fell over the class. Everyone turned around and stared at me. Murzin almost fell off the podium. He steadied himself, then grabbed a glass of water and took several sips.

"Let me clarify my question," I said. "If we, as members of the Communist society, reach such a high level of social awareness that the government structure will no longer be necessary, then should it not follow that society will run itself and there will no longer be any need for a Communist party?"

Murzin glanced about wildly, as though looking for some suitable answer from the walls or ceiling, downed the rest of his water, and cleared his throat. But by then, two students were laughing and another produced an ear-piercing whistle. Within seconds, the students had gotten to their feet and broken up into small groups to discuss the question.

I always felt sorry for the little man lost there on the podium, and he seemed to sense my sympathy. On those rare occasions when I attended classes, he would seem to be delivering his lectures solely for me, and, at the end of the school year, when I made a mess of the final exam, confusing dates and names of the various heroes of the October Revolution, he still gave me a passing mark.

I had forgotten all about him until my present predicament brought him back to mind. After having written myself a glowing recommendation and having typed it impeccably, I went in search of Murzin, with the full intention of having him sign it.

The little professor had no authority to sign such a paper; only Silantiev's signature carried any weight with the authorities. But I told Murzin that even though I would have the full blessing of Silantiev, I would deem it a great honor to have his recommendation as well, since I considered him an esteemed and honored Marxist philosopher. I somehow thought of him, I said, as a kind of godfather who had guided me politically into the realm of Soviet science.

With the broadest smile that probably had ever crossed his face, he took pen in hand and signed the paper with a flourish.

I felt slightly ashamed at my duplicity, but I knew that this was not the time for soul searching. It was time to move to Phase Two.

What I needed next was the signature of the party secretary. Since I knew he would never give it to me without Silantiev's signature, subterfuge was my only recourse. I studied the office hours of the president, the secretary, and the assistant secretary of the local party office and discovered that at a certain point in the afternoon the secretary left, putting his assistant in charge. Precisely at that moment, I entered the party office and knocked politely on the assistant secretary's door.

"Come in!"

I blustered in, spread my papers in front of him, and began a rapid-fire monologue.

"These have to be in the president's hands in ten minutes," I said, "and over at the Kurchatov Institute first thing in the morning. It's only a formality. I gather the secretary's not in, so you'll have to sign for him."

The poor assistant secretary almost fell off his chair. He had never laid eyes on me before and had no idea what he was doing or how to handle the situation.

"I can't sign this without the approval of the Marxist-Leninist section," he said.

"Of course. I have it right here," I said, shoving in front of him the paper Murzin had signed. "Please," I said, "the president's waiting."

His eyes ran down the page. "Excellent student . . . great

integrity. . . . Active and morally sound builder of Communist society." How could he go wrong?

"Fine," he said, taking out his pen. He too signed on the dotted line with a flourish.

Two down and one to go. I charged into the office of the president, a man named Kirillov-Ugriumov who was not a bad fellow, and handed him my papers. Seeing that the assistant secretary had signed, he added his name to the lot and handed the document to his aide, who stamped it with the official seal of the Soviet Union.

Later that week, the Academic Council of the Physical Engineering Institute had recommended me for graduate studies.

But bureaucracy had not had its last word.

A few days later, I received a summons to appear before the public prosecutor to whom the KGB officer from the State Examination Commission had given my case when I had refused to accept the job at the sewage disposal laboratory.

I was received by an amiable young man who had the unpleasant task of informing me that I would have to report for sewage disposal duty or suffer the legal consequences.

I produced the papers showing the Academic Council's approval of my graduate studies at the Kurchatov Institute. He looked at them in disbelief.

"These people are crazy! On the one hand they lodge a complaint against you, and then they sign these papers. The whole thing's absurd!" He regained his composure and said, "The only thing I can suggest is that you go see the head of the laboratory to which you have been assigned and have him write us a letter saying he can live without you."

The person in question was a man named Joseph Strizhevsky, whom I telephoned immediately. He listened to my story, then said in a quiet and reassuring voice, "Why don't you come right over."

Strizhevsky is a man I shall remember as long as I live. Utterly suave, and with the long nose of a born strategist, he heard me out, then smiled, placed a hand on my shoulder and said, "Your high aspirations do you credit. Your love of theoretical physics, your desire to collaborate with Professor Tigrov, all that is praiseworthy. The only problem is, I have other plans for you here. I need young physicists of your caliber. For years I've been fighting with the Ministry of Communal Living to send me some people just like you. People who can come up with new ideas. You'll spend the three years required by law to fulfill your State obligations right here with me, then you can go back and work for your Tigrovs and Kurchatovs. But if you have any sense, you'll write your doctoral dissertation here, and if you do, we'll give you such a magnificent laboratory that you'll never want to leave."

His smile made me sick, but I decided to control my temper. "I'll sleep on it," I said, "but I don't think you ought to count on me."

"Whatever you say," he smiled unctuously, "but if you decide against it, we'll see you in court."

We parted coolly. My situation was becoming desperate. My complicated plot with Murzin and the party functionaries had just been shattered.

I was beginning to despair when there occurred one of those unexpected little miracles that can change the course of a life. One of my friends who was getting married introduced me to his future mother-in-law, who turned out to be the personal secretary of Anatoly Aleksandrov, the director of the Kurchatov Institute who later became president of the Academy of Sciences. In fact, she had even worked with Kurchatov himself. In any case, she intervened on my behalf with Aleksandrov, who immediately called the general prosecutor and formally requested that I be left alone. He then called his own personnel department and told them to see that I was admitted to the institute. The next day, he telephoned to congratulate me.

For once, bureaucracy had lost if not a battle, at least a skirmish.

A few months later, I ran into Strizhevsky on the street. His tone was just as oily and his nose just as pointed. He took me by the arm and said effusively, "How nice to see you. And to know you got into the institute. Really . . . you know, you almost got me into a real bind." He shook a finger in my face. "You never told me you had connections in high places. When you failed to show up to work for me, I went to see the director of security at the Kurchatov Institute, a retired KGB general, and I told him about you. Not very nice things, I might add. Told him you refused to work where you'd been assigned by your country. 'This Lopansky,' I said, 'this fellow Loshmansky or whatever his name is wants to worm his way into the institute. I trust you'll take proper measures to keep him out.' 'Don't you worry,' the general told me, 'I'll take care of him.' Well, when I called a few days later to find out what labor camp you'd been sent to, he had ice in his voice. 'I suggest you leave Lozansky alone,' he told me. 'We've accepted him here at the institute.' I couldn't believe my ears. I looked like a fool. But never mind, I'll forgive you if you'll only tell me the name of your friend at the top."

I leaned over and whispered in his ear. "I can't tell you his name, but I can describe him. He's tall and thin, wears glasses, and looks like a crow. That give you a hint?"

His eyes widened in disbelief, for the person I had described was Mikhail Suslov, an arch-Stalinist, chief ideologue of the party, and a member of the Politburo.

"Are you serious?"

"Yes."

"Well, I have to be going," he said, releasing his grip on my arm. And he hurried down the street muttering, "My God! I can't believe it! Mikhail Suslov! Oh, my God!"

It wasn't true, of course, but the "connections" part of my story was. Without it, all my wild stratagems would have been for naught. The old adage "It's not what you know but who you know" may be true in most societies, but in the Soviet Union it's the gospel.

Ironically, not long after I enrolled in the institute, I learned that my friend whose mother-in-law had gone to bat for me had gotten divorced.

It seemed that after all my tribulations in search of an academic career in science, everything would end well. My thesis adviser was a remarkable scientist and a fine man to boot. I made many friends at the institute and loved my work. What more could anyone ask?

When I entered the institute, nuclear weapons research was not the only area in which its scientists were concentrating. My section, the Department of Plasma, studied thermonuclear reactions on a controlled basis. Physicists were attempting to control the fusion of the light nuclei that had led to the production of the hydrogen bomb. If they succeeded, it would mean an almost inexhaustible source of energy, since the fuel is deuterium and tritium, which are isotopes of hydrogen found in vast quantities in water.

It was still only a dream, since there are a number of almost insurmountable obstacles remaining to be hurdled, the foremost of which is that light nuclei can only be fused at incredibly high temperatures—around 100 million degrees centigrade. In the hydrogen bomb, this temperature is attained with the preliminary explosion of an atom bomb. It is theoretically possible for scientists to attain this temperature, but nature provides us with no materials that can withstand such heat, so we cannot construct chambers in which these reactions can occur.

At one point during their leadership of the project, Sakharov and Tamm came up with an ingenious idea. At heat measured in millions of degrees, all matter is in a plasma state—that is, it consists of gases made up of electrons along with nuclei that are not assembled in the usual way into atoms and molecules. Sakharov and Tamm envisaged a special ring-shaped chamber, the center of which would contain a strong magnetic field so that the hot plasma would be compressed in the middle and would not touch the walls.

The idea seemed so promising that a number of countries other than the Soviet Union started building plants based on Kurchatov's Tokamak facility. In due course, a group of scientists from our department analyzed the results of the experiment and came to the conclusion that it was time to move forward from the theoretical to the practical phase of the project.

But a few days later, their hopes were dashed. They found

that within the magnetic field, the plasma contracts to a certain point and no farther. When the pressure reaches a critical point, it produces an explosion that ejects the plasma from the magnetic field and thus burns the chamber walls. The scientists concluded that the problem was a good deal more complex than they had thought, and that only a concerted effort on the part of the world scientific community could solve it.

At an international congress in Geneva in 1956, Kurchatov proposed such a cooperative effort, which most of the delegates accepted. It takes a long time, however, to turn a vote into reality, and it was not until ten years later that foreign scientists, principally British and American, arrived at the Kurchatov Institute of Atomic Energy, a mysterious place isolated from the rest of the world by an immense network of walls topped with barbed wire, and protected by every conceivable kind of electronic security device. As is so often the case in the Soviet Union, however, this ultrasophisticated system was complemented by an ultraprimitive one: A horse continually plowed a strip of land all around the walls of the institute, so that the tracks of any intruder could immediately be detected.

Now, the KGB agents who were trained to pull their guns and assume a position of combat whenever they heard the word *Westerner* were obliged to smile politely at these foreign scientists and wave them through the main gate. I have often wondered how many sleepless nights some of our hard-line staff members must have spent during this period. But they soon came to realize that some benefits were mixed in with the risks: expanded staff, higher pay, better equipment. In my department, for example, the arrival of three British scientists created openings for three more KGB agents, at a time when it was impossible, for budgetary reasons, to hire even one more research assistant.

The number of horses on duty, however, remained the same.

The subject of my thesis was not directly related to the Tokamak project. I was working on an electric discharge theory as part of my investigation into plasma formation in gases. In the course of my research, I found that this theory could be used to explain complex processes that occurred in the chambers especially designed to register elementary particles. After working for three years on this problem and publishing several papers on it, I submitted my thesis for defense to the Joint Institute for Nuclear Research in Dubna.

Around that time, I got married. It was a mistake, which both my wife and I realized almost immediately. We were young, naive, and poor. More important, it became apparent that our goals and aspirations, as well as our priorities, were very different. So we agreed to separate. I will not pretend that our divorce was not painful, for failures are never pleasant, but the fact that we had come to the realization quickly and acted on it almost at once, made it somewhat easier. And, thank God, there were no children.

In the course of those years marked by a sense of well-being and progress in the world of science, a number of political events influenced me enormously.

One was the 1967 Six-Day War in the Middle East, which triggered a campaign of violent anti-Semitism in the Soviet Union and made me realize, once again, my special vulnerability. Then, in 1968, Soviet troops invaded Czechoslovakia, an event that clearly heralded a much harder political line. Indeed, there was considerable speculation at the time that the party was about to put Stalin back on his pedestal.

Because of my youthful experiences with Soviet racism and bureaucracy, I had always been a skeptic, but I had come to what I might call an "accommodation." I had made up my mind that the only enduring and permanent values on this earth were art and science. This conviction wrapped me in a comfortable philosophy. Everything else, especially politics, was vain and empty, and I was glad to leave it to others. Even though I had always sympathized with the dissidents and devoured their clandestine writings, I had never belonged to any active movement or group. However, whenever my country's authorities planned or committed what I considered an outrage at home or abroad,

I never kept my opinion to myself. But such disapproval was only verbal, opinions delivered generally to my fellow students or scientists. I was not alone in this; most people in my situation were not reticent about voicing candid opinions.

Little by little, however, I realized that my easy philosophy was nothing more than an escape valve. It was impossible to hide in my self-made cocoon. An immense feeling of rage and frustration would grip me whenever I heard that some of my fellow citizens had been arrested, though I knew they were innocent of any "crime"; whenever the press, radio, and television would spew forth their anti-Semitic venom; whenever thousands of Russian tanks rolled into a tiny and helpless country like Czechoslovakia. A friend of mine, a Czech physicist who had returned home to Prague after having completed his research with us at the institute, used to write to me frequently. In May 1968, I received an ecstatic letter from him. "We are going through a great, an exhilarating time. For the first time I am going to vote freely for a president. There are *several* candidates. Can you imagine what this means?"

I felt genuinely happy for the Czechs and wished them well. Perhaps if their "revolution" succeeded, it would blow some warm spring air into the frigid climate of the Politburo and make some of its senile leaders sit up and think. How naive could I be! My friend's letters stopped coming. Then one day there was a final letter. "I hate your country, where so many people live like animals. Yet your leaders stick their swinish snouts in everybody else's business and force their own barbaric ways onto civilized people." The letter was unsigned.

I could have dismissed his letter, chalking it up to the shock of the August invasion, and rationalizing that as soon as things settled down, he would take a reasoned view of things. But I didn't. His letter went straight to my heart. And I realized then, if I had not before, that an individual is responsible for the sins and misdeeds committed by his country. At that point, only two solutions seemed possible: flight or fight. Both struck me as impossible. Out of some protective instinct, I hated the notion of getting involved in some sort of political activism. As a result, I felt totally trapped.

A second incident, which occurred toward the end of 1968, proved my undoing. Mikhail Alexandrovich Leontovich, the director of our department's theoretical section, signed a letter addressed to the Central Committee, supporting the people who had demonstrated in Red Square against the invasion of Czechoslovakia. In those days, a number of intellectuals still harbored illusions left over from the Khrushchev era and believed that this kind of political protest could have an effect on the government. As a result, not just scientists but writers, painters, scholars, performing artists, all signed numerous petitions on a wide variety of issues. This period has come to be known as "the era of the signers."

Leontovich was a thoroughly decent and honorable man. The authorities decided to make an example of him. It was time to put a stop to these intolerable petitions. A three-stage anti-Leontovich campaign was set into motion. The whole thing was a masquerade, but nonetheless effective.

Act I: *Leontovich would be obliged to confess his misdeed in the presence of the party activists at the institute.*

Act II: *He would be confronted by the "workers," in this instance the seamstresses at the Trekhgornaya Textile Factory. Fiery speeches had been prepared for them to read from the podium. All these tirades attacked Leontovich, demanding to know how he, as a member of the Academy of Sciences, a man highly paid by the Soviet State, could betray the interests of the workers and peasants, thereby serving the interests of Western imperialists.*

Act III: *The culmination was to take place in public, where the accused would be made to confess and repent, in the purest Stalin tradition.*

I was then working in Leontovich's section, and when I got word of these plans, a number of my colleagues and I decided we should do everything in our power to prevent this wonderful old man from suffering such humiliation. We drew up a strongly worded petition addressed to the party committee of the institute, protesting the harassment of this outstanding scientist. Since all the duplicating machines were under the control of the KGB, we made several carbon copies, which we sent to the other sections of the institute for their approval.

The administration, the party committee, and the KGB were aghast. Never had anything of this sort ever happened at the Kurchatov Institute, this sacrosanct place where the future of the country was being assured. The next day, the party called an emergency meeting of all members of the Department of Plasma. The first secretary of the party, a man named Legasov, was present, together with the local head of the KGB and several members of the administration. Fortunately for us, before the meeting we had managed to collect an impressive number of signatures from well-known scientists, including some who had worked directly with Kurchatov himself. In addition, our petition had been read and approved by the academician Boris Kadomtsev, who at that time was Leontovich's deputy. Because of the depth and breadth of this lineup, the party realized the dangerous possibility of a major scandal, and they were obliged to make a few concessions.

At the meeting, Legasov was calm, almost jocular. Avoiding all mention of Leontovich, he ranged over a wide variety of subjects with unusual candor. When one of our group asked him about the anti-Israel campaign in the press, he smiled smugly and said, "What do you think? That we love the Arabs? Don't be stupid. Why do you think we're spending billions there? For one reason only: oil. We need Arab oil for the satellite countries, my friends, because Russian oil we need for ourselves."

When someone else posed a question about the lack of hard news in the Soviet press, he replied, "What do you want, stories of crime in the streets, rampant alcoholism, poverty and misery? Suppose the press focused on all that. What would it lead to? Nothing but unrest, maybe even rebellion. Is that what you want, gentlemen?"

I must say that Legasov's tactics worked. Taken aback by

the bluntness of his remarks, we didn't know what to say. Then, having won the opening gambit, he announced his concessions. Through his own personal intervention, and that of Aleksandrov, Leontovich would not have to go to the textile factory. On the other hand, his appearance before the party committee could not be canceled, but it would be kept internal. In our theoretical section, only two scientists were party members. They alone would attend the meeting. Later, both were reprimanded for allowing the petition to be written and circulated.

Legasov called Leontovich and ordered him to come to the meeting. The old man refused. "I refuse to relive the purges of 1937," he said. "Settle your own miserable little squabbles among yourselves. I have no intention of getting involved."

One of my colleagues who attended the party meeting reported to me what had gone on. Red-faced and averting his gaze, he said, "It was terrible. Legasov ordered me to say all kinds of abominations about Leontovich . . . and I did. Last night I went home and found it impossible to look my wife and children in the eye. How can I live with myself after that?"

I had no answer.

Two weeks went by, and the tension seemed to have subsided. I assumed the whole episode had been forgotten, but suddenly I received a notice to report to the security office. I was greeted by two men, both of whom were extremely polite. Then I heard a blunt question for which I was not prepared. "Who initiated that petition?" one of them asked.

I mumbled some answer—that I couldn't remember, that it had all happened simultaneously, that several people had had the same idea at the same time. Who they were, I couldn't recall.

"You can't recall? You have a damned poor memory for a physicist. Speaking of which, when is it you're due to defend your thesis?"

I tried to remain calm. "You yourselves realized how pointless it was to take Leontovich to the textile factory," I said quietly, "which implies that you agree with the sense of the petition. Anyway, all that's water over the dam. Let's forget it."

There was a long silence. Then one of the men murmured, "All right. By the way, where do you plan to work after you've defended your thesis?"

"Right here at the institute. My thesis adviser has already offered me a post, and I've accepted."

"Your thesis adviser, eh? That's most interesting. All right, you can go now."

I was upset by that interrogation. What did they have up their sleeves now? But I quickly decided it was a waste of time to worry, and in 1969 I defended my thesis at the Institute for Nuclear Research at Dubna. In Russia, three external examiners are named to the panel, and, after questioning me for several hours, all three gave me a positive evaluation, with honors.

It was over.

The following day I received several phone calls from a number of laboratories and institutes, offering me jobs at twice my salary at Kurchatov. The man from the Electro-Technical Institute even offered to put me in full charge of a laboratory. I refused them all, without hesitation. Nothing could have made me move from my post at the Kurchatov Institute, which I found both challenging and exhilarating. To my mind, the privilege of working alongside such men as Tigrov, Leontovich, and other giants of Soviet science far outweighed any other considerations.

Once again I had to change my tune.

After due consideration, the institute's personnel department turned me down, doubtless because of the Leontovich petition. The official reason was: no openings. Period.

It seemed that I had no choice but to call the Electro-Technical Institute. The man who had offered me the job gave me a grand tour and showed me my future laboratory. I was then taken to the personnel department, where I filled out all the forms. The director recommended that I be hired as a senior scientist, at a remarkably high salary compared to what I received at Kurchatov. I felt like a young gigolo being married off to a rich widow.

My remorse was short-lived. The director phoned me a few days later. "I've just had a big fight with my personnel department," he said. "I'm afraid they're dead set against your coming here. What in the world could they have against you?"

"I have no idea. Maybe you should ask the party assholes."

"I'm really sorry. I was looking forward to having you here."

I began calling all those who had made me offers after my thesis. Each time the scenario was the same. "Great idea. Come right over." Tour and form-filling. "Very sorry. Our personnel department has turned thumbs down."

Two months went by, two terrible months. Clearly the KGB was taking a special interest in my case. The combination of negatives finally got to me: my divorce, my inability to find a job, my lack of money, and even no roof over my head. I roamed the streets of Moscow like a dog with rabies. Then one day I realized I was on the verge of a nervous breakdown. In desperation, I picked up the phone and called an English physicist who was working at Kurchatov on an exchange program. I asked him if he could arrange a meeting for me at the British Embassy. The Englishman hardly sounded enthusiastic, and I knew I was putting him on the spot, since it could jeopardize his status, but I remained adamant.

Soviet citizens are formally forbidden from entering any foreign embassies. Stationed outside each embassy is a militiaman, a person particularly adept at remembering faces. If he suspects that the visitor is a Soviet citizen, he can ask to see his papers and arrest him on the spot. I knew all that. But still I was determined to take the chance.

Flanked by the British physicist and his wife, I approached the embassy. The militiaman made no move to stop me, although he looked at me intently.

Inside, the consul, a Mr. Banks, received me coolly but politely. He rose from his chair and asked what he could do for me.

Actually, I wasn't quite sure, but I blurted out, "I want to go to England."

He looked at me even more closely, as if to make sure he was not dealing with a madman.

"Why England?" he asked.

A good question, for which I had no ready answer.

"Because," I said at last, "because England has always been for me the country of democracy and freedom."

Mr. Banks looked at me pityingly. He was still not quite sure whether he was dealing with a lunatic or an idiot. Still, he was obliged to do his duty. He took out some paper and began asking me questions, noting my answers. He said he would transmit the request to London, where he was sure it would be given careful consideration. The nature of his reply gave me reason to hope. We shook hands warmly at the door; in parting, I launched a mild joke. "See you in Piccadilly," I said.

He smiled wanly, gave me a sympathetic look, and turned to go inside.

My English friends had long since departed from the embassy. How was I going to leave discreetly? There was no choice but to walk out with my head held high. At the gate stood two militiamen. I strode past them. They studied me closely but made no effort to stop me. I wasted no time leaving them behind.

On an impulse, I stopped in a store and bought a map of Europe. I sat down on a bench and began studying it, still caught up in the crazy idea of finding some way to get across the border. The chances were less than minimal. The Finns, I knew, sent refugees back across the frontier. Going to Norway was about as practical as going to the North Pole. Turkey seemed more likely. For a fleeting moment, I considered calling my ex-wife and asking her to go with me. I had the notion that with a pretty woman on my arm, I could con some ship's captain into taking us as stowaways. As I said, I was pretty far around the bend.

I'm sure I would have undertaken some crazy action had I not received a call from the head of one of the laboratories at the Institute of Nuclear Physics at Moscow University. He offered me a job. "It's only temporary," he said, "but that way we don't have to clear anything with the KGB. We can keep you for a year, by which time I'm sure you will have found something permanent."

How could I have had such good luck at such an opportune moment? Then I learned how.

"By the way," the man said, "you can thank Leontovich. He arranged everything."

When it rains it pours. Within days I had also found, thanks to the mother of a former student, a lovely room in Starokoniushenny Lane, just across from School 59.

Slowly I resurfaced and began seeing old friends and acquaintances.

All this happened in the late 1960s, and many of us sensed that the country was on the brink of major changes. Moscow was filled with rumors about letters of protest signed by the most prominent names in science, literature, and the arts. The bottle that Khrushchev had uncorked was being sipped by a lot of people, and there was a tang of hope in the air. The Russian leaders were appalled by it, and were not quite sure how best to recork the bottle.

Almost every day, a group of us met in someone's apartment to drink and talk and exchange the latest antigovernment stories. It's not even peculiarly Soviet; it's an old Russian habit. Any time there is a party, however small, politics is the center of discussion.

We all exchanged opinions with remarkable freedom. In our group were not only scientists but also psychologists, philosophers, writers, and theater people. They helped me to articulate and clarify my own thoughts, and I came to realize more and more that the political system was not only ruining Russian agriculture and industry but also destroying the political, cultural, and intellectual life of the country. It was not all the fault of the Soviets: The roots went deep, but what the October Revolution and the regimes that succeeded it had done was to create the conditions under which everything most base, trivial, and absurd in Russian traditions was allowed to flourish and prosper.

They would discourage all that was good in man and foster what was bad.

Years later, when KGB agents confronted me, they quoted long passages from the discussions we had had during those heady days.

Once again, there had been a traitor in our midst.

2
Tatiana

Word of my success with the students at School 59 had spread throughout Moscow. Many parents used to call me to ask whether I would tutor their son or daughter, to help them prepare for their university entrance exams. Since I did not now need the money and tutoring didn't interest me, inevitably I refused. One woman, however, was more stubborn than the rest. She was so insistent that finally I said, "All right, madam, bring your son down for a little talk."

"It's a daughter. . . ."

"All right, bring your daughter."

Several days later, shortly after four o'clock, my doorbell rang. I opened the door, and what I saw I can describe only as a vision. I remained there like the village idiot—my mouth open, my arms dangling helplessly at my sides, dumbfounded, flabbergasted, speechless. A vision? No, a miracle. It was her smile that first caught my attention. Then her gray eyes, her soft, fair hair, her face with cheeks slightly flushed. And her smile—it was the most beautiful smile I had ever seen. I stood transfixed, and finally this miracle could endure the village idiot no longer, and she broke out laughing.

"Hello. My name is Tatiana Kozlova. I've come for tutoring with Professor Lozansky. Is your father in?"

"But . . . but I'm Professor Lozansky."

"You? My mother told me I would be studying with a famous professor. I . . . I guess I expected an older man."

I pulled myself together and asked, with as much dignity as I could muster, "Does that mean you're disappointed?"

"No. Why should I be? All that matters is that you're a good teacher."

"Well, do come in. Let's get started."

The hour went by in a flash. Tatiana was looking at her watch and saying the lesson was over. All I could think of was that there was no way I was going to let this creature leave so soon. But all I could manage to sputter was, "Let's go on for a while longer. I can spare the time."

"But I can't," she laughed. "People are waiting for me. But I'll be back soon."

"May I conclude," I said portentously, feeling for all the world like some crazy old man courting a girl far too young for him, "that you approve of my tutoring?"

"Yes, indeed. You explain even the very complicated things very clearly and simply." She laughed brightly.

"Thank you. May I expect you tomorrow?"

"No, not tomorrow, but in three days."

"Three days? But why wait so long?"

Again she laughed and left, just like that, taking every bit of light and life with her, as though she had never been in the room.

I closed the door behind her, not daring to look out and see who might be waiting for her—some dandy, no doubt, with an English suit and a car. As for me, what did I have? A temporary room and a temporary job. Plus a fat file with the KGB. I bet that young jerk picking her up had no KGB file. And a father in some high position. Damn him. I was already jealous, insanely jealous, and I had only known her for one hour.

Again I figured I must be cracking. *Look, fellow,* I told myself, *a girl like that's not for the likes of you. Forget her. Anyway, you're ten years older than she is.*

Easy words.

The next three days were the longest I had ever spent. I could do nothing except pace the floor of my room. No, I did do a couple of other things. I went to one of the best barbers in Moscow and got a proper haircut. And I bought myself some new shirts.

Please don't let her cancel, please make her come, I said over and over again, as though that magic incantation would have an effect.

At the appointed hour on day three, the doorbell rang. Haircut, new shirt. She noticed all right, but made no comment, unless her slightly raised eyebrows were a sign of approbation.

"I'd like to work a little longer today, if you don't mind, Edward Dmitrievich," she said. "Does that pose any problem?"

"No, no, of course not. Three hours. Four, perhaps?"

She laughed, and it was a knife stab in my poor heart. "I meant only an extra half hour," she said.

Even the idea of that extra half hour sent waves of elation through me, and suddenly I realized—I'll never figure out why it had taken so long for me to understand—that I was simply madly, hopelessly in love with Tatiana Kozlova.

From then on, I lived from one lesson to the next, waiting impatiently for those twice-a-week afternoons when my doorbell would ring and life would begin again.

She was an apt student, and she solved the problems I gave her with increasing ease. Soon we became friends, and Tatiana would sometimes stay after the lesson to talk and listen to music.

One day she arrived with a bag of groceries. I thought nothing of it, assuming her parents had asked her to pick up some things along the way. But at the end of the lesson, she asked me where the kitchen was. I showed her the little corner where, behind a curtain, there was a gas burner. She put on an apron, checked to see what pots and pans were available, began taking the food out of the bag, and sent me out to buy some spices. When I came back, the table was set and the room was awash with wonderful aromas. She stirred some of the spices into the wonderful dish she had concocted, and we sat down to dinner.

The proverbial fly on the wall would have looked upon us

as the perfect young Russian couple—which was all I was dreaming of. But I had learned the hard way that it's best not to dream. I was afraid of frightening her away, of saying something that would cause her never to return. And yet I knew that she did like me, that her feelings for me transcended those of a student for a professor. That realization filled me with joy, but it also filled me with an abiding terror. How could I aspire to such a creature? What could I offer her except a dreary existence compared to the kind she had every right to expect? Wasn't I sure to make her unhappy?

There was no other way: I had to put an end to this relationship before it went too far. I would call her mother and inform her that I could no longer tutor Tatiana. My work at the university had become more demanding; my outside commitments no longer allowed me enough time to tutor. Anything. A simple telephone call and all would be over. One simple call. And yet I felt myself incapable of making it. I also felt myself incapable, despite my resolutions, of talking to Tatiana. Each time after she left, I said to myself, *Next time she comes, I'll speak to her.* But every time I opened the door again and saw her smile, all my resolutions went up in smoke.

If only I had been able to find a job that would have guaranteed me real independence, that would have offered me the opportunity to give Tatiana a decent life. Another dream. There was no place for me in the Soviet Union. There never would be.

If only I could take this wonderful girl with me to England, to America, to France, to any country where personnel departments were not all-powerful. . . .

To leave or not to leave. That was not really the question, for leaving was quite out of the question. They would never allow me to leave the country. My only attempt, simply to travel to another satellite country, had ended in failure. While I had been working at the Kurchatov Institute, I had sent a paper to the organizing committee of an international conference on ionized gases that was being held in Bucharest. As a result, I had been invited to attend the meeting. Armed with the official invitation, I went to the foreign section of the institute and requested permission to leave the country for a few days to attend the conference. Two months later, my request was denied, without explanation. I went to plead my case with the director of our section, the academician Lev Artsimovich, who interceded on my behalf. The response was that the budget allocated for the Soviet delegation was too small to allow for another person. "Otherwise," the reply went, "we'd be only too happy to accede to Edward Lozansky's request." At that point I proposed paying for my own trip. All right, that might be possible. Please fill out all the following forms, including medical certificates, photographs, and other documents. It took a month to get all my papers together. The conference was scheduled for August. By June I had heard nothing. When I called the secretary of the foreign section of the institute for an update, she responded coldly that she had no idea who I was or what I was talking about. For a week I tried to reach the head of the foreign section, without success. As a last resort, I went to his office and camped out, swearing to his secretary that I would not leave until he had seen me. Finally he agreed to see me . . . for a few minutes. He seemed confused and upset.

"I don't understand what has happened. Your file must have been misplaced," he said.

That was one of their favorite ploys. But I took him at his word. Two weeks later, I had reconstituted the entire "lost file" and given it to him—only a month before the conference was slated to begin.

To make sure my file was not lost a second time, I telephoned every day for the next three weeks. August arrived, and still I had no reply. Eventually, perhaps because they couldn't bear to receive another phone call from me, the functionaries of the department prevailed on the director to grant me a hearing. A secretary showed me into his office, saying that he would be with me in a few minutes. I saw my file on his desk. I opened it and read: "In reply to your request, this is to inform you that we regard Edward Lozansky's voyage to Bucharest as undesirable."

I saw no point in waiting. I took out a piece of paper and wrote a message on it, which I left on top of the file folder. It

said simply, "Go fuck yourself." In English. Unsigned. Then I
left the office. The secretary saw me leaving and said, "Where
are you going? He'll be with you in just a few moments."

"Tell him I'm busy and can't wait. Tell him, too, that he's
already two minutes late, and if there's one thing I can't bear,
it's people who are late. I suggest he be more punctual next
time."

Thus ended my first "trip" to Bucharest.

When I related my story to Artsimovich, he smiled and said
compassionately, "Don't worry. That same thing happened to
me, only worse. I was supposed to take the plane. Everything
had been arranged. I had my passport and plane ticket. Even a
few dollars that had been allotted to me. I was actually *on* the
plane when a voice came over the loudspeaker saying, 'Comrade
Artsimovich is requested to disembark and report immediately
to the documents desk.' When I did, they confiscated all my
papers and my trip was canceled. Yet I'm an academician, not
simply a graduate student like you, Edward, with all due respect. . . ."

He was right.

Thus my dream of taking Tatiana abroad, to some free country, wherever it might be, was only that: a mad illusion.

I still could not bring myself to speak to Tatiana about my concerns. We were spending more and more time together, going
to the theater, the cinema. Once I was able to get tickets for
the Vakhtangov Theater, where they were playing a melodrama
entitled *Warsaw Melody*. I stood outside the theater with a little
bunch of flowers in my hand, trying to spot Tatiana as she arrived. A black Volga automobile pulled up to the curb. The door
opened and I saw Tatiana emerge, after which the car pulled
away.

I had a sinking feeling: Ordinary Russian citizens do not run
around in chauffeured black Volgas. I took that car to be a sign,
a symbol of the impossibility of our situation. *So she's one of
them,* I thought. *I must put an end to all this. Before it's too
late.*

But Tatiana was not privy to my dark thoughts. She ran up

to me, took my little bouquet, and kissed me on both cheeks. She looked radiant. That kiss sealed my fate. Nothing would ever come between us. Nothing.

And yet I couldn't refrain from asking, "Is that your car?"

"No, Edward Dmitrievich," she said. She had been calling me that for a year, despite my efforts to make her adopt less formal usage. "After all," she would say, "you *are* my professor. We must respect protocol." In any case, she responded to my loaded question with a dismissive wave of her hand, saying that the car belonged to some friends. Whether it was true, or whether her feminine intuition made her realize that the accursed Volga could become a cloud over us, I do not know. But I immediately put the car out of my mind.

During the performance, I took Tatiana's hand in mine. She made no attempt to withdraw it.

The play was about a Polish singer who was studying at the Moscow Conservatory, where she fell in love with a young Russian. War broke out, and he was shipped off to the front, where he fought bravely and returned home with a chest full of medals. He and the Polish student, who had waited faithfully for him all those years, decided to get married. But no: Soviet law forbade marriages between Russians and foreigners. Brokenhearted, she returned home to Warsaw.

Twenty years go by. The Polish student has become a famous singer. Her Russian boyfriend has also attained a prominent position. One day his work takes him to Poland, where with some trepidation he decides to call her. Both are married and have families, but it is clear as they evoke their youthful times together that their love has never died.

A real tearjerker. But Tatiana and I followed their every word as though their story were our own. At one point, I saw a tear trickling down Tatiana's cheek.

After the play, as we walked along the sidewalk from the theater, Tatiana said, "I don't understand why they didn't fight for their love. They could have told their story to the press, gone to the party regional committee to plead their cause. . . ."

I stopped, turned to face her, and kissed her tenderly several times.

"What about you?" I asked. "If you were separated from the man you loved, would you fight?"

"You bet your life I would," she said.

Neither of us had any idea how prophetic that brief exchange was, how many battles we would have to fight in the years to come.

We walked and walked, stopping at every corner to kiss, and by the time we had reached her house, it was 1 A.M.

"Your mother is going to be furious," I said.

"No, she won't. She's not home. She and my father went to Kiev, so I'm alone with my grandmother."

"Are they on vacation?"

"No. My father's in the army and has just been assigned to Kiev. We will be moving there as soon as I've finished my studies."

My heart skipped a beat. "Kiev? You're moving to Kiev? Not if I have anything to say about it. Tatiana, I'm not going to let you leave. You're going to Moscow University, and you might as well know it right now."

"Really?" she said, smiling broadly. "That's wonderful news. I can't wait to call my mother and say that Edward Dmitrievich intends to kidnap me!"

I couldn't bear to let her go inside. I kissed her, then kissed her again. Finally, she pulled away and said, "Edward Dmitrievich, I don't know what's come over you. If you don't stop, I'll begin to believe you're trying to seduce me."

And so saying, she turned and ran up the steps into her house.

Spring came, and I was still working "temporarily" at the Institute of Nuclear Physics. There was still no sign on the horizon of anything permanent.

One day a friend called and asked if the idea of going to Vladivostok interested me. There were plans afoot to open a Far East branch of the Academy of Sciences there. The salary was good, an apartment would be included—perks to try and tempt scientists to that remote city, which was as far from Moscow as New York is.

"Call the chairman of the geography department of Moscow University," my friend said. "Kapitsa's his name. He's the son of Peter Kapitsa, the Nobel Prize physicist. I've already spoken to him about you, and he's interested."

The possibility of having a real job in an institute, of occupying a real apartment, seemed very tempting, even though it would be at the end of the world. I sensed that this was a turning point in my life and realized I had to apprise Tatiana of the situation and let her decide for herself where we stood. I decided to write her a letter and tell her about everything, including my marriage and divorce. I spared no detail, revealing the truth about the precarious nature of my position at the institute, and added that in a few weeks, when my year was up, I might well be destitute. I also told her about my plans for possibly leaving Russia, going to England or the United States. I told her that I was madly in love with her but that I did not want to ruin her life, and I suggested that it would probably be best if she forgot me. The only thing I did not mention was the possible job offer in Vladivostok. It had never occurred to me that she would agree to go with me to the end of the earth, and I had made up my mind to go there alone in the event she did break off our relationship. If nothing else, I had the impression it would be easier to slip across the border to freedom from there than it would be from western Russia.

I concluded by saying that at a specified time I would be sitting on our favorite bench near the university. "If you do not come, I will understand," I wrote. "I'll know that it's all over between us and that we'll never see each other again."

I walked to the bench like an automaton, scarcely able to see or think. I was prepared to wait there for some time. I hadn't determined how long—maybe an hour, maybe forever.

No more than a minute after I had sat down, a pair of delicious hands covered my eyes. She had come! We kissed and burst into tears, laughing and crying at the same time. We both had the feeling we had just invented love.

When at last we had come to our senses, I looked at her and asked if she realized what it really meant if she joined her fate to mine.

"Of course I do," she said. "I also believe that virtue is rewarded. You'll find work. And we'll live happily ever after."

In a bantering tone, I said, "And just suppose I found work in . . . say, Vladivostok. Would you come with me?"

I expected one of her lighthearted answers to which I had grown accustomed over the past year, but her murmured response went right to my heart.

"Do you really want me to come with you?" she asked.

"With all my heart."

"Then I'll come. I'll talk to my parents about it. After all, there is a university at Vladivostok."

I felt as though every burden I was bearing, every worry and concern, had fallen away in a second. It was the most intense moment of happiness I had ever felt.

The following day I called Kapitsa, who agreed to see me immediately. I had an hour-long conversation with him, during which he painted a glowing picture of life at the other end of the world. He said that he had checked into my record and that the responses had been uniformly enthusiastic. Within a short time after my arrival, I would have my own laboratory.

As I was preparing to leave, he handed me a bunch of forms to fill out. I noticed he gave a quick glance at the *Nationality* line, but he made no comment. Could it be that that was not a problem out there on the edge of the Sea of Japan? Or was it possible that this was the way the authorities cleared undesirable elements out of Moscow? In any case, Kapitsa promised to call me within a month.

Anna Ivanovna Kozlova arrived back in Moscow from Kiev for a short stay, and Tatiana arranged for us to meet at their apartment. It was a large, tastefully furnished place, with no sign of ostentation. A comely woman of forty or so, Anna Ivanovna exuded energy and ambition. I sensed that if indeed there is a woman behind every successful man, she undoubtedly had had a great deal to do with her husband's success. She seemed determined to attack the successive rungs of the Soviet hierarchy, to move up the social ladder, and above all to make sure she never slipped back. I had a feeling she did not know the word *hesitation*, and that she had never experienced anguish in her life.

Like her daughter, Anna Ivanovna's hair was blond. Her smile, which was forthright, had none of the charm of Tatiana's.

Our first contact was all positive. She was impressed that I was a physicist. If the thought of my "nationality" crossed her mind, I had no sense of it. I told her my parents lived in Kiev, and the coincidence that her husband had just been assigned there somehow brought us closer together. It turned out that they would be living on the same street my parents did, and that Tatiana's younger brother, Mitya, was in the same class as my nephew Dima. After all this small talk, I took a deep breath and plunged ahead. "Anna Ivanovna," I said, "I would like to ask for your daughter's hand in marriage. I love her very much and have reason to believe she loves me too. We want to marry and plan to move to Vladivostok, where I have been offered a good job. Tatiana can enroll in the university there."

My words had come streaming out, and, as suddenly as it had begun, the torrent stopped. I knew that, despite all the pleasantries we had exchanged, there was a serious social gulf between us. Everything about her, from the way she looked and dressed to the apartment where we were conversing, bespoke that difference. My new shirts had proved less sturdy than I had hoped, and I knew that if she looked closely, she would see that the collar was slightly frayed. She was so poised, and I knew my scars of past battles must have showed at some point during our exchanges. As the seconds ticked by, I knew that her response would be polite, for she clearly had good breeding, but I also knew that it could only be negative.

I was totally wrong. Anna Ivanovna's eyes widened as she heard my declaration, her face seemed to freeze for a moment, then she burst into tears.

Her daughter rushed over to her and tried to console her. "Mama, please don't! There's no need to cry!" But she appeared inconsolable. When at last she raised her head, her cheeks were streaked with mascara.

"Please forgive me," she said. "I've just realized that Tatiana is no longer a child. She's become a woman. It also means my own youth is past—without my ever being aware of it. We've led such a peripatetic life that I somehow never noticed how quickly time has gone by. And here we are, my husband and I, heading toward our golden years."

I found her words somewhat incongruous, for she was a handsome woman in the prime of life. "How can you talk like that?" I said. "You're a young woman. You have your whole life ahead of you. After all, Tatiana's still only a child, so you shouldn't think of yourself as old."

I wished I could have taken back that last sentence, but it was too late.

"You're right," she said. "Tatiana *is* only a child. Eighteen is very young to get married. Why are you in such a hurry?"

I tried to worm my way out of it. "Of course we could wait," I said, "but my departure for Vladivostok is imminent, which is what precipitated matters."

"But why are you leaving? I understand you have a very good job right here in Moscow."

So Tatiana had told her nothing. I glanced at her, and she simply gave a slight shrug. I smiled even more broadly. "I could, of course, stay in Moscow, but the opportunity in Vladivostok is hard to turn down. I'll have my own laboratory, which would take me years to achieve here."

The argument seemed to hit home. As the wife of an army officer, she understood the need to go wherever the opportunities for advancement lay.

"I don't know quite what to say," she murmured. "I think this is something you should discuss with my husband next time he's in Moscow."

I breathed a sigh of relief. At least I could conclude that Anna Ivanovna was not *a priori* against the idea of her daughter marrying a physicist of well-known origins. The absence of racism was reassuring in a woman of her background and station. I left, feeling more hopeful than when I had arrived. I hoped that we could move ahead with her parents' blessing. But I also knew that even without it, Tatiana would never change her mind.

Tatiana graduated and needed to apply to a university. But which one? I still had not heard from Kapitsa, so I advised Tatiana to apply to Moscow University and transfer to Vladivostok later. By now we were inseparable, which apparently Anna understood, and she suggested I move in with Tatiana and her grandmother in the Leninsky Prospekt apartment. I was flattered by the suggestion, but I thought it prudent to decline.

In September, Tatiana began her studies at Moscow University. I still had not heard from Kapitsa, and when I tried to reach him, his office told me he was in Vladivostok. I wrote and urged him to expedite matters.

Tatiana and I had only one desire: to go down to the Marriage Registration Bureau and fill out all the forms. But we wouldn't do that until we had her father's consent.

At last the mysterious army officer arrived in Moscow and immediately invited me to dinner.

Armed with a bottle of Cognac and two bouquets of flowers—one for Anna and one for Tatiana—I rang the Kozlovs' doorbell. Tatiana answered. The apartment was filled with wonderful aromas of cooking, together with the smell of wax and military uniforms. Through the half-open door to the living room I could hear laughter and the murmur of conversation—mostly men's voices, which put me on my guard. I took off my coat, and, as I was about to hang it up, I saw the coat rack filled with military coats, all bedecked with stripes and medals. High-ranking coats. My mouth went dry. So Father was not just an army officer. He was a goddamned general! Tatiana had never mentioned it. And I had never thought to ask. All right, I thought, let's go face the music.

At that point the door opened, and General Kozlov appeared. I was surprised at how young he was. Certainly under fifty. Stocky, his dark hair close cropped, he had a strong, square-jawed face. He extended his hand and said, "I'm delighted to meet you." He struck me as open and friendly and unpretentious. He ushered me into the living room and introduced me to his guests. In addition to Anna and his mother, there were three other generals, all older than he.

"This is the young man," the grandmother said. She, unlike

Anna Ivanovna, made no attempt to conceal her peasant origins.

The generals, resplendent in their uniforms, rose to greet me. I bowed. Is that what one does to generals? Aside from Sasha Polyakov's parents, I had never been in such exalted company. I felt stiff, timid, and slightly on my guard. But they quickly put me at ease. Tatiana's father offered me a glass of vodka and proposed a toast, and everyone relaxed. Even me.

"Have you heard the latest?" the youngest of the three older generals began. I realized they had been telling jokes before I arrived. "Brezhnev has fallen in love."

"With whom?" another general asked.

"A young girl who's leading him on without ever letting him touch her. Brezhnev is going crazy. He keeps making her insane proposals. Finally he says, 'I'll give you anything you want. Just name it.' She pauses for a moment and says, 'Anything?' 'That's right, anything.' 'All right,' she says, 'then open up the borders.' 'Ah,' says Brezhnev, 'I always knew you wanted to stay here alone with me.' "

They all roared with laughter. The oldest general was holding his sides. He fished out a notebook and a pencil. "That one I'll have to remember," he said.

I couldn't believe my ears. Russian generals telling jokes. Russian generals with senses of humor. More jokes were told, more vodka poured. Tatiana's father seemed in especially fine form. I felt pretty good myself. I downed another swig of vodka and said to the oldest general, "I know a pretty good joke."

"Go ahead. Let's hear it."

"Some children were visiting the museum and paused in front of a painting entitled *Lenin in Poland*." The name *Lenin* had a magical effect, and everyone fell silent. I went on with my story with all eyes fixed on me.

"The painting portrayed a tent with two pairs of feet sticking out. Underwear was strewn about all around the tent. One of the children asked the guide who the feet on the right belonged to. 'They belong to Nadezhda Krupskaya, Lenin's wife,' the guide said. 'And what about the feet on the left?' the other child asked. 'Those feet,' the guide said, 'belong to Comrade Dzerzhinsky, the head of the secret police.' 'Excuse me,' said the first child, 'where is Lenin?' 'Can't you read, child?' the guide said, pointing to the title, 'Lenin's in Poland.' "

The general with the notebook laughed loudly, but no one else did. Throughout my story, Tatiana had been trying desperately to catch my attention, shaking her head and making various signs for me to desist, but I was enjoying myself too much to notice. Suddenly I realized what a terrible mistake I had made. The silence was so thick you could have cut it with a saber. Grandmother was coughing. Kozlov was looking at me through narrowed eyes. And I could see Tatiana biting her lips.

"Let's have another," the old general was saying, his shoulders still shaking with laughter.

Now it was my turn to laugh. Then I smiled brightly at my glum-looking public. So I made a blunder. So what? What did I care about these generals? I was going to marry Tatiana and leave for Vladivostok. That was all that mattered. The hell with propriety. The hell with Russian generals. I was ready to take on the whole damned army, the world if necessary.

Kozlov touched me on the sleeve.

"Come," he said, "it's time for us to have a little man-to-man talk."

I followed him into his study, feeling not at all meek or afraid. Rather cocky, in fact.

The general got right to the point. "Tell me more about your work," he said, "your present situation."

"It's not exactly what I would call brilliant," I said, deciding to level with him. "I'm going to have to leave Moscow for Vladivostok."

"Why Vladivostok? There must be plenty of opportunities in Moscow."

"That may be so, but not for me."

"What does that mean?"

"It means I have good contacts, excellent references, and terrible relations with personnel departments."

"Judging from the jokes you tell, I think I may know what the problem is."

"I'm not the only one to tell such jokes."

"I know, I know. In Russia today, too many people talk first and think afterward. . . . Where will you live?"

"They promised me an apartment in Vladivostok."

"And if Vladivostok doesn't come through?"

"I haven't the foggiest notion. But in that case, General, you needn't worry. I'd feel that I had no right to ask Tatiana to marry me."

Kozlov paced the floor for a minute or so, then looked me straight in the eye.

"If you were to become a party member instead of spending your time telling jokes, maybe you wouldn't have to go to Vladivostok."

I gaped at him in disbelief. Me? Join the party? I wouldn't have been more taken aback if he had asked me to go up in the next space shot.

He saw my consternation and said, "What's so wild about that? You're a grown-up. By the way, how old are you?"

"Twenty-nine."

"Eleven years older than Tatiana. That's a lot."

"She doesn't think so."

"What does she know? She's still only a child."

"What do you mean by that?"

Our conversation was moving onto slippery ground. I wanted to end it before I turned an ally into an enemy. Again I decided to opt for candor.

"Listen, Pyotr Ivanovich. I want very much to be on good terms with you, and I'd appreciate your hearing me out. I love your daughter, and I'll do everything in my power to make her happy. Since I can't do that in Moscow, I decided to try my luck in Vladivostok, where I may have a real opportunity. Tatiana has made up her mind to go with me. We ask nothing of you, and I hope that you will not ask anything impossible of us."

He raised an eyebrow. "Have I asked you for anything?"

"No, that's true. But you've asked me to do something I can't—namely, to join the party."

"So what? Any schoolboy will tell you that if you want to make it in this society, you'd better join the party."

"The party can't help me reach my goals."

"Nonsense! If you were a party member, you'd find work in a second. Your own laboratory. Right here in Moscow. And within a few years, you'd be the head of some institute."

"But even assuming what you say is right, how could I ever become a party member when the KGB is making sure nobody will even employ me?"

"Let me handle that. Just stop telling off-color political jokes denigrating Lenin and keep your nose out of politics. Focus on your physics or mathematics, whatever it is, and stop meddling in things that don't concern you. Leave politics to the idiots!"

I couldn't help thinking that the general's philosophy and attitude toward the political system was not all that different from mine. There was also a basic contradiction in what he said, which I couldn't refrain from pointing out to him.

"How can you advise me on the one hand to stay out of politics," I asked, "and on the other suggest I join the party? If I became a party member and went to meetings, I would feel obliged to give my opinion on all sorts of matters."

"Maybe so," he said, "but follow the herd. A lot of party members almost never attend meetings."

"In other words, you're suggesting I say things I don't really believe, and applaud all kinds of stupidities?"

"Once a month, that's not a big deal."

"The problem is, if I were to join the party as you suggest, I would be unable to make Tatiana happy."

"What do you mean by that?"

"I would become another man, a man she would neither love nor respect."

"I see. . . . So we're all shits, and you're a saint."

"No, but you have your convictions and I have mine. That's all I mean."

We were turning in circles, getting nowhere. I got up to leave without having said what I came for, which was to ask formally for his permission to marry Tatiana. But the propitious moment had passed, and it would be awkward if not impossible to do so now.

Tatiana accompanied me to the door. "Don't worry," she said, "everything will turn out all right."

I wasn't so sure.

A few days later, a tearful Tatiana came to tell me that her father had returned to Kiev, and before his departure, he had pronounced himself against the marriage until such time as I had joined the party.

"Tell him you'll do it," she pleaded. "It's not all that important. It doesn't mean you have to believe in Marxism or all those other stupidities. Do you think my father does? Of course not. But he has to go along with it because of his career. Can't you see that?"

"No," I said, more dryly and loudly than I had intended, "I'm afraid I don't."

Tatiana looked at me in amazement. It was the first time I had raised my voice to her. She began to cry. I took her in my arms and asked her forgiveness. She smiled through her tears.

"You know what I think?" she said. "I think we should go down to the Marriage Registration Bureau and fill out all the forms. Once we start things rolling, no one will try to stop them. And besides, if Kapitsa ever writes to say that the job has come through and we have to leave right away, there won't be any delay."

What she said made a great deal of sense. We went down to the Leninsky Prospekt and duly requested the marriage forms. As they handed them to us, they told us that there was a long waiting list, hundreds of couples, and that we should not expect our turn to come before the following February. *In Russia*, I thought, *you even have to stand in line to get married!*

The long-awaited letter from Kapitsa arrived two weeks later. It said that he was still doing his best to find a job for me as promised, but that for the moment there were simply no openings. Period. Meanwhile, my contract in Moscow would run out in a month. It seemed to me there was nothing to do but climb to the thirty-second floor of Moscow University and jump.

This latest blow was almost as hard for me as my rejection at Moscow University. I locked myself in for several days, refusing to answer the phone, brooding and fuming. Finally I brought myself to write Tatiana. I told her that my Vladivostok job had fallen through and thus I did not feel I had any right to marry her. I released her from her promise and closed by saying that I hoped that she would find someone else who could make her happy.

I went out to mail the letter, the first time I had been out in almost a week. It was late December, and the feeling of the approaching New Year was in the air—a time of warm hearths, exchanges of special greetings, good cheer. Even though it was very cold, there was bright sunshine. I should have felt renewed and reinvigorated. The sunshine and the laughter of children throwing snowballs at one another should have had a therapeutic effect. But they did not. I wandered through the streets, tossed a few snowballs at some kids, and eventually crept back home, feeling miserable. Nothing seemed to matter anymore.

I found someone waiting for me in front of my door. It was my first wife.

"I've come to tell you I'd like to give our marriage a second chance," she announced.

I didn't ask her what had prompted her decision, but blurted, "Listen carefully to me. I want to leave this country. I'm going to escape to the West. Do you want to come with me? We can go to Odessa or Murmansk, and from there try to smuggle ourselves on board some foreign ship."

She looked at me as though I were out of my mind. But then I made it even worse. "You should also know that I'm in love with Tatiana Kozlova, but we've just broken up. So if you still agree to come with me under those circumstances, I'm willing to give it a try too."

"You're crazy," she said, "stark, raving mad. You're almost thirty and you still act like a child—which is maybe why you fall for young girls. Well, I'm not a child; I'm a full-grown woman!"

And with that, she turned on her heel and fled.

Later I learned that she went straight to the Kozlovs' apartment. How she knew where it was, I never found out, nor would Tatiana ever reveal the substance of her tirade, except to say that she told them of my mad plans to leave Russia.

The following day, Tatiana received my letter. That, plus the emotional visit from my ex-wife, was all too much for her. She went into the bathroom and swallowed the contents of a bottle of sleeping pills. When her grandmother noticed her absence, she went in and found Tatiana unconscious. She called the neighbors for help, and Tatiana was rushed to the hospital in an ambulance—none of which I knew till many months later.

On December 30 the phone rang. It was Tatiana. She came right to the point.

"Are you still living with your ex-wife?"

"What difference does it make?"

"Just answer me: yes or no?"

"No. But that doesn't change anything. The point is, I can't live here anymore. I'm going crazy. I hate them all!"

"Hate who?"

"All those people who are keeping us apart."

"You're the one who's keeping us apart."

"That's not true. Don't you understand?"

"You're the one who wrote that awful letter. You're the one who refuses to make any compromise."

"What compromise? You mean joining the party?"

"Precisely."

"I loathe your party!"

"It's not *my* party any more than it's *yours*. But it exists, and there's nothing you can do about it."

"How old are you?"

"What does that have to do with it?"

"You're talking like one of those old farts who run this country. Compromise. Resignation. Nothing we can do about it. I know how to compromise, but not when it means losing my own self-respect."

There was a pause on the other end. Then she said, "I respect you. I've always respected you."

Another pause. "I love you. I need you."

"It's impossible to love someone who doesn't respect himself. Someone who . . ."

She cut me off. "Do you love me?" she whispered.

"Yes."

"Then do me a favor. Come and spend the New Year with us."

"With your parents?"

"Why not?"

"No, thanks. I don't want to see them."

"Then take me away somewhere."

"I can't."

"Why? You promised to take *her*. She's only your mistress. I thought I was your fiancée."

"Tatiana, my darling, what's the sense of seeing each other when there's no future in it? No future for us. No future for me in this country. Can't you see? I have to leave."

"And you promised to take *her* with you, true?"

"Yes."

"So you two have a future, and you and I don't, is that right?"

"No, that's not right. It's just that I have to leave."

"I know," she said, her voice suddenly gentle and distant. "I tried to leave too."

"What does that mean?"

"Nothing. Just take me somewhere to celebrate the New Year."

"What do you have in mind?"

"Nothing. What I had in mind I've already done."

I wasn't sure I understood what she was saying, but I suddenly felt cold, as though my heart knew. "Tatiana, promise me you won't try anything foolish."

"It's already over and done with. Let's drop the subject."

She was making it all up, of course. My sweet Tatiana was too positive, too much a life force ever to try anything like. . . .

"Tatiana, you must forget me. Put me behind you. Get on with your life. I don't want you to suffer. . . ."

She hung up.

I spent the most miserable New Year's Eve of my life. I was invited to a party by a group of friends. I drank, I sang, I laughed. I felt dead. All I could think of was Tatiana. What was she doing right now? Who was she with? What was she thinking?

Two interminable weeks went by. Then I received a letter

from Tatiana—I recognized her beloved handwriting. I trembled as I tore open the envelope. It began:

If you are happy, tear up this letter. If you aren't, read on.

I read on.

I love you. If you still love me, we can get married on February 27. Forget all that nonsense about joining the party. My parents have no objection. I'm ready to confront any problems and hardships that might emanate from our marriage. Probably because I so earnestly believe that everything will work out in the end. You were right to challenge me in your letter to make up my own mind. Well, I have. So, if you love me as you say, then I cordially invite you to "our wedding."

I read the letter, over and over, tears streaming down my face. I knew that from this day on, nothing, no force on earth, could ever keep me from taking this step—in retrospect, a fateful step. Another, stronger man than I would doubtless have acted differently. He would have replied, as I did, "Yes, I will marry you," but would have demanded at the same time that her parents leave us completely alone. No strings attached. But I was emotionally spent, incapable of making demands on anyone. All I wanted now was to let events take their course.

I dialed the Kozlovs' number. It rang only once. Tatiana picked it up. She recognized my voice.

"Have you made a decision?"

"I have."

"And may I know what it is?"

"I would be delighted to accept your invitation to attend the marriage on February 27 of Tatiana Kozlova and Edward Lozansky."

I thought at first that she was laughing. Then I realized she was sobbing her heart out.

I felt nothing but sheer happiness.

Love had impelled me to my decision, and had, as the saying goes, found a way. But love also had its consequences. From that day forward, I became, almost overnight and through no merit of my own, a member of the privileged class in our classless society. I was still a Jew, but now it was forgotten or qualified by the more meaningful qualification: son-in-law of General Pyotr Kozlov, Chief of Staff of the Kiev Military District. Past barriers came tumbling down. Past obstacles were swept away as though they had never existed. Past frowns were replaced by broad smiles. I was respected, envied. My friends would say, "He's made it." My parents would walk a little taller. I would still feel more than an occasional pang of conscience, a lingering bitter taste in my mouth, born of a mixture of complicity and compliance and seasoned with a touch of betrayal. But this time love was stronger than all my reticences and inhibitions. We were too happy to think about anything else.

It was to be a proper, lavish marriage. White wedding gown, dark suit, exchange of rings, full-fledged banquet.

I called my parents to break the news and tell them to start preparing for the February trip to Moscow. I wanted them present. Even though I was marrying into luxury and starting a new life, I had no intention of ever turning my back on my roots. Quite the contrary, in fact.

Two days before the wedding, General Kozlov called and suggested that we meet. I was sure he was going to pressure me again to join the party, but he had more practical considerations in mind.

"Where are you two going to live?" he asked.

"In my bachelor quarters, at least at first," I said. "Then we hope to buy a cooperative apartment."

"With what money?"

"I have some savings, plus what I expect to earn this summer in Siberia."

"Doing what, if I may ask?"

"Logging. I'm told there is always a demand for loggers."

"You mean you're prepared to leave your wife and run off to Siberia?"

"Why would I leave her? She's coming with me. I'm told there's also a demand for cooks."

How does that sit with you, Comrade General? I couldn't help thinking.

Actually, it had been Tatiana's idea. Strike out on our own without worrying about what anyone else wanted for us or expected from us. Raise our children as we saw fit, how we saw fit.

But the general and his wife had other ideas.

"Forget Siberia. And the cooperative apartment. As for your savings, you can use them to help furnish your *Moscow* apartment."

I stared at him, wide-eyed. "What Moscow apartment?"

"Just a minute," he said, and dialed a number.

"Kozlov here," he said. "Give me the head of military housing, Moscow." After a few seconds' pause, he said, "Hello, my friend. I think I may have mentioned that my daughter is getting married shortly. What can we do to help these two lovebirds find a roof over their heads? All right. Hold on a second while I get a pencil."

He scribbled something on a piece of paper.

"Many thanks," he said, "and don't forget to come and see us in Kiev."

He hung up and handed me the piece of paper.

"Here are the addresses of three available apartments. We'll take a look at them tomorrow and see which suits you."

And so it was. A single telephone call had swept away years of sharing one's lodging with strangers, of waiting on interminable lists, of struggling to have a place of one's own. I had become, with one wave of the general's magic wand, a member of the elite. That simple gesture was one of the most important in my life. If I had refused that apartment—the symbol of all the privileges that henceforth would be mine—if I had vigorously defended my independence, my future would surely have been different. But for someone who has known poverty, it is difficult to resist the temptation of ease and comfort. So I gave in. And I paid the price.

It is fair to say that our tragedy—Tatiana's and mine—began

that day. But I was too weak, or too weary, either to understand the implications of the situation or to find within me the strength to say no.

The next day, the general, Anna, Tatiana, and I were chauffeured in the official military automobile to all three apartments. I liked them all and was therefore useless in making a choice. Tatiana and her mother finally opted for the apartment in Lefortovo, a building occupied primarily by the military. Our apartment consisted of two huge, sunny rooms, an oversized kitchen, and a bathroom big enough to ride a bike in. I had trouble believing that all this was for only the two of us.

"Now don't rush out and buy furniture," Anna admonished. "Remember that we can order it more advantageously through military suppliers."

So we did not rush out. In fact, the next few days seemed to me like a dream. Every morning a car would come to pick me up, either to take me to meet some VIP the Kozlovs thought could sometime be useful to me, or to whisk me to a furniture or clothing store I had not even known existed. Ordinary citizens passed by their doors thousands of times without ever suspecting the panoply of riches that lay behind them: imported clothing, television sets, hi-fi equipment, appliances manufactured in the West, exotic liqueurs and alcohol from around the world. I saw, purchased, ate, and drank foods and beverages that until then I had seen only in the movies.

I moved my miserable belongings from the room on Starokoniushenny Lane to our new home. I spent hours wandering through it, turning the lights on and off, stroking the doorknobs as though they were made of solid gold. All this for only the two of us. And yet I kept thinking something was missing. Finally it dawned on me: We had no telephone.

I made up my mind on the spot that I would take care of that by myself, with no special pull. After all, I had to contribute something to the dream. I felt like a little boy desperately wanting to emulate the grown-ups.

Delighted by my initiative, I went down to the telephone office the next day. A girl handed me a stack of forms, which I duly filled out and handed back. She then tossed them into a large cardboard box without even glancing at them.

"Excuse me," I said, "but what day do you think they'll come to do the installation?"

"Installation of what?" she asked, as though she weren't listening.

"The telephone, of course."

"Oh, that. Listen, young man, would you mind stepping aside? Can't you see I'm busy? Look at that line of people behind you."

I could hear some snickers in the long line behind me. One man called over to me and pointed to a notice on the wall. "Better read that," he said.

I walked over and read the sign:

CURRENT REQUESTS FOR TELEPHONE SERVICE CAN EXPECT TO BE FILLED SOME TIME BETWEEN 1978 AND 1980. KINDLY REFRAIN FROM BOTHERING THE STAFF WITH QUESTIONS ON THIS SUBJECT.

This was 1971, for God's sake! A seven-to-nine-year wait?

That evening, I couldn't help mentioning my morning expedition to the general, who exploded and began to pound the table with his fist.

"Now what have you done? When are you going to stop making everything more complicated?"

I learned that he had written the day before to telephone headquarters formally requesting that a phone be installed in our apartment under his name. He stated that he needed the phone for professional reasons. I, of course, had failed to mention that he was living with us, which placed him in an awkward position. He put in a call to the communications office and asked them to clear up the mess. But it was too late. The discrepancy between our two applications had already been noted, and the general's request had been turned down.

Furious, the general launched an immediate counterattack. He called army headquarters and ordered that some military phone be disconnected and turned over to us. The next day, we had a whole platoon of soldiers stringing miles of telephone line over the roofs of Moscow to our apartment. Don't let anyone ever say that there is no room under the Russian system for personal initiative! That very evening, we had a functioning telephone.

When my parents and sisters arrived in Moscow, I introduced them to the Kozlovs. Although my parents were, and still are, simple people, the Kozlovs received them graciously and apparently took a liking to them. My family was duly impressed with the bearing and lifestyle of their future in-laws. All in all, the meeting went well, considering the sharp distinction in social rank between the two families.

At last the great day arrived. Early on the morning of February 27, a long line of official cars began arriving at our apartment house. From them emerged an impressive array of broad-shouldered officers with oversized caps, and sober-suited functionaries, elderly gentlemen who by their dress and demeanor would not have been wholly out of place at Buckingham Palace. They were accompanied by a bevy of plumpish women and a collection of adolescents who were, I must say, impeccably behaved. My own family observed these lofty creatures with awe, not knowing quite what to think. I was feeling stiff and awkward in my new close-fitting suit. Tatiana, who also seemed slightly intimidated, smiled demurely under her veil. The neighbors stood at a polite distance, whispering or murmuring comments not for our ears, or watching from their windows with nodding heads.

I took my place next to Tatiana in the first car, and all of a sudden my stiffness vanished. I felt relaxed and happy. At the Marriage Registration Bureau, I listened intently as the party functionary gave his set speech, ending with: "And may this new Soviet family contribute to the best of its ability to the edification of Communist society." At this point there were polite coughs and applause from the honored wedding guests. Anna Ivanovna wiped a tear from the corner of her eye. The general kissed his daughter and shook my hand.

It was over. Tatiana and I were man and wife, for better or for worse.

The wedding banquet was held that evening at the Arbat Restaurant. The toasts went on forever. The old general of notebook fame was there, jotting down new jokes as they were told. The laughter grew louder and louder, more hearty and unrestrained. Eyes glistened and cheeks glowed as some friends of mine sang to the accompaniment of a guitar. I could not help joining in. The songs were "ideologically suspect," and at one point I saw General Kozlov shaking his head with dismay. Finally he came over and suggested, as gently as possible, that I cease and desist.

"If I were you, Edward," he said, "I would let these Decembrists* go their own way. No good can come from associating with them."

I was in no mood to argue, but I did say, "The songs aren't really that bad. Anyway, everybody in the country knows them."

"That may be so," the general said, "but it's also the way your friends sing them. They seem to put their heart and soul into them. They care about those songs. And that is what's dangerous."

Dangerous for whom? I thought. *Him or me?* But of course he was right. I realized that the general was far less obtuse than I had thought originally. For a moment, I almost felt sorry for him.

Seated near us, Tatiana overheard our conversation. She leaned over and said, "Daddy, you promised you wouldn't discuss anything like that today."

The general shook his head, turned, and walked away. Well done, Tatiana. You're only eighteen, but you're solid as a rock. And you know how to use that wonderful smile of yours to devastating effect. I squeezed her hand, filled with a new surge of love and admiration. I knew I was in good hands.

The following day, my parents and the Kozlovs returned to Kiev. For the first time, Tatiana and I found ourselves alone together in our wonderful new apartment.

---

*A group of Russian aristocrats who, in December 1825, attempted a coup against Czar Nicholas I. Most of them ended up in Siberia.

Fifteen years have gone by. I still don't understand how General Kozlov and his wife ever agreed to let their daughter marry someone as dubious—at least in their eyes—as me. For even though Tatiana had gone on record that she would marry me even if they refused to give their consent, there was no way, at age eighteen, that she was ready to break off relations with her parents.

All those who know the background of our story constantly ask me: How could the general ever have made such a tactical error?

One possible answer to that question lies in the fact that, in truth, the general did not give us his benediction. All he did was ratify his wife's decision. For a long time, he remained reticent and tried to impose his conditions on me—namely, that I join the Communist party. At best, he viewed the marriage with a total lack of conviction. He possessed a sort of sixth sense and knew that nothing good could come of this marriage, at least from his point of view. It was a premonition I shared. We often talked about it later on. He frankly admitted that the only things he liked about me were my desire to fend for myself and my refusal ever to ask for any favors. Everything else—my "nationality," my age, my precarious situation, the facts that I was not a party member and had been married before—was against me.

Anna, however, viewed things in a very different light. Everything about me that displeased her husband she dismissed as inconsequential. She preferred to focus on what she considered my good qualities: my education, my degree in science, and my enormous appetite for work. It may be that she also saw me as a door leading to another world that had hitherto been inaccessible to her: a circle of writers, artists, and musicians. This new world might have helped her forget the old, familiar world of her husband's, the military with its emphasis on discipline, its heavy drinking and morbid humor. She was tired of competing with the wives of the Soviet generals and hoped to broaden her horizons by coming into contact with what she called "the Moscow intelligentsia." I got a sense of that the first day I sat down at the Kozlov piano and banged out a few amateurish notes. You would have thought Rachmaninoff had come to dinner!

Contrary to her husband, too, Anna would have preferred me to be less independent. She would have liked me to be more flexible, more willing to take advantage of the Kozlov connections to work my way up in the world. But she was also a realist, and she knew that perfection was not of this world. She decided that, since Tatiana loved me, there was no strong reason for her to contest her choice. In any event, she figured that with time she would be able to tame me. Besides, Tatiana's marriage suited her for another very practical reason. Her husband's ascension had been very fast. He had just received another star and been assigned to a more exalted post in Kiev. Anna had contributed in many ways to her husband's success. What mattered now was that nothing negative happen to mar the future. To be sure, it would have been nice to have their daughter with them in Kiev, but it was important to think of her future, too, a future that only studies at a prestigious university such as Moscow could ensure. So, they concluded, the child would surely be better off safely married and ensconced in an apartment than left to her own devices in a university dormitory.

All this, of course, is only pure conjecture on my part. But Tatiana concurs that it is probably not far from the mark. In the Kozlov household, it was Anna who ruled. The general put himself in her hands, knowing that she had rarely if ever made a mistake, that her intuition was virtually infallible.

In fact, his confidence in her had always brought him luck. Without Anna, without her constant support and counsel throughout his career, would he ever really have ended up that day, in the autumn of 1970, in Marshal Andrei Grechko's office, where he had received his second star? It was on that day, too, that he had been given the Order of the October Revolution and transferred to the Ukraine, to head the most important military district in the Soviet Union.

The Vice-Minister of Defense, General Sergei Sokolov, had been present at that promotion ceremony, and he walked Kozlov to the door afterward.

"Believe me," he said, "this promotion is only the beginning

for you. Mark my words, one of these fine days you're going to
be nominated as Chief of Staff of the Soviet Armed Forces.
They've already talked about it at the Politburo. I wanted you
named to the General Staff immediately, but some members
felt the move was premature. The Politburo felt, finally, that
two years in Kiev will give you added experience and stature.
In any event, you should know that you're on the Politburo list
of those for whom the most brilliant future is predicted. And
you can be sure your name will be constantly in our minds
whenever we discuss new promotions."

That day was not only a triumph for Kozlov. It was also a
day of triumph for Anna. Her ambition, her patience, and her
obstinacy had finally been rewarded. After many years of poverty, problems, and, yes, humiliations, she had at long last,
through the intermediacy of her husband, reached the summit
of power.

Both Anna and the general had come a long way. At age
nineteen he had been a simple laborer on a collective farm
outside Moscow. On several occasions he had tried to leave his
village and move to the city, without success. In those days no
one could leave his or her post without special authorization,
and any unauthorized departure was punishable by imprison-
ment. Only World War II had saved Pyotr Kozlov from his
hopeless situation.

Called into service, Kozlov was assigned to the infantry. He
fought bravely, was decorated several times, and was sent to an
officer-training school. At the end of the war, he was a captain.
While he was a student at the War College in Moscow, he met
Anna, a student of Russian language and literature, who lived
with her mother in a communal apartment. They married.
Kozlov graduated from the War College, and thus began the
long years of living in provincial garrisons, with all the unpleas-
antness they had to offer: miserable, sparsely furnished lodgings;
colleagues who drank too much; endless card games; officers'
wives who spent their mindless days gossiping and backbiting.

Without his wife, chances are that Kozlov would have ended
up as a neurasthenic. But Anna would not allow it. Every night
when he came home, she demanded a detailed breakdown of

his day—exactly what had happened, whom he had talked with, what he had done, what he had heard, down to the slightest detail and rumor. Then she gave her opinion on all counts: who he should see more of, who he should avoid, who they must invite to dinner. With Anna's help and advice, Kozlov became increasingly known as a solid, respectable officer. In 1964 he was summoned to Moscow and informed that he had been chosen for advanced study at the War College—an unhoped-for opportunity, the dream of every officer. What it meant was that Kozlov would one day make general.

In addition to his own intrinsic qualities, Kozlov's peasant background was partly responsible for his success. The party has always encouraged the promotion of officers with rural backgrounds. The regime considers them rock-solid, faithful servants who are not in the habit of asking too many questions. The privileges that generals enjoy are in such stark contrast to the harsh life of the collective farms from which they come that the party has every reason to believe that officers with peasant roots will be wholly devoted to the regime.

Anna made up her mind early on to renounce her own ambitions and devote herself exclusively to her husband's career. She had hoped to become a teacher of Russian. Henceforth she would be General Kozlov's wife and the mother of their two children, Tatiana and Mitya.

Kozlov's stint at the War College was without incident. If he was less than brilliant in the scientific area, he was without peer on the battlefield. His considerable experience as a field commander and in logistics impressed everyone. During maneuvers, he inevitably came up with original solutions to tactical problems that impressed his professors and earned him the highest marks.

After his graduation in 1966, Kozlov was named Chief of Staff of the operational sector of the infantry. Although he was still only a colonel, the post normally was filled by a general, and indeed Pyotr received his first star the following year.

The Kozlovs moved to a new three-room apartment on Leninsky Prospekt and enjoyed the luxury of an official car (though Pyotr, at this point, could use it only to go to work). New doors

were also opened to them in those special stores that only the
Soviet elite could frequent. Still, theirs were one-star doors;
they were still refused access to the doors through which walked
two-, three-, and four-star generals.

They had barely had time to grow accustomed to their new
life when an unexpected event propelled the career of Pyotr
Kozlov to heights that neither he nor Anna could ever have
expected.

Spring 1968, the "Prague Spring," as it came to be known. For
the first time since the October Revolution, there seemed a real
hope among many of us that a people who had been subjected
to the harsh oppression of Communist rule might be able to
throw off its yoke. In Moscow, all anyone talked about was the
situation in Czechoslovakia. I remember a huge party given by
the academician Leontovich at his dacha outside Moscow. There
must have been at least 200 people present, most of them scientists. The July evening was warm and moist, but there was a
kind of unaccustomed lightness in the air. I had never seen so
many smiling, happy faces. For one brief moment, the distant
breath of freedom seemed to have lent my colleagues and friends
a real sense of hope, a childlike belief that the Czechs might
really regain their liberty. I am sure that many thousands of
other Russian citizens were thinking the same thing. That was
something the Soviet leaders could not endure. For them, the
virus of freedom was more frightening than the notion of nuclear
holocaust. It had to be eliminated. Immediately.

There were no Soviet troops stationed in Czechoslovakia. As
for the Czech Army, it could hardly be relied upon: Chances
were that it had been affected by the same anti-Soviet virus as
the rest of the population. Years later, when I was teaching at
the Military Tank Academy in Moscow, a general told me that,
as early as May 1968, plans had been drawn up in the strictest
secrecy at Ground Forces Headquarters for the invasion of
Czechoslovakia. My father-in-law had been a key figure in drawing up those plans.

Then came summer. August 21, to be exact. On that date,
a Soviet transport plane apparently in trouble asked the control

tower at Prague Airport for what appeared to be routine permission to land. The control tower gave its immediate OK. The plane landed and taxied to the far end of the runway. There its door burst open and out came a line of armored vehicles, followed by a contingent of crack commandos. Within half an hour, Prague Airport was in Soviet hands, and wave after wave of Soviet transport planes arrived, each filled with men and matériel. At the same time, Red Army troops crossed the Czech border at several places simultaneously and moved toward Prague, without meeting any serious resistance. The fate of Prague Spring was signed and sealed.

At a Politburo meeting devoted to the long-term plans and strategy of the armed forces, the decision was made to move some younger officers into positions of key importance. The defense minister submitted a list of the most capable Soviet generals. Kozlov, who had conducted himself especially well during the invasion of Czechoslovakia, was high on that list. As a result, in 1970 he received that second star, awarded by Marshal Grechko himself, and was assigned to Kiev, with, as mentioned, the promise of even brighter things to come.

The Kiev post was a real plum. It was filled by direct decision of the party's Central Committee, and thereby indicated that Kozlov was now truly a part of the *nomenklatura*. His new rank conferred solid political authority on Kozlov, a distinction confirmed shortly thereafter when he was "elected" a member of the Presidium of the Supreme Soviet in the Ukraine. As such, he became Moscow's eye in that part of the empire.

The only shadow in the picture: Ordinarily, in order to make sure that their Russian appointees do not become too closely allied to the local authorities, Moscow tends to keep its military chiefs in a region for no more than two or three years. Kozlov spent seven years in the Ukraine. It is quite possible that I was in part responsible for Pyotr Kozlov's unexpectedly long tour of duty in Kiev.

The first three years of our married life were delightfully serene. Nothing from 1971 to 1974 gave any hint of the tempestuous

events that were to follow. At first I had some difficulty finding
a job, but then General Kozlov had a quiet chat with the KGB
section that had my file and persuaded them to leave me alone.
After all, I had committed no crime, so the general was not
exactly risking his neck in my behalf. In all likelihood, he also
promised the KGB that he would keep an eye on me. But, as
he pointed out, I had to be able to support my family, and that
was impossible as long as I kept running into their endless road-
blocks.

The computer operator at KGB headquarters made a few
discreet corrections to my file, and, presto! in no time at all I
was approached by the directors of several laboratories who not
too long ago had refused to employ me because their personnel
departments "had a problem with my case." Ah, the miracles of
modern science!

Our daughter Tania was born in December 1971, so at this
juncture I had to consider carefully whether I could enjoy the
luxury of joining a lab as research assistant, where the pay was
insufficient to support a family of three. I finally opted for a
teaching post at the Military Tank Academy, which was offering
a salary twice that of the laboratories for a two-day work week.
That would give me a chance to spend the rest of my time
working on scientific projects for the Institute of Atomic Energy
and the Institute for Nuclear Research in Dubna. I signed contracts with all three institutions.

My initial contact with the Military Tank Academy is worth
relating. After meeting with the school's director, Marshal Oleg
Losik—whom my father-in-law had of course telephoned several
days earlier to smooth my reception—I headed for the personnel
department to fill out the proper forms. I knocked discreetly at
the door. A voice called out that I should come in.

"What can I do for you?" growled a moustachioed *muzhik*,
his voice a mixture of barbed wire and vitriol. He turned out to
be the chief of personnel.

"I've come to fill out some forms."

"Forms? What forms?"

"I've just been given a job here."

"A job? What kind of job?"

"A teaching job. In the physics department."

"Hold on just a minute. Who sent you here, anyway? Let me see your passport."

I realized that no one had told the poor man anything about me. With a certain degree of pleasure, I handed him my passport. I saw his eyes run down to the *Nationality* line. For several seconds, he seemed so taken aback he was at a loss for words. Then, articulating each syllable with painful clarity, he said, "I regret to inform you that no such opening exists at this institution at this time. You must have been wrongly informed. Here, take your passport back. And please excuse me. As you see, I'm a very busy man."

I felt sorry for him. How was the poor man going to extricate himself from the trap he had just walked into? At that moment, the telephone rang. Waving me to leave, he picked up the phone.

"Yes, Comrade Marshal. (*Silence.*) Yes, he's here with me. (*Long silence.*) Of course, Comrade Marshal, I'll take care of it immediately."

He gently laid down the phone and took a deep breath. He raised his eyes and graced me with a wheedling smile. Suddenly his voice was as smooth and suave as that of a nightingale.

"Well, Edward Dmitrievich, I must say that you failed to introduce yourself properly. This is, as you know, a military school, and here we do things by the rules. We can't be too careful, as I'm sure you know. Here are your forms. Take them with you and fill them out at home. We look forward to seeing you tomorrow, Edward Dmitrievich. Without fail."

He seemed in a great hurry to get rid of me. I had the impression that if I had told him I couldn't fill out the forms because I didn't know how to read or write, he would have replied, "Don't worry, Edward Dmitrievich, we'll fill them out for you."

Ultimately, I found him touching. Later on, we became good friends. One day he told me, after considerable hemming and hawing and discreet coughing, that his nephew was graduating from officer-training school in Kiev and had been assigned to the Chinese border. He wondered, assuming of course that it was no bother, in which case of course he would understand and never raise the subject again, he was wondering that is if I would mind terribly mentioning it to my father-in-law, in the hope that the general might put in a word for his nephew, since that duty was not only so far away but also dangerous and it would be wonderful if there was any way he might be reassigned to some place less remote. By the way, he concluded, was I aware that the post of head of the physics department would soon be vacant? "Your name is being mentioned, Edward Dmitrievich," he nodded. "I thought you might like to know."

In fact, the head of the personnel department did not have sufficient influence to affect that nomination one way or another, but I did mention the conversation to General Kozlov, who did make the necessary phone call and had the *muzhik*'s nephew reassigned to a Ukrainian garrison.

"You may be right," was the general's rationale, "he probably doesn't have any influence. But you can never be too careful in life. Might as well have the man in our pocket."

My friend the *muzhik* was deeply grateful. As he passed me one morning in the hallway, he took my arm and pulled me aside. "You know, Edward Dmitrievich," he said as though revealing a state secret, "I've never been an anti-Semite myself. I want you to know that. But now, if I ever hear anyone insulting a Jew in my presence, I swear to you I'll hit him on the spot!"

I enjoyed my work, both the teaching and the research, especially the opportunity to collaborate again with Tigrov, Leontovich, and their colleagues. I resumed my experiments with the Department of Plasma, trying to formulate a complete theory on the electrical discharges in gases under atmospheric pressure, which included the mechanism of the formation and propagation of lightning. I published a dozen articles, some written in collaboration with Tigrov and the Dubna group. Later Tigrov and I decided to write a book summarizing the results of our work. I threw myself into the project with enormous enthusiasm.

At the Military Tank Academy there was, in fact, increasing talk of my becoming the head of the physics department. But there was still the same old obstacle: I was not a party member.

Still, my life was a dream. No more lines in front of stores, no more crowded subways or buses. Each week, when we did not fly down to Kiev on a military plane to visit Tatiana's parents, they would send us huge packages filled with foodstuffs from the special stores and neighboring farms that provided for the military of the region.

One day, out of curiosity, I visited one of these model farms that specialized in fruits and vegetables. The director took me on a tour and proudly showed me the latest equipment, mostly from the West, that graced his farm. At the end of the visit, he took me into a large building staffed by girls in spotless white blouses who were busy measuring tomatoes with a ruler, then consigning them to various crates.

"These tomatoes are being hand picked for the families of the Soviet military here," he said. "As you can see, the largest, plumpest ones are destined for the top military brass and their families." That "brass," I later learned, consisted of only four people: the commanding general, his deputy, his chief of staff, and the top political commissar of the region. "Those slightly smaller and less plump," the director went on, "are of course for the lower-ranking generals, their administrative staffs, the censors, and the attorney general."

The stratification of the *nomenklatura* was as strict and precise in all other areas as it was in the case of the large, ripe tomatoes. The commanding general of the Kiev Military District had a seven-room apartment, a two-story dacha set in the midst of an immense garden, an eight-room house on a lake thirty kilometers outside the city, and another large house at the seashore, with a pool and a tennis court and an army of servants. In contrast, General Kozlov, the Chief of Staff, had only a five-room apartment, a dacha with a considerably smaller plot of land, a house on the lake with only six rooms, and a seaside villa that was only one story tall and staffed with fewer servants.

One of the basic problems, in my view, with the Soviet system is that that stratification is responsible for the stagnation that has beset the country—socially, economically, and politically—for decades. Those with power and privilege are terrified of taking any risks, trying anything new, for fear it might fail and bring them down. For if you fall, your privileges fall with you.

And yet in all fairness, the *nomenklatura* is less harsh today than it was in the past. High-ranking officials who fall from grace never lose all of their perks. No matter what, they never descend to the rank of ordinary citizens again. Even if they have committed crimes, they rarely if ever move down more than a few rungs on the *nomenklatura* ladder. Sometimes, their movement is even lateral. For example, the president of the Chamber of Nationalities, one of the two chambers of the Supreme Soviet, was a woman named Yadgar Nasriddinova, who spent her leisure hours running clandestine and illegal liquor factories, from which she made millions. After she was found out, she was demoted— all the way to vice-minister!

Another case: Vassily Mzhavanadze, first secretary of the party Central Committee in Georgia, together with his deputy, Vassily Churkin, combined to bring corruption in that republic to heights—or depths—unprecedented even by Soviet standards. Ministerial posts, regional party secretaries, deputies of the Supreme Soviets—all were bought and sold in the best tradition of the free market. At the same time, these gentlemen's wives were just as busy, running an extensive underground operation in hard currency and diamonds. When, for reasons still unclear, Leonid Brezhnev decided to crack down, and the "Georgia gang" was caught red-handed, only the small fry went on trial. The chiefs were simply shifted to other positions in the *nomenklatura*, without even losing their precious party cards.

Even while Brezhnev was cleaning up the corruption in Georgia, he was well aware that his own daughter Galina was the head of a gang running an extortion racket, also specializing in hard currency and diamonds. Aside from her father's protection, Galina knew she could count on two other highly placed members of the gang: her husband, General Yuri Churbanov, who was Deputy Minister of the Interior in charge of fighting corruption and economic crimes (no less!), and Semyon Tsvigun, who was first deputy head of the KGB but also Brezhnev's brother-in-law. As for the Minister of the Interior, General Nikolai Shcholokov, he had devised what was perhaps the neatest setup of all. Soviet artists and performers who wanted to go abroad needed his department's approval, and many was the time when the minister struck a deal that served a dual purpose: It enabled the performers to travel abroad as they so ardently desired, and it filled the coffers of the minister. Shcholokov got a cut of everything the customs officials confiscated from departing Soviet citizens, which was quite a take. During his term of office, the minister managed to accumulate four Mercedes limousines as well as ten other Western automobiles, in addition to a considerable store of hard currency and a fortune in diamonds. If only Tatiana and I had known how open to corruption Shcholokov was at the time, we might have saved ourselves six sad years of separation. Unfortunately, the revelations came only after Brezhnev's death, too late to do us any good. Yuri Andropov, of course, knew what was going on, but when he came to power, all he did was replace Brezhnev's Mafia with one of his own. He "advised" his former deputy Tsvigun to commit suicide. But the others fared far better: Churbanov was simply transferred within his own ministry to a post in Murmansk; Galina Brezhnev was left completely alone; Shcholokov, according to rumors, was going to be brought to trial. In the beginning of 1985, he died under mysterious circumstances.

This kind of corruption in high places has been part of the Soviet system since its beginning, and it will end only with the demise of the Soviet Empire. But it is worth noting that while crooked and incompetent officials do remain part of the *nomenklatura* after their fall from grace, relations among members of the party elite are such that being remanded to a lower caste or discharged from an exalted post is deemed to be the most humiliating punishment anyone can suffer, a terrible shock, a loss of prestige from which many never recover.

When Yekaterina Furtseva, Minister of Culture and a member of the Politburo, was accused of stealing State property, she was ousted from the Politburo but was able to keep her ministerial post. Yet the humiliation she suffered was such that she went into a deep depression and began drinking heavily, which precipitated her premature death. As for Shcholokov's wife, she was so distressed by her husband's fate that she committed suicide.

I have also heard that there is an unusually high rate of heart attacks among high-ranking members of the military who are demoted or forced into early retirement. For them the tragedy is not so much the imposed idleness or the loss of privilege as the fact that they become the laughingstock of the very people who only a short time before had bowed and scraped to them. That is one of the most disconcerting constants of Soviet life: You are a hero one day and dirt the next. In the West, people talk of hierarchies and a pecking order, but I have never seen anything in Europe or the United States that even faintly compares to the servility and autohumiliation in the Soviet Union. I have witnessed high-ranking officers castigating and humiliating their subordinates only to turn around and cower, minutes later, before their superiors.

Such tensions can only have the most disastrous psychological effects on people, even those who are basically independent and respectable. Thus, a completely new kind of human being has emerged over the years: *Homo soveticus*, a person devoid of honor, dignity, and pride; a person ready to lie and betray, to grovel and cringe before his superiors while heaping insults and indignities on his subordinates. The apparent solidity and imperious nature of *Homo soveticus* is only a mask. When you have a chance to talk to these people in private, you find they are frightened and insecure. Some ex-prisoners of Russian *gulags* told me that the most pathetic people there were the KGB officers, who, after persecuting and torturing innocent victims, turned out to be the most pitiful and repulsive prisoners in the camp when they in turn became victims of their own system and were arrested for some crime or other.

The *nomenklatura* is surrounded by and catered to by a powerful bureaucracy whose job it is to make sure that the right people get the right clothes, the right food, the right books, the right appliances—all the right privileges from the special agencies set up solely to distribute them. The employees of these agencies have precise instructions in all areas. They know exactly what officials are entitled to enter which hospitals, sanitoriums, or rest homes; who is entitled to receive this or that rare medicine; who gets tickets to concerts or the restricted screenings of Western movies.

One summer I was able to see this bureaucracy in action. Tatiana, Tania, and I were spending our vacation at a resort near Yalta reserved for the families of high-ranking military officials. The daughter of the Commander of the Kiev Military District was also there with her husband. As befitted their rank, they were assigned to the largest suite, which was outfitted with a refrigerator, color TV, and telephone. We had a smaller room, with a refrigerator, a black-and-white TV, and a phone that didn't work. Nonetheless, we had the beach, and we were happy to be there.

One afternoon we returned from the beach to find our room empty. Stripped. While we were standing there, gazing in disbelief at what had been our quarters, trying to figure out what kind of a practical joke had been perpetrated on us, the manager arrived, all out of breath, apologizing profusely.

"Please do forgive me," he pleaded. "We had to move you into the commander's room." He took me aside and lowered his voice. "Just between us," he confided, "we just got word yesterday that the commander has been dismissed, and the rumor is that your father-in-law will get his job. So we had to take appropriate action. I'm sure you understand."

I was so shocked that I told him I was sorry but I didn't understand, and furthermore, I wanted our things brought back to our room immediately.

"I'm afraid I couldn't do that," he said, looking crestfallen. "You don't want me to lose my job too, do you?"

"And what about the daughter of the commander and her husband? Where are you going to put them?"

"Don't worry," he said, "it's all been taken care of. This morning I explained the situation to them, and they've already left for Kiev."

In all fairness, things have improved since Stalin's day. People in high places no longer have to fear being "eliminated" when they are fired or fall from favor. In the case of the commander, he was simply assigned to a lesser post in Moscow. As General Kozlov noted ironically, now he would have to do his shopping in a third- rather than first-category store—which is a far cry from rotting away in Siberia or in the basement of Lubyanka Prison.

Thus Soviet society today is a universe marked by distrust and disdain, both of which have been erected since the October Revolution as twin pillars of virtue. In the Soviet Union, as well as in the satellite countries, communism has managed not only to freeze society but to pervert human nature as well. Under Stalin, for instance, spying and informing were considered "heroic," even if the victims were close friends, relatives, members of your own family. All it took was an accusatory letter sent to the KGB, and the target of such a letter inevitably would be arrested. Often, too often, these "ideological" or "patriotic" denunciations were neither more nor less than the settling of old grudges.

There is a story about two prisoners in the same Soviet cell. One prisoner asks his cellmate, "Tell me, what are you in for?"

"For telling a political joke. What about you?"

"I'm in for being lazy."

"Ah? What happened?"

"I was with a group of friends. Someone told a political joke, making fun of the party. I had every intention of informing on him that same evening, but I was too tired, so I decided to wait till the following morning. But, unhappily, another member of the same group was quicker on the draw and went that night to the KGB to turn in the joker. I was arrested and sentenced to ten years for being dilatory."

Unfortunately, it was more than a joke. During the Stalin era, people were thrown into prison or sent to *gulags* for less than that. An arrest also affected the victim's family, which was henceforth tainted with the stigma of being "a relative of an enemy of the people." Here the sad result was a whole series of repudiations, as wives turned their backs on husbands, children on parents, brothers on sisters. An atmosphere of complete paranoia developed. Even today, school curricula continue to pound into children's heads the notion that love of party is far more important than love of family and friends. Tens of millions of school children have been brought up on the story of Pavlik Morozov, a fourteen-year-old boy who reported to the KGB that his father, a peasant, had hidden some grain that should have been turned over to the State. His father was shot, and Pavlik became a national hero. Poems were written about him, songs composed in his honor. Thousands of Young Pioneer organizations were named after him. And Pavlik is only one of thousands of Soviet "heroes" whom the State calls upon its citizens to emulate in their daily lives.

The result is that over the decades normal relationships have been undermined or perverted. Friendship, love, respect, and a sense of kinship count for less and less. Feelings have been repressed; respect for the law is everything. To be sure, Soviet citizens, like people everywhere, fall in love, have friends, respect their parents. Human nature is stronger than any ideology. But the fact is, feelings and reactions that elsewhere are normal are clandestine and repressed in the Soviet Union. Soviet citizens have to conform to the dictates of a group of morose and mediocre marionettes who call themselves leaders, men who have theories where they ought to have hearts. Instead of encouraging spontaneity, enthusiasm, and sincerity, Soviet society has only one goal: standardize, standardize as much as possible, and always to the lowest common denominator.

Woe to the Soviet man or woman with an original idea or concept in the realm of economics. Unconventional thinking is dangerous, and all those who harbor new notions must be eliminated. The Great Terror under Stalin was not, as is often stated, an aberration imputable to the ravings of a madman and tyrant, but a logical extension of the system itself. And it did not cease because the leadership of the country changed or because the nature of the system was modified, allowing for a more humane attitude at the top. No, it ceased because the terror was no longer necessary. The behemoth had done its job and done it well. There was no one left at the pinnacle of power who posed any threat to the system, no one who, motivated by a desire to improve society, would question its stagnation. The "true" Communists, who genuinely believed in Marxist ideals and really wanted to bring about justice on earth, had been liquidated. The internal logic of Marxism results in a paradoxical situation: Its most ardent defenders are the worst enemies of the order that engendered them, and must therefore be destroyed. I doubt that there is anywhere in the world an ideology that so ruthlessly devours its young!

Today, people say, things are better. Political murder no longer exists, at least in as systematic a way as under Stalin. But this does not mean that violence no longer exists. Nationalists, religious dissenters, and other dissidents are all victims of what one might properly call a Minor Terror, which translates in various ways: internment in *gulags* or plain old-fashioned jails, confinement in psychiatric hospitals, loss of jobs, exile, or breakup of families.

The Red Army's history offers a good example of how this works. The 1917 Revolution produced a whole constellation of talented military leaders who were truly national heroes. Stalin wasted little time in eliminating them, trumping up a wide array of absurd charges: treason, espionage, sedition. Since then, the Red Army has allowed no popular national heroes to emerge. Very simply, they are far too dangerous.

During World War II, heroism was anonymous. There was only one key figure, one object of cult worship to whom all glory and honor was given: Joseph Stalin. The astounding exploits of the Red Army were attributed solely to Stalin's genius, whereas in truth they were due to the courage and sacrifice of millions of unknown soldiers. The Red Army was a depersonalized mass with ingrained patriotism. After Stalin's death, Khrushchev tried to take some of the credit for World War II, and later on Brezhnev tried as well.

Today, Soviet heroes come with strings attached. Their ratings depend on the positions they hold and the tactics of the regime. If you want to be a hero in modern Russian society, you must forget all about bravery, initiative, individualism, and or-

ganizational ability. The story is often told of Stalin's warning to
Lenin's widow, Nadezhda Krupskaya: "Madam, if you continue
to give me trouble, I shall have the statutes revised and find
someone else to be Lenin's widow."

Today's heroes are fabricated, made to order—often overnight. When the authorities decide to launch some campaign
for increased productivity, for example, a particularly photogenic
worker is selected and ten other workers are assigned to help
him fill his incredible "quota."

A committee was appointed to select Russia's first space hero.
The choice seemed obvious: Yuri Gagarin, the modest cosmo-
naut with the winning smile, who was known and liked throughout the world. And yet clearly the committee had not thought
things through sufficiently. One of my friends who worked for
the Soviet space program told me that Khrushchev was furious
and almost fired the entire committee. It seems they had completely overlooked the fact that Gagarin was the name of an old
Russian aristocratic family. The Soviet press was quickly brought
into play to set the matter right. It ran a series of articles proving
that Yuri Gagarin had nothing to do with any aristocratic ancestors and was a genuine product of the working class.

Today, even that kind of hero is anathema. Statistical heroes
are greatly preferred: the hundred-thousandth visitor to an
exhibition or the millionth inhabitant of a given city. Such
gift-wrapped heroes appear regularly on television or in the
press.

But surely, one might well argue, there still must persist in
a large segment of the Soviet Army a basic belief in the ideals
of communism. I strongly doubt it. At least since the end of
World War II. For all intents and purposes, the army has become
a troop of mercenaries, lacking both in ideals and esprit de corps.
Officers think only of their good pay and perks, as well they
might. A twenty-year-old lieutenant fresh from military school
earns twice as much as an engineer, teacher, doctor, or scientific
researcher. The highest pension a civilian can look forward to
after twenty-five or thirty years of work is 120 rubles a month,
whereas a retired colonel gets 300, and a general obviously more—

after ten or fifteen years less service than their civilian counterparts.

Western officials and foreign correspondents who have admired the impressive, goose-stepping units as they parade past
the viewing stands on Red Square have seen only one side of
the military picture. I know from my five years of living among
the military elite that the notion that the Russian soldier's heart
beats with pride, loyalty, justice, duty, and honor, and that he
is dedicated to the nation and the party, is far from the truth.
At best, it is outmoded.

In the army, inner conflicts can be tragic and run deeper
than is the case with members of the Soviet intelligentsia. At
least intellectuals can vent their feelings to friends over an evening meal, give voice to their frustrations. But army officers,
who have trouble putting their thoughts or convictions into words,
who have been brought up never to question the system, often
do not know how to articulate their fears and resentments. As
a result, they sink into cynicism and drink themselves into
depression. And the political controls to which they are subjected constantly only increase their resentment and rage.

In the armed forces, the political commissars are known as
priests, not a complimentary term. In pre-Communist times,
the village priests were often illiterate drunkards who repeated
the same pet phrases over and over. Today, the political commissars do much the same, repeating ready-made slogans believed by no one, probably not even the commissars themselves.
At best, the "flock" swallow their gobbledygook apathetically; at
worst, it is a constant irritant and a source of disdain for the
priests who spew it.

And yet the Red Army is so structured that no key decision
can be made without the approval of the political commissar.
How often have I heard generals complaining bitterly about the
"politicos" who stick their noses into major strategic and tactical
discussions about which they know nothing. A general once
voiced his bitterness to me about a particularly obnoxious commissar: "The damned fool hasn't a clue, but that doesn't keep
him from offering his two kopeks at every opportunity! The son-

of-a-bitch can't stop filling our ears with the party-this and the Marxism-that. Well, if you want to know the truth, that bastard's only ideology is licking Yepishev's* ass!"

A surprising number of generals I knew felt much as I did about party dogma. Yet all of them, starting with my father-in-law, never failed to remind me how important it was that I join the party. They were genuinely perplexed at my reluctance to take what seemed like an obvious, and simple, step. "With your education and the general's connections," they kept telling me, "you can land any job you want: director of a major institute, department chairman, embassy attaché—you name it. But without that little red book in your pocket, forget it!"

At first I was shocked by their cynicism. Then I got used to it. But one question continued to haunt me: If all these people truly don't believe in anything, what do they have left? How can they behave like normal human beings?

One day I was invited to a gala reception where a famous general gave a speech about World War II. As he was recalling the Battle of Stalingrad, he suddenly burst into tears. Why? I had trouble believing he was insincere, that his tears had been faked or forced, that he was only trying to impress his audience. Suppose, then, that he was sincere. What did it mean? That he couldn't forget his fallen comrades? That he felt guilty for having survived? That he was crying for all the years he had lost because of the war?

Actually, the answer is much simpler. The Russian people seem to have a profound, tender, almost religious feeling about World War II. Despite its horrors, it was a wonderful time— a time when everyone loved one another, helped one another, shared concerns and sorrows. People then had a goal—to survive—which united them, gave them strength, kept them aglow. During the war, something akin to human relations surfaced for the first time since the nightmare years of the Great Terror. The best books, the best films, the best music had to do with the war. Why? What was so appealing about this terrible time, which

*Alexsei Yepishev was head of the Central Political Directorate of the Soviet Army and Navy.

took the lives of millions of Russians? Why was it only in wartime that a psychologically healthy climate appeared, a flowering of the human spirit?

These questions touch on one of the basic anomalies of Russian culture, and it is a tragic one. In what other country is there such an overwhelming nostalgia about the war? It is not that Russians are warmongers, not that they are anxious for another war, having tasted the horrors of it. The Russians are neither fanatic nor stupid. But the sad fact is that in time of peace, life seems to lose all meaning for them. Only a war, apparently, can bring it back. It is not only the natural reaction of repelling an invader, but the triggering of some cultural mechanism that results in the Russian people being uplifted spiritually. To other people whose sole desire is to be left in peace, this may appear incredible, but my own experience and reflections lead me inexorably to this conclusion. The party theorists got there way ahead of me, and they skillfully exploit this national characteristic for the party's own ends. The Communist leaders need national unity, and war or the threat of war provides it. Thus, from a very early age, Russian citizens are imbued with a *need* for war, as opposed to a readiness to repel an aggressor.

One of the great unifying factors of the Russian national consciousness is the existence of an ever-present enemy. The external world is fundamentally hostile to the Communist experiment, therefore to the Soviet people. "Russia is ringed with enemies" has been a rallying cry ever since the early days of the Bolsheviks. The Soviet Union has always found enemies, both internal and external: the bourgeoisie, the *kulaks*, the priests, the party renegades, the nationalists. All are collected under the general heading "Enemies of the People," and they can be cited at any convenient time as those responsible for the misfortunes and disasters that befall the country.

That obsession goes a long way toward explaining why the Soviet Union now controls about one-sixth of the earth's surface. The conquest of each new square mile of territory can be justified by the fact that it pushes the "enemy" farther from the central regions of the country and its major cities. In schools, teachers proudly explain how Peter the Great "opened a window on

Europe"; how Siberia, Central Asia, and the Caucasus were conquered; and how the Baltic states—along with part of Finland, the Western Ukraine, Byelorussia, South Sakhalin, and the Kurile Islands—were "liberated." There is a story about a Russian teacher who asks a pupil what countries the Soviet Union borders. "It borders whatever countries it wants to," was the child's reply.

To attain its expansionist goals, the Soviet Union resorts to a mixture of demagoguery, hypocrisy, and lies. The most cunning technique is undoubtedly that of exploiting the huge Russian losses in World War II. How often have we heard Soviet spokesmen reiterate: "We lost 20 million people in the war. Every family had men killed or missing in action. How can anyone truly believe that this country is ready to inflict that kind of horror on its people again?"

It takes a courageous soul to give the answer: "What are 20 million deaths to you, who sent twice that number to their doom in prisons and *gulags*? Who punished you for that? You helped start World War II by invading Finland, the Baltic states, and Poland. You sent in troops to crush any bid for independence and freedom in those countries you seized and subjugated. Today you are committing genocide in Afghanistan. You arrest your own citizens for the 'crime' of calling for the respect of your own constitution. You will not hesitate to institute another 'Great Terror,' with all it implies, including another 20 million deaths if necessary, if it means holding on to power."

Western leaders are generally too polite or too unsure of their facts to challenge the Soviet leaders in this way. Many are genuinely impressed by the apparent sincerity of the Russian leaders with whom they deal. Once back in Moscow, the Kremlin's envoys break out the bottles of vodka and toast the gullibility of the Americans, the British, the French, or the Germans, who can be taken in so easily.

It is a dark picture of today's Russia that I have painted. Yet it represents the truth as I saw it and lived it. For five years I preferred not to see it, to turn my back on the truth, to accommodate the system and enjoy the fruits of my privileged position. But there was no way it could last.

Today dissidents are part of the Soviet political landscape. Even when I was a member of the Russian elite, thanks to my Kozlov connections, I always looked upon them with sympathy and respect. But even though I was fully aware of their existence, though instinctively I shared their aversion for the system, read *samizdat* literature, and talked about them with my friends, my opposition to the regime was still personal and emotional. If, for instance, I had heard about the demonstrations being planned for August 1968 in Red Square to protest the invasion of Czechoslovakia, I would have participated without hesitation. For the time being, however, I remained faithful to my basic apolitical philosophy, which placed art and science above any political system.

I had no wish to become a dissident myself, and in this I was not alone. People can in all honesty adopt this position because they are not interested in politics or because they do not feel mature enough to make sound judgments. Or simply because they are afraid. However, one does have to survive in the Soviet system. How? That is a question I pondered for a long time, and finally I came to the conclusion that such people should either do their best to emigrate, or, failing that, try to preserve their spirit of independence by insisting on their rights and refusing to be bullied or cowed by the authorities. I argued with myself that every time a person fulfills himself in some way, or manages to get some fun out of life, he automatically delivers a blow to the system. And he who manages to remain outside of it, so that he is left alone, is in a very real sense outwitting it.

With such superficial arguments did I try to quiet my conscience, telling myself that I was minding my own business, that I was doing nothing reprehensible by simply enjoying the fringe benefits of the ruling class. But I was naive to think that this comfortable existence could go on for very long. Some day I would have to pay for what I had received, but meanwhile I would just keep my head down and try to convince myself that everything was fine. There was only one dark cloud: Every once in a while, Tatiana's parents would badger me to join their stupid party. I staved them off with pat answers and vague promises.

"In a few years, once I've finished my book," I would respond. "But for the moment I don't consider myself sufficiently versed in Marxism to become a good Communist."

Such replies sent General Kozlov into a rage. He would bite his lips, turn on his heels, march out of the room, and slam the door behind him. But such unpleasant scenes did not faze me. As long as matters went no further, I remained unruffled. As a result, the early years of our marriage were happy.

Tatiana and I were both busy, she as a student in the chemistry department of Moscow University, I teaching and deeply involved in my research. Tigrov and I were making good progress on the manuscript of our book, and we had a contract with a leading scientific publisher, Atomizdat. I wrote a mathematics textbook intended to help upper-school students prepare for their university entrance exams. This was a task I enjoyed immensely, especially because it was a text I wished I might have had a few years earlier when I was preparing for the exams myself.

Tatiana and I never stopped marveling at the luxury of our apartment, with its contemporary Finnish furniture, its rugs and appliances. We would sit together in the evening for hours, sipping tea as we discussed the day's events and talked of our plans for the days and weeks to come. I helped Tatiana with her studies, and she made drawings and sketches for my books. Both Tatiana's grandmother and my mother came frequently to Moscow, to help raise Tania, which made our social life so much easier. We went to all the latest films and plays, entertained friends for dinner, and were often invited out by a growing circle of people we came to know and like. By government order, we were able to buy the latest books, most of which were not widely available. Through friends, we were also able to get any *samizdat* books we wanted. These we would read late into the night, sometimes till dawn, since the works were in great demand and could only be kept for a short time before being passed on to the next privileged reader.

I cannot say that Tatiana took much part or even interest in our political discussions. "We can't really change anything," was her stock answer. "I don't intend to spend my life hitting my head against the wall. And I warn you," she would admonish me, "I don't intend to let you do it, either." She remonstrated if any of our guests ever went so far as to suggest direct political action—none of which, I might add, ever went beyond words. But Tatiana was afraid I might somehow take it into my head to turn these verbal resolutions into action.

Her fears were groundless. Despite my passion for the writings of Aleksandr Solzhenitsyn, Robert Conquest, and Abdurakhman Avtorkhanov, and the sometimes extreme positions I postulated in political discussions with friends, my viewpoints were unchanged: Leave politics to the politicians. And yet each day I became increasingly aware of the strange ambiguity of my situation.

After having stayed up all night reading Conquest's *The Great Terror*, I boarded a military plane the next day for the Crimea, where Tatiana and I spent the day lounging on a beach reserved for the use of high-ranking military officers. I who had sincerely sympathized with the Prague Spring watched my daughter splashing in the pool with Marshal Yakubovsky, head of the Warsaw Pact troops. I who had despaired at seeing my country's agriculture being systematically ruined was also on the receiving end of delicacies reserved for the happy few.

The conflict was growing, and I knew that sooner or later it would explode, bringing with it an end to our pleasant and peaceful existence. Sooner or later we would be asked to pay for our privileges, whether it was to denounce friends, betray our ideals, or collaborate with the authorities. For the time being, however, no such demands were being made. It was silly, though, to think that *they* would really forget me, leave me alone. Still, I remained passive. Even if I was tempted from time to time to emigrate, usually in the wake of the departure of one of our friends, I would say to myself, *As long as nothing happens, let well enough alone. If and when they rear their ugly heads, then we'll see.*

Which is tantamount to leaving your head buried in the sand.

In 1970, a group of desperate men decided to hijack a plane to Sweden after giving up all hope of ever receiving official approval

to emigrate to Israel. Their attempt failed; in fact, they were
arrested even before they reached the airport. But the authorities were clearly alarmed. No one had ever made so bold an
attempt before. They decided to make an example of the ring-
leaders, Edward Kuznetsov and Mark Dymshits, both of whom
were tried and sentenced to death. The outside world was shocked
at the harshness of the sentence. Throughout the trial, the world
also learned that emigration was a major problem in the Soviet
Union. Finally, if their intention had been to deter further flow
of applications for emigration, the authorities were in for a rude
surprise: The number of requests multiplied immediately.

Kuznetsov and Dymshits would have lost their lives had it
not been for the timely intervention of both President Richard
Nixon and Secretary of State Henry Kissinger. It so happened
that several Basque activists had been sentenced to death by
the Spanish courts at roughly the same time, and the White
House was quick to seize its chance. The Americans pressured
Generalissimo Franco into commuting the sentences, which he
eventually did. Brezhnev had no choice but to follow. Communism's leaders could not come off looking harsher in the world's
eyes than a fascist dictator!

The "Jewish question" loomed large, especially because of
the crushing military victory that Israel had won in 1967 over
an enemy vastly superior in numbers and equipped with the
latest wonders of Soviet weaponry. The Six-Day War had stirred
the hearts of Soviet Jews as nothing had ever done before. For
the first time, they were proud to be Jews. Until then, most of
them dreamed of only one thing—integrating, becoming as Russian as possible—so much so that substantial sums of money had
been paid to have documents falsified and personal biographies
altered, with the cherished goal of seeing the word *Russian* or
Ukrainian or *Byelorussian* written in their passports where the
word *Jew* once had been. In the case of children of mixed par-
entage, the choice was almost automatic when one reached the
age of consent: The nationality of the non-Jewish parent was the
one chosen. And at census-taking time, many Jews did their best
to hide their origins.

Israel's lightning victory changed all that. Nor did the change have anything to do with religion. Most Soviet Jews had long since given up the religion of their ancestors and undergone the usual agnostic training of contemporary Russia. We simply felt our kinship with the Israelis, with a people who had just conducted themselves in what seemed to us exemplary and heroic fashion. When the Soviet press launched its vitriolic attacks against Israel, it only fueled the fire. Even the most integrated and sophisticated Jews began to contemplate the possibility of emigrating. The Israeli government, which had long dreamed of a major influx of Russian Jews, did its best to encourage that new frame of mind. As a result, the number of applications surged to flood level. Caught short, the Soviet authorities lost their cool and panicked. They imprisoned activists agitating for a quick departure and terrorized those who had already applied for exit visas by removing them from their jobs. Meetings were held that subjected Jews to all kinds of indignities. Almost every day there was an anti-Semitic article in the press. Again, the campaign proved counterproductive. Instead of intimidating Russian Jews, it made them believe, with good reason, that a full-scale pogrom was in the offing, and any method of getting out was now worth trying. Many wrote to friends or relatives in Israel begging to be "invited" to visit. (OVIR* required such an "invitation" before even considering a request for emigration.) Most of the requests for exit visas were summarily refused, without explanation. A few, mostly from the Western Ukraine and the Baltic states, were allowed to leave, mainly because the local leaders were glad for an excuse to rid themselves of "their Jews."

Those whose visa requests were denied without explanation were known as *refuseniks*, and their numbers grew steadily day by day. Most of them were out of work, had nothing but time on their hands, and were not afraid to voice their demands. Each time one of them was arrested, the news was passed to the West. It traveled around the world and made its way back to Russia via the Voice of America, the BBC, Deutsche Welle, and the Voice of Israel.

*OVIR is the Soviet government agency in charge of emigration.

At this juncture, the Soviet authorities had another fear: that the *refuseniks* would join forces with the dissidents. The KGB and the Central Committee were convinced that the roots of the dissident movement were largely Jewish. Official propaganda played on the basest instincts of the people, stressing the fact that most of the well-known dissidents were Jewish. For the Kremlin, the notion that there was a nationwide network of determined, intelligent, and courageous "subversives" was a nightmare. To allow any rapprochement between *refuseniks* and dissidents would be nothing less than catastrophic. They remembered all too well the important role that the Jewish intelligentsia had played in the October Revolution. They knew that many of Lenin's coworkers and comrades were Jewish, and that they held key posts in the early Soviet governments. The thought of seeing history repeat itself, this time at their expense, haunted them—so much so that they saw the long arm of the Jews in the events in Czechoslovakia in 1968 and Poland in 1970.

So convinced were the Polish authorities of this nefarious Jewish influence that once peace had been restored, they systematically exiled the country's Jewish population. And when the uprising of the Polish workers in 1981 shook the very foundations of the regime, the leaders accused the "Zionists" of creating the problem, even though only 6,000 Jews were left in Poland.

One of my colleagues at the Military Tank Academy, a general, put it this way: "All these Prague Springs, these workers' revolts, these economic reforms, and all such nonsense are the result of a vast Zionist conspiracy. The proof is obvious. Do you think it was by chance that Dubček wanted to establish diplomatic relations with Israel? Believe me, I have it from impeccable sources: It was the Zionists who instigated the Polish workers' insurrection."

"Then why don't you let the Jews leave the Soviet Union?" I asked, playing dumb.

"If it were up to me," the general muttered, "they'd already be gone. But the Politburo doesn't want to create a precedent. If the Jews go, the Armenians will follow, then the Ukrainians, and before you know it, all our Ivans will want to go, too. In which case, who will be left to build socialism?"

That reminded me of a story, which I told the general. "Brezhnev was complaining to Kosygin. 'What are we going to do, Alexei? Since we authorized the possibility of emigration, everyone and his cousin is leaving the country. Pretty soon, we'll be the only two left.' At which point Kosygin looks up and says, 'Speak for yourself, Leonid!' "

The general laughed heartily, then took out his little black book and made note of the joke, to be sure he remembered it at the next party.

But what he said reflected the Communist party line. The Kremlin could not let this explosive situation continue much longer. The fuse was lighted, but they could not risk an explosion.

It was during this tense period that the attempted hijacking to Sweden took place, multiplying the demand for exit visas. The Politburo, caught between a rock and a very hard place, decided it had to slightly lift the iron curtain. Quite rightly, they thus hoped to separate the Jewish emigration movement from the mainstream dissidents.

At the same time, the Soviet leaders were using the theme of emigration to enhance their image throughout the world. It was publicized as a concrete gesture of goodwill, proof of the regime's new liberal line, a meaningful step in the context of détente. Détente was key, and a means to several ends: recognition of the status quo in Europe, extension of the Soviet sphere of influence, and a means to increase the flow of economic aid from the West to Russia.

A decade later, it is clear that even though Soviet diplomacy has suffered setbacks in certain areas, the notion of détente has brought Russia a number of very important pluses: new technology, credit, computers, and scientific and technical exchanges. Détente also enabled the Soviet Union to make great strides militarily. In 1973 Brezhnev told a Warsaw Pact meeting, "Détente will enable us to achieve in a very short period of time what long years of confrontation failed to obtain from the West. You may rest assured, comrades, that within the next decade or two, we will have the means to impose our will wherever we find it necessary."

I would be curious to know whether partisans of détente in the West have pondered the full implications of that statement.

The official organs of propaganda played a key role in the outburst of anti-Semitism following the liberalization of Jewish emigration. "Soviet Jews who leave their country," they proclaimed, "are traitors and deserve to be treated with contempt and scorn." But there was another, hidden reason for this: jealousy. For the ordinary Russian citizen, a trip abroad is an impossible dream. Those who have traveled, especially in the West, are surrounded with an aura of prestige. It means they are more intelligent, more patient, more supple, and above all more wily than their fellow citizens. All of a sudden, the Jews can stroll away, their hands in their pockets, leaving Ivan behind the iron curtain, never to see London or Paris or New York. It's shameful! Goddamned Jews!

The authorities also played their part in fanning the flames. Today it is virtually impossible for a Jew to get into a university or find a decent job in the Soviet Union. The argument they use is irrefutable. "Look," they say, "we can't give you a job. How do we know you won't just pack up some day and leave the country?"

All this said, the bureaucracy continued to function in its own inimitable and unpredictable way. Some who applied for exit visas were turned down, because, OVIR informed them, they had "access to secret State data." This hardly explains why taxi drivers and hairdressers were also refused.

A sociologist friend of mine made a study of these cases and came to the conclusion that the authorities chose families at random for rejection, giving the most absurd reasons for the turn-down. In fact, the more absurd, the better. That "voluntary absurdity" created among the applicants a climate of fear and uncertainty. Anybody could be turned down. The hope was, among the Soviet authorities, that this fear would cut down on the number of requests. After all, a *refusenik* was henceforth branded as a marginal member of society, if not a criminal, and subject to arrest or incarceration in a psychiatric ward at any time.

Once again, however, the Kremlin leaders were mistaken. The lines in front of the OVIR office did not, as the authorities had expected, grow shorter. They grew longer day by day.

In that climate, I too should have been in the OVIR line. But two obstacles stood in my way. First, I had worked at the Kurchatov Institute of Atomic Energy and the Institute for Nuclear Research in Dubna. Second, I was teaching at the Military Tank Academy. In the eyes of the authorities, I had to be in possession of State secrets. Fortunately, my classification for access to restricted information was not "top secret" but only what is termed "second category." Still, anyone even in that lower category was obliged by law to remain in the country for five years after leaving these areas of sensitive employment, so that, in principle, the secrets they possessed could become outmoded. I would gladly have left my job and waited for five years. But there was a third and far more serious reason why even that would not have worked: An applicant for emigration had to obtain a letter of consent from his or her parents before submitting the forms. To think that General Kozlov and his wife would give us such a letter was a utopian dream.

So I tried to put the whole idea out of my mind. Besides, I did not want to upset Tatiana. But the thought kept coming back, until it became almost an obsession. The general's pressures on me to join the party were also increasing, and sooner or later I was going to have to deal with that.

One day the general arrived at our apartment unannounced during a big dinner party. At one point, Tatiana took him aside and whispered, "Papa, you should be proud of us. Among our guests tonight is Alexei Fedoseyev, the son of the academician." Alexei's father was one of the most reputed Soviet ideologues. "He's become one of our closest friends," she added with a disarming smile. The general beamed and congratulated Tatiana on her choice of a new friend. "It's time you two were seeing decent citizens rather than those anti-Soviet bums you used to hang out with," he said.

Two days later, the phone rang at dawn. It was the general

calling from Kiev. "What are you trying to do to me?" he screamed. "Kill me?"

I was still half asleep and couldn't figure out what he was talking about, so I handed the receiver to Tatiana. "What's the matter?" she asked calmly.

"Last night I was listening to the Voice of America," he said, "and what do I hear but that your Fedoseyev has defected. Not only that, he's ranting and raving about the USSR and the inevitable fall of socialism. If you go on seeing that kind of person, we're all going to end up in Siberia, I warn you. I think you're both crazy! Out of your minds!"

It was sensational news, all right. The president of the Academy of Social Sciences, head of the ideological section of the Central Committee, a defector! I found it hard to believe. I immediately called Alexei to find out what had happened.

Without even saying, "Good morning," I blurted out, "So, is it true?"

"Is what true?" he asked.

"The story about your father."

"My father?"

"Stop playing dumb," I said. "They announced it on the radio last night."

"Announced *what*? What in the hell are you talking about?"

Something stank in the kingdom of Russia.

"Don't tell me you don't know that your father has defected. . . ."

"Are you joking? My father's right here. In his study."

"I'll bet he's not."

"Hold on a minute. I'll go check. Unless he's defected in the last half hour."

In a few seconds, Alexei was back. "My father," he said, "is not only in his study but is reading an article announcing that he's just been awarded another Order of Lenin. At least he *looks* like my father. Where did you hear all this?"

I told him, and Alexei burst out laughing. "That's another Fedoseyev," he said, "some electronics specialist who defected during an air show in Paris. And by the way, Edward, that's old news. It happened quite a while back."

Poor General Kozlov. He had almost had apoplexy over the wrong Fedoseyev.

One day I ran into one of my former students in the street. He had just graduated from the army's translator school, following a tour of duty in Syria, where he had completed his on-the-job training in Arabic. He was only passing through Moscow, on his way to his new post. I asked him where that was, but he was reluctant to answer. Finally he said, "My job is preparing Arab-language broadcasts for the Middle East."

Intrigued, I asked him for more details, but again I had the feeling that he preferred not to answer. Still, I was his old teacher, and little by little managed to worm it from him. The party, it seems, had decided to step up its propaganda program to the most sensitive political areas of the world. In the Arab countries, the Soviet influence seemed to be waning. To help reverse that decline, new transmitters had been built on the southern borders of the country, with the intention of flooding the Arab countries with Soviet propaganda. My former student worked in the editorial room of one of these stations.

"You don't seem exactly overjoyed by your work," I said.

He shrugged. "It's a job," he said, "and it pays well. But I have to confess I find most of the programs we put out pretty strange."

"Strange? In what way?"

Again he hesitated, shifting from one foot to the other. Then, as though making up his mind to level with me, he said, "Oh, what the hell. . . . But I trust you'll keep this to yourself. To take one example, during the Yom Kippur War, we were urging the Arabs to mount a holy war against Israel, calling on them to wipe the country off the face of the earth. You should have heard the text: 'Brothers, fellow Muslims: the Zionists have stolen your lands and your homes! Dishonored your women! They have desecrated the Koran! Death to the ungodly!' And so on and so forth. You can imagine how I feel reading that crap out loud from morning till night."

I'm naive, and always have been. I found it hard to believe

what I had just heard. "No government radio station would broadcast that," I said, shaking my head.

"I don't think you understand," he said. "We make them think we're Arabs ourselves. We imitate the style of the mullahs. We were specially trained for the job."

"But that's illegal!" I exclaimed.

"I suppose it is," he said.

I wanted to know more, but seeing how upset I was by his revelations, my ex-student made some excuse and hurried away.

It was the first time I had heard of these "pirate radio stations." I know that today they are becoming more and more aggressive. During the American hostage crisis in Iran, Soviet programs were aired for the express purpose of undermining negotiations that might have led to the hostages' release.

What my ex-student had said had so appalled me that I phoned my father-in-law in Kiev and asked him if I could see him right away. He told me he would be in Moscow the following week and we could get together then. We set a date, and I showed up a minute ahead of time. After the usual amenities, I blurted out my "news." "Are you aware, Pyotr Ivanovich, that there exist, on Soviet soil, pirate radio stations broadcasting propaganda around the clock and specifically fomenting war, aggression, and murder? All of which is forbidden under Soviet law?"

Maybe I was talking too fast. In any event, it was apparent the general didn't know what I was talking about. Then, after he made me repeat my question more slowly, he looked at me suspiciously. "Who told you about these stations?"

"It doesn't matter. I just happened to learn about them. Do you know about them, yes or no?"

"Listen, my boy," the general said sternly, "I have only one piece of advice to give you. Keep your nose out of such things. You're dealing with State secrets, and the less you know about them, the better."

So he *did* know. Given his position, how could he not have?

"How could you stoop to such methods?" I said accusingly. "How can you appeal to people's basest instincts, play on their ignorance in that way? Don't you have any self-respect? Where are you people leading our poor country?"

The general was not used to being talked to this way. His eyes widened, he blanched visibly, and in so many words he told me to mind my own business, to take care of my family and keep out of politics.

"You're a stupid son-of-a-bitch, and all I've had from you to date is trouble. I've been asked several times to curb your anti-Soviet activities. You have no idea what might happen if you don't shape up."

"I only speak my mind in the privacy of my own home," I said bravely. "Am I to infer from what you just said that they've bugged my apartment?"

I was amazed. Why should the KGB be even vaguely interested in a man who was not a dissident, whose dreams of changing the world remained within the four walls of his own home? Maybe there was an informer among my friends. Or else the general was exaggerating, trying to score a point or find out from my reaction if there was any truth in what he had said. In any event, I was furious at not being able to confirm my suspicions about the pirate radio stations, and I decided to let the general have it straight out.

"Frankly, I don't see what's wrong with expressing my own opinion. I've heard you criticize conditions here dozens of times: how the problem of alcoholism is getting worse, not to mention productivity. How many times have I heard you go on about the laziness of the peasants on the collective farms? How students and workers and engineers, not to mention whole army divisions, have to be sent out to bring in the crops? I've also heard you go on about the five-year plans that aren't working, about the army that's going to hell in a handbag, and God knows what all."

"You're right," the general said calmly, "I did say those things, and I would say them again, because we have to fight against such conditions. There are too many drunks and backsliders among us. But instead of accusing the party of all the evils in the system, we should work to change and improve things. There are two ways of criticizing: one as a friend who wants to better the situation, the other as an enemy who is delighted by the problems."

"Pure demagoguery!" I said. "And who's going to educate the people? The party for which you have nothing but contempt? Name me one member who you can say in all sincerity is honest and decent, with ideals, and able to carry them through on a practical level? Just one! You keep pestering me to join the party when you know very well I consider its methods criminal."

"You don't know what you're saying, Edward. I was trying to talk to you like a normal human being. I thought you understood that I wanted to help you. I care about Tatiana's future, and Tania's, too. Yes, and even about yours, Edward. But all you care about is not getting your hands dirty, isn't that true, comrade?"

"Why keep coming back to my problems?" I asked. "We were talking about general problems that I consider very important."

"Stuff your general problems!" he said. "Of course we have shortcomings. But who doesn't? Look at America—with millions of people unemployed, a soaring crime rate, racism, recurring recessions. You think everything is a bed of roses over there?"

As usual, the general was falling back on the familiar Communist ploy of shifting the conversation onto wholly new ground. I should have let well enough alone. But I couldn't refrain from replying.

"We weren't talking about America but Russia," I said. "Why are you sticking your nose in other countries' affairs? Why impose your barbaric methods on them? Instead of squandering billions to satisfy the imperialist ambitions of the old farts in the Politburo, why don't you clean up your own backyard first? Then people wouldn't have to stand in line for hours waiting to buy a few pounds of rotten potatoes, or travel for hundreds of miles to get their families some meat. At least the Americans have enough to eat."

"Don't try to tell me you really care about the people, Edward! You don't know what you're talking about. And as for your earlier question, yes, we do go sticking our noses in other peo-

ple's businesses sometimes, because if we didn't, the Americans
would have long since been occupying Red Square. Our policy
is to oppose American imperialism wherever it appears, and
that of their allies when they get out of line, too. It's them
or us, Edward. And I think it's high time you decided whose side
you're on."

What the general didn't know was that I already had decided.
The only problem was how to get to the other side. From the
way he seemed intent on trying to knock some sense into me,
I felt that at least for the time being, the general did not suspect
anything.

But from that day on, there were many such clashes between
us. After each, I realized that I was fast coming to a turning
point in my life. All of my philosophical reasons for remaining
aloof were crumbling. I could no longer go on living as I was,
feeling as I did on the one hand and profiting from my privileged
status on the other. That, too, was a crime.

I had to talk to Tatiana, to share with her my secret thoughts,
to find out what she thought. As always, her advice was wise
and to the point. "You can't feel responsible for other people's
crimes," she said. "If people knew that you were suffering because of the way the Soviet government is acting, they'd laugh
in your face. There might be a few who would understand you,
but believe me, there wouldn't be many."

"I don't care whether or not they understand," I said. "The
point is, I can't stand it here any longer. I can't read their
newspapers without flying into a rage. Whenever I hear the oily
voices of the radio or television commentators extolling the virtues of the latest working-class victory, I feel like throwing up.
The same is true when I hear our leaders mouthing off. Darling,
one can't live constantly in a climate of hate. I'm at the end of
my rope."

Tatiana heard me out without saying a word. Then she put
her arms around me and tried to comfort and calm me. "You
may be right," she said, "but don't forget that you have Tania
and me. Try to be happy and forget the rest. Let them do what
they have to. It's no concern of ours. In a country like that, we
have to live for ourselves. That's the only solution."

"That's what I've been telling myself for months," I said, "but I no longer believe it. And we have to face up to the fact that they won't leave us alone. They'll try to force me to join their stinking party. And that will only be the beginning."

"So what should we do?" she asked quietly. I could see she was fighting back tears. I could not stand to hurt her, but in fact we were caught in an absurd, and seemingly inescapable, trap.

"Maybe I could ask my father to let us go work abroad for a few years," Tatiana murmured.

The poor girl still believed in miracles. But her voice was so filled with hope that I suddenly had a crazy idea. Why not join the party after all and then get myself assigned to East Germany, where the Military Tank Academy had an annex. Once there, we could climb the Berlin Wall.

"Abroad?" I said. "Why not? Of course we still have to find a way over the Wall."

Again Tatiana's eyes filled with tears. I couldn't bear it any longer. I had to find a solution. What could I do? Divorce her? Did we really have any other choice? I pronounced the word. Tatiana clapped her hands to my mouth. "Never," she said. "Don't ever say that word again."

Her determination gave me strength, but it did not lessen my obsession. I asked my friends for advice. Some told me, "By all means join the party. The more decent people there are in the party, the better chance of making things better from within." Others said that if ever I joined the party they would never speak to me again. Still others held a middle ground, saying that they had been caught in the same dilemma for years without knowing how to resolve it.

All of which advanced me not one inch. To avoid sinking into apathy and depression, I threw myself into my work. I finished my first book and completed several chapters of another. I had brought my theory of electrical discharges in gases to a point where its verification required the use of computers. Meanwhile, I enrolled in some advanced courses in biophysics at the university, to advance my knowledge in that area. The work exhilarated me. It also altered my relationship with Tatiana. She had majored in biochemistry and organic chemistry and quickly became my teacher, scolding me in the same way I had done to her when I had been her tutor. At the same time, we both started teaching Tania to read and were amazed by her progress.

So life resumed its course, and, little by little, the dark ideas that had beset me disappeared.

Several months later, in the fall of 1974, as I was leaving the Military Tank Academy amphitheater after a lecture, two faceless men accosted me.

"Edward Dmitrievich Lozansky?"

"In the flesh. What can I do for you?"

"Please follow us," said one of them, flipping open his police credentials. "State Security," he added, but I knew it before he opened his mouth. Strangely, I felt relieved. *It had to happen,* I said to myself, though I didn't quite know why. After all, I had done nothing wrong.

"Can I call my wife? I don't want her to worry."

"That won't be necessary. We won't detain you for very long."

So I was not being arrested. These were relatively liberal times, and people were not arrested, with rare exceptions, for mouthing off against the regime in private. I was only going to be interrogated. I probably should have been worried, but for some reason I wasn't. In fact, I found myself looking on the whole episode with a certain humor. I had often wondered, as I was reading *samizdat* writing, how I would act during an interrogation. I always identified with the man being grilled, and I used to think up devastating and sarcastic phrases that the men in the books had not had the presence of mind to think of on the spot. But thinking up such clever and original phrases while reclining on the couch in the comfort of your home, with your wife only a few feet away, is not quite the same thing as dealing with the situation when it occurs.

Flanked by the two KGB men, I crossed the courtyard of the academy, which had originally been a castle built by Catherine the Great. Every time I walked through the courtyard, I admired the imposing architecture, and even now the same thoughts filled my mind. Outside, a Volga was waiting for us. We headed toward the Kuznetsky Bridge and then on to KGB headquarters.

During the trip, one of the agents said nothing, but the other tried to get a rise out of me by relating my life in surprising detail. He knew where I had studied, who my friends were, how I spent my leisure hours, even where I had been on such and such a date.

I was impressed, and I nodded as he went down the list. When I corrected a few technical terms he had misused, he smiled and nodded in turn.

The car stopped, and they led me to an office in which was seated a relatively young man. He rose as I entered and introduced himself: Andrei Petrovich. It was he who conducted the interrogation, the two others remaining silent throughout, though I noted that from time to time they jotted something in their notebooks.

"Well, Edward Dmitrievich," Petrovich began, "you've really got yourself in a bind, haven't you?"

"I'm afraid I don't know what you're talking about."

"You have no idea why you were brought here?"

"Not in the least."

"Let me refresh your memory."

Andrei Petrovich opened a file on the desk in front of him. He pulled out a sheet of paper and began to read.

Attempted to get into the trial of Sinyavsky and Daniel. *
Anti-Soviet agitation during the events of Prague, and
of the Middle East. Sent a telegram of congratulations
to Solzhenitsyn for winning the Nobel Prize. Involved
his students in the above-mentioned matter. Mentioned
Sakharov's name on several occasions during his classes
at the Tank Academy.

*Andrei Sinyavsky and Yuli Daniel were two Soviet writers tried and sentenced in 1966 to long prison terms for having allowed their works to be published in the West.

"I could go on, Edward Dmitrievich, but I think that should suffice for the moment."

"I still don't understand what you're getting at," I said. "The trial of Sinyavsky and Daniel was public—at least that's what *Pravda* said—so I went out of curiosity. But I never actually got in. The militia stopped me at the door. What's the crime there? What I said about Czechoslovakia and Israel was in the privacy of my own home. Solzhenitsyn? I did send him a telegram, but I never involved anyone else. The students who signed it did so on their own initiative. As for Sakharov, I mentioned him in a lecture on thermonuclear synthesis, since as you may or may not know, he made a series of important discoveries in this area. But my mention was totally in a scientific context. In fact, in that respect I was defending Soviet science, so I fail to see what harm you could find in that."

Andrei Petrovich smiled slightly. "Don't get so excited," he said. "We only brought you here for a little talk, not to quarrel."

"I'm not getting excited."

"Good. I assume you're aware that the directors of the Tank Academy would like you to join the party. That candidacy is for the moment on hold. In fact, given your position regarding Czechoslovakia, it would seem that party membership seems . . . how shall I say? . . . unlikely."

"Let me try to reply," I said. "As far as the party is concerned, I frankly haven't made up my mind. As for Czechoslovakia, I recognize that I was wrong."

"Ah?" Petrovich murmured, raising an eyebrow. "Wrong in what way?"

"Well, I thought the Czechs were what you might call sincere Communists, that they were trying to find the original purity of Marxist ideology. I was wrong. If we had not invaded Czechoslovakia, there wouldn't be a trace of communism left in the country, of that I'm now convinced."

"Fascinating," Petrovich said. "Go on."

"That's all," I said.

"I want more."

"I said I made a mistake. I thought the Czechs wanted to construct a new model of socialism. Actually, all they wanted was to revert to a multiparty system and a free-market economy."

"Where did you get this information?"

"It's a simple deduction."

"Fine. And what do you think about it now?"

"I told you. I was mistaken."

He looked at me closely. Then he took out a blank piece of paper and said, "Would you mind writing down everything you have just said?"

My knowledge of *samizdat* literature warned me that under no circumstances should you put anything in writing for the KGB. But I had said nothing blameworthy. On the other hand, I could see no possible harm in doing as he asked. I took the piece of paper and, virtually word for word, wrote down what I had said.

After Petrovich read it over, he looked up and said, "There's one point on which your position is not very clear. Did Czechoslovakia need our help or not?"

I smiled ambiguously. "That is not for me to say. If the Czechs really asked you to save them from the danger they were facing, as *Pravda* stated, then everything is fine."

"If the Czechs really asked *you*, Edward Dmitrievich? Why *you*? Are you dissociating yourself from all this? Don't you feel involved?"

"Of course," I said, "but nobody ever asked me for my opinion. I never saw the request from the Czech government. I suppose you did?"

"All right," he said, ignoring my question, "let's turn to another subject, Sakharov. You say you mentioned his name solely for scientific reasons. But tell me: Do you share his political ideas?"

"I don't know what his political ideas are. For me, Sakharov is first and foremost a great scientist. I've never met the man."

"You've never met him?"

"No."

"Didn't you attend any seminars at the Lebedev Institute?"

"Several. And I did see Sakharov there. But as I said, I never spoke to him. I'm sure he doesn't even know I exist, unless he has seen an article or two of mine in some journal of physics."

Petrovich leafed through my file. "According to our information, you went up to Sakharov several times and he handed you anti-Soviet literature."

It was a lie.

"Your information is wrong. Your men are doing a lousy job."

"I happen to believe otherwise. Be that as it may, you still haven't answered my question. Do you or do you not intend to continue defending Sakharov to your students? That's an important question, Edward Dmitrievich. Your students are the cream of the crop, those who will be the future military leaders of the country. They are the pride and glory of the Soviet Union, and we have to take every measure to protect them against pernicious influences."

"If they are your pride and glory, then you don't have to worry about them. But I would be happy to correct my views if they are wrong. Perhaps you could enlighten me: Did Sakharov make the scientific discoveries I mentioned in my lectures? After all, discoveries don't just happen. If Sakharov did in fact *not* make those attributed to him, I'd be only too happy to tell my students."

Petrovich snapped shut my folder. "We have no intention of joking with you. Several people have commented negatively about your behavior, Edward Dmitrievich. You are a professor. You use that post, and the authority it conveys, to the detriment of government interests. This is something we cannot and will not tolerate."

The man's apparent good nature had completely vanished, and his voice took on a metallic timbre. He handed me another piece of blank paper and said dryly, "I would like you to admit the subversive character of your past activities and agree that in the future you agree to cease and desist from circulating ideas detrimental to the Soviet State."

Now I was scared. Soviet authorities do not take accusations of propaganda and subversion lightly. Sentences can be as heavy as seven years in prison. And witnesses can always be found to swear to anything. I knew it was out of the question for me to write anything on that sheet of paper. All I could do was play dumb.

"How could I tell a dangerous idea from one that isn't? I'll bet there isn't a person in the Soviet Union who can tell the difference."

"Let's be practical. Write that you agree not to mention Sakharov's name again at the academy. The man is clearly a traitor, or on his way to becoming one. By praising him in your classroom, you can cause great moral damage to your students."

I found myself disliking this man Petrovich more with every passing minute.

"I refuse to write any such thing, at least until such time as you can find someone capable of convincing me that by telling the truth about who made what discoveries in science I am threatening the security of the State."

Petrovich's fingers beat a tattoo on the desk. He reached for the telephone. "We're about finished, Nikolai Vasilievich," he said into the phone. "If you have any questions for Lozansky, would you please join us now?"

He put down the phone and took a deep breath. "It is most unfortunate, Edward Dmitrievich. We had hoped that you were a very different kind of person, one who was simply under the influence of persons of doubtful character, whereas you were really one of us, an upstanding Soviet citizen. I'm afraid we're going to have to reconsider our opinion. Anyway . . . we think you ought to have some time to think. Our hope is that you will realize how far your delusions have taken you. At least I hope so, I sincerely do."

At that point, the door opened and in strode a short, balding man. He had a beefy face and darting eyes. "Good morning, Edward Dmitrievich. Allow me to introduce myself. My name is Nikolai Vasilievich. If you don't mind, I'd like to spend a few minutes with you to find out if you might be able to help us."

I couldn't believe what I was hearing. Were they trying to recruit me? I tried not to smile. Maybe they wanted to send me

to England on a top-secret assignment. Just what we were
dreaming of. I'd give Tatiana just time enough to browse through
all the English shops, then we'd go over to the nearest bobby
and announce that we were defecting. I almost burst out laughing. "At your service," I said, with more enthusiasm than I had
intended.

Nikolai Vasilievich beamed, as though convinced he had a
new convert. "Good," he said. "I don't need to tell you that we
live in perilous times. Some Western leaders dream only of
returning to the Cold War era. They're doing everything they
can to stir up trouble inside Russia, using a network of backsliders, criminals, and whatever other dregs of society they can
unearth. We must react against this situation."

I sensed that what he was about to propose had nothing to
do with a free trip to London. In all probability, the KGB needed
another informer, nothing more.

"What exactly do you want from me?" I asked.

"All that in due time. I'll get in touch with you in the very
near future. Meanwhile, if a possible collaboration is of interest
to you, we'd like to give you something that will enlighten you
about the problems we face. Here's an article on Sakharov by
the well-known historian Molchanov. I think you will find it
most interesting. But don't show it to anyone. It hasn't been
published in the Soviet Union. It has only been broadcast over
Radio Moscow to the West."

I knew Molchanov by reputation. I had recently read an
article by him in *The Literary Gazette* on Solzhenitsyn. In it he
tried to prove that Solzhenitsyn was both an anti-Semite and a
Jew, that he was descended from aristocrats and dreamed of
bringing back the old regime, and that he had sold his country
down the river for a pocketful of coins. The title of that article
had been "One Who Sold Out." I had no desire to read the same
kind of drivel about Sakharov.

"Keep the article," I said. "I know what's in it."

"That's strange," said Nikolai Vasilievich. "You claim to know
nothing about Sakharov's political opinions, yet you refuse to
read an article that would enlighten you on the subject."

In all honesty, I was disappointed by the KGB. I had always heard that the KGB used methods that were as subtle as they were diabolical. But, I figured, I was small fry in its eyes, and doubtless second-raters were assigned to my case. I must have been scowling, for Nikolai Vasilievich added, almost apologetically, "There's nothing terrible in this article. Next time we'll show you something much more instructive. That will be all for today. You can go."

"Needless to say," Petrovich interjected, "we'd like to ask you not to mention this meeting to anyone. Not even your wife."

"That's rather impractical, isn't it," I responded dryly, "since everyone already knows about it? Several officers at the academy saw me leave accompanied by your two colleagues."

"No matter. If anyone asks, tell them it was a routine matter. As for your superiors, none of them knows anything. In fact, they're very pleased with your work and have no idea you mentioned Sakharov in your classes, which we learned about through our own channels. So don't be worried. Go on about your business, but try to bear in mind our little discussion today."

Outside in the street, I took a deep breath of fresh air. The moment I had long feared had finally arrived. The comrades of the KGB had left me alone for many years. Now, I was sure, they would leave me alone no longer.

Needless to say, despite the warning of my interrogator, I told Tatiana everything the minute I got home. At first she was upset and frightened, but when I said I thought they were trying to recruit me, she thought it was hilarious.

"That's too much!" she exclaimed. "I'll be Mata Hari, you'll be Philby, and Tania will be Major Pronin.* Let them send us abroad. We'll ferret out all of capitalism's deep, dark secrets. And since we all know those secrets are closely guarded, it will take us a long time to find them!"

We spent the rest of the evening joking and fabricating scenarios in which we figured as master spies. All very funny. But deep in my gut I still carried the memory of the day's interrogation, and of the repercussions that were sure to follow.

*Major Pronin is a Russian spy character similar to James Bond.

One of my friends was a man named Vanya Petrov. A psychologist and sociologist, he had once confided to me that the KGB had tried to recruit him. "But I finally shook them off with a few well-chosen tricks," he concluded.

Vanya was a strange duck. Short, virtually bald, and constantly wrapped in a scarf no matter what the weather, he was enormously erudite, equally well versed in literature, music, and art. Despite this, he never struck me as either arrogant or haughty. He would always peer benevolently and questioningly over his wire-rimmed glasses, as though he were dealing with first-year students scared to death at the prospect of making a mistake in responding to their professor. He usually positioned himself in the middle of the room so that he was able to follow several conversations at the same time and respond to all, rather like a chess genius playing several boards simultaneously. His comments and advice were always interesting, even if one did not agree with them. At parties, he always turned up alone, without his wife, which only added to the aura of mystery that surrounded him. But at this juncture of my life, he was the man I wanted to talk to. I called him and set up an appointment for the next day.

He opened the door at my first knock, as though he had been standing there waiting for me. The inevitable scarf was in place. Before I could say a word, he put a finger to his lips, gestured for me to come in, and tiptoed to the telephone. He turned the dial slightly and secured it with a coin. Then he explained that the KGB had just put into service a very sophisticated new eavesdropping device purchased from the United States—or at least that was the rumor circulating in Moscow— that enabled the agency to overhear conversations through telephone lines even when the phone was on the hook. This eavesdropping, apparently, could be countered by rotating the dial a few degrees. Vanya said it was becoming commonplace in Moscow that, before you told an anti-regime story or talked freely at a party, the host would go to the phone and, using a coin or matchstick, outfox the KGB with this simple method. I suggested that as soon as the KGB realized the countermeasure, they'd quickly place another order for an even more sophisticated de-

vice. At which point the dissidents and intellectuals would find
a new antidote.

I then told Vanya what had happened to me the day before.
He listened, his eyes closed, nodding every now and then. When
I had finished, he said, "Before commenting, I'd like to know
what your plans are. Do you simply want to get rid of the KGB
agents or do you want to leave the Soviet Union? What are your
ultimate goals?"

I decided to level with him. "Vanya, I have only one desire:
to leave the country, with my wife and daughter. The idea of
leaving all my friends behind is hard to accept, but I also know
that someday, sooner or later, many of you will do the same. In
any case, all I know is that if I don't leave the country soon, I'll
go crazy."

My voice had become more and more emotional, but Vanya
did not flinch. Still, he seemed to take my case seriously. More
seriously, in fact, than I did.

"I understand," he said, "and the fact is I'd like to do the
same myself. But unfortunately I haven't a drop of Jewish blood
in my veins. I suppose I could divorce my wife and marry a
Jewish girl. . . . Anyway, we're not here to talk about me. Let's
look at your problem. You want to emigrate, and obviously you
want to do it legally. What are your problems? You have a
security clearance, I presume? You work for three official institutions at the same time. Your father-in-law is a general and a
member of the Presidium of the Supreme Soviet. What does all
that add up to? Not much, I'm afraid. But first a cautionary note:
I'm going to ask that you not mention our little talk to Tatiana.
Not that I don't trust her, but you never know. She just might
make some innocent slip to the wrong person without realiz-
ing it."

"All right. I won't say a word."

"I need time to think. Let's see each other again in a week."

Exactly seven days later, Vanya called and suggested we
meet in Gorky Park. There were lots of people out strolling,
and I felt comfort in numbers.

"I think I've found a solution for you," he began, "but I must

warn you that I think the chances of success are slim and the
risks enormous. Shall I go on?"

"Please do."

"First, let me say that I think you're crazy as a loon. Second,
you're in an almost impossible situation. So far so good?"

"I can't quarrel with the diagnosis," I said.

"Third, I have my own reasons for handling this case. If you
do succeed and reach the United States—I assume I'm right in
saying that's where you intend to end up—then I expect that
you'd help me get started if ever I made it there. Any problem?"

"None whatsoever."

"All right. Let's begin."

"Please. The suspense is killing me."

"I have to tell you that you and Tatiana get the credit for
what I'm about to suggest. You gave me the idea."

"We did?"

"You told me, jokingly of course, that you and Tatiana had
once entertained the idea of becoming Soviet spies. They want
to recruit you as spies, so why not spy?"

"Are you serious?"

"Absolutely. You must be aware of one key point. If you
want to 'take' them, you have to realize that they won't let you
leave without any strings attached. First you'll have to gain their
confidence."

"If that means joining the party, forget it."

"If that's your position, it will just make things more complicated. But first hear me out."

I had no intention of cooperating with the KGB, but still I
was curious to know what Vanya had in mind. I was also naive
enough to think that I could "take" the KGB and somehow get
it to send me abroad without first having proved myself.

We spent hours going over every aspect of my future behavior. I was astonished to know how well versed Vanya was
about the KGB, its structure, its methods, even its key personnel. From then on, our relations took on a new dimension, for
if he was putting himself on the line for me, I also realized more
and more that contact with Vanya was also dangerous for me. I

listened to his every word. After all, this was the first time that anyone had come up with a concrete plan for awakening me from my nightmare and making me a free man.

I met with Vanya several times. As promised, I never mentioned our meetings to Tatiana. It was bad enough to know that I was implicating her in this crazy adventure. The closest I came was to ask her if she would come with me if ever I found a way to reach the West. She had a moment's hesitation, then said, "Of course I will. How could you ever think otherwise?" Her voice carried a tinge of reproach. "I know that ever since the KGB has taken an interest in you, your life is finished in the Soviet Union. I have only one goal," she went on, "and that is to keep our family together. Since our country is making that difficult, if not impossible, we have no choice but to leave."

How simple. How logical. Her words, her candor, and her clear determination gladdened my heart. But even if everything worked out the way Vanya had planned, I knew we had a long, hard road ahead of us.

Vanya had explored all the possible variants of my situation with computerlike precision. He had also ascertained that my summons and interrogation by the KGB was not an isolated case. For months, apparently, the KGB had been concentrating on "the Jewish problem," in an effort to control what had essentially become a near-anarchic emigration process. They used various techniques: Some people they tried to frighten and others they tried to coopt and turn into propagandists against emigration. Still others were enlisted as agents, working within the country or abroad (primarily in Israel), where it was possible to blend with the other Soviet émigrés without arousing suspicion.

According to Vanya, as many as thirty or forty percent of the émigrés were contacted by the KGB before their departure, and about half of them signed up, out of either fear or concern that otherwise their visas would be denied. Virtually all of these would-be agents owned up immediately upon their arrival in Israel. The KGB was aware of this but deemed that quality was preferable to quantity and that even though most of the recruits were lost, it was still worth the effort if one in a thousand remained faithful.

Thus the problem Vanya was analyzing: How could Tatiana and I get on the list of a group emigrating to Israel without the KGB tying us up completely? He was also trying to find out about the psychological criteria for selecting recruits. All he knew—from having been asked to join—was that there was a special psychological section whose job it was to study each candidate. The problem was that mine was a unique case, one that did not fit any known criteria. On the one hand, the KGB agents should never have contacted me, for they knew that the general would be furious if he found out. On the other hand, they could not allow me to continue what they called my "anti-Soviet activities." It was not only the mention of Sakharov's name in my classes. It was also, as Vanya pointed out, that there were a number of foreigners, officers from Third World countries, in my classes, and these people were considered key couriers of Communist propaganda when they returned home. My influence on them was considered to be especially pernicious. For all these reasons, Vanya was of the opinion that the KGB had not yet made up its mind quite how to handle me. The plan probably was to see how I reacted to my "warning," observe which bait I might take. It was clear to both Vanya and me, however, that for the moment the KGB had no intention of sending me to Israel. But anything was possible. If I were to behave "properly," I still could wind up on the list of "correspondents." But just what "properly" consisted of, I did not know.

Vanya promised to check with some people who had already worked with the KGB in this way and enlighten me. I was sure he wouldn't have far to look. I knew I wasn't the only person he was advising. In fact, there were times when I wondered whose side he was really on. In any case, he ordered me to change my ways immediately, to shape up and stop acting like an arrogant prig, and to listen to the KGB's next proposals calmly and patiently. Sooner or later, they would show their true cards.

Three months went by. Nobody called. I must confess that I was slightly disappointed. I was hoping that something would happen to get the ball rolling. But they seemed to have forgotten me. Then, toward the end of 1974, Nikolai Vasilievich phoned and asked if I would meet him at one of Moscow's major hotels.

Tatiana accompanied me as far as the lobby, hugged me, wished me luck, and left.

Vasilievich had told me to come to a room on the third floor. He opened the door with a friendly smile and invited me in. He asked me about my family, my work, my vacation plans. When they are interviewing potential agents, the KGB can be as smooth as silk. Then he got down to business.

"For several years now," he said, "so-called Sunday Scientific Seminars have been held at the home of a well-known Zionist, Aleksander Voronel. As you might expect, they are attended for the most part by a bunch of turncoats, mostly Jews who have been refused exit visas. I might add that the people attending these seminars are less concerned with matters of science than with anti-Soviet activities. Also, foreigners are sometimes invited, mostly American agents and Zionists. We would very much like to know precisely what goes on at these gatherings."

As he talked, his eyes darted back and forth, unable to meet mine, and his voice sounded odd and different. When he had concluded, he gave me his best smile and said, "So, what about it?"

"Frankly, Nikolai Vasilievich," I said, "you disappoint me. I'm surprised you bother me with such trifling matters. Here I thought you were going to ask my help in uncovering a group of saboteurs planning to blow up the Kremlin, or the Moscow subway. But if I understand you correctly, all you're looking for is one more petty informer."

Vasilievich flinched, and smiled wanly. "It's not so petty, Edward Dmitrievich," he said. "We are truly concerned about the people who attend these seminars."

"So why don't you let them leave for Israel?"

"We can't. Most of these people have access to classified security information."

"Not all of them, I'm sure. And even those that do generally don't have high security clearances. I for one have a security clearance, yet I have no confidential information of any real value. I warrant that ninety-five percent of all scientists with clearance are in the same boat."

Nikolai Vasilievich's eyelids fluttered, and he slumped slightly in his chair. "Edward Dmitrievich," he said reproachfully, "you promised to help us, and look how you're reacting."

"First of all, I didn't promise you anything," I answered. "I simply said I'd hear you out. As for your proposition, I can't really help you. But I should point out that these seminars are open. Any one of your people could go without any problem. If they do, I suspect you'll find that these scientists you're apparently so frightened of represent no danger whatever."

His eyes finally found mine for a moment, and he said evenly, "You are quite wrong, Edward Dmitrievich. They *are* dangerous. We have proof that they are in contact with foreign agents and that they are spreading anti-Soviet propaganda across the country." He paused. "You say these seminars are free. But I assume you would not attend for nothing."

I wasn't sure I followed what he was saying.

"What I mean is, we're all materialists. We would make it worth your while."

Ah, so that was it. . . . "Nikolai Vasilievich," I said, "I'm afraid I'm going to have to lodge a complaint against you with Comrade Andropov.* I thought you might have something interesting for me, but I can see I'm wasting my time. You're trying to buy me for a few kopeks, as you might do with any petty criminal. If you don't mind, I have some urgent business to attend to."

I rose casually and started for the door. "Don't leave," he cried, "please don't go. You're wrong. I didn't mean to insult you. I wasn't trying to 'buy' you, as you put it. All I meant was that we would cover your expenses—restaurants, taxis, that kind of thing."

Now I felt I had the upper hand and decided to exploit it to the hilt. "Nikolai Vasilievich, let's get to the point. I have no intention of becoming an informer. Do you really want to know why I consented to come here today?"

He nodded expectantly. "Boredom," I said, reciting the speech I had rehearsed. "Yes, boredom, Nikolai Vasilievich. I was hop-

*Yuri Andropov was at that time head of the KGB.

ing you might come up with some dangerous, fascinating mission, filled with spine-tingling chases and female agents in slinky dresses. The real thing."

He smiled sadly, as if to indicate that he too would not mind a few encounters in a Hilton Hotel room with an agent with stunning legs and long blond hair. Instead of that, his job was to try to lure stool pigeons.

"All right," he said, "what precisely do you want?"

"I'm not sure," I said, playing hard to get. "Your role should be to propose, mine to dispose."

I wished at that moment I had had a hidden camera. Rarely had I seen someone so upset, so uncomfortable. Clearly he had been given precise instructions, with carefully defined limitations, and beyond that, he could not venture. So he had no place to go.

"All right," he said finally. "I'll report the details of our little conversation and get back to you."

That evening I met with Vanya and gave him a full report. But he wanted to know more, every tiny detail, until finally I lost patience and said, "Why everything? Are you writing a book on the subject?"

"Never mind," he chided, "I'm simply gathering information."

"You are crazier than I am," I said. "Just imagine if they learn that you are following their every move like a bloodhound."

"Don't worry about me," he said. "I can take care of myself."

"I hope so. Well, what do you think?"

"I think that if they had a brain in their head, they would drop you. But since they're not smart, and they value Nikolai Vasilievich's work as a recruiter, chances are they'll come back to you."

A few days later, the deputy commander of the Military Tank Academy called me into his office. He was a friend of General Kozlov and had always been solicitous toward me. He told me that the ministry had just signed an order restructuring the curriculum in military academies. As a result, less time was to be spent on physics, chemistry, and mathematics.

"Don't worry," he said, "your post is not in jeopardy. Still,

I would suggest that you try to come up with a new course, perhaps one on basic physics specially oriented toward modern weaponry. The minister would like that. That way we could transfer you to another section and keep you out of trouble when the inevitable arguments arise about who is to stay and who is to go."

I spent the next two weeks working up the special course, including up-to-the-minute subjects such as new energy sources, lasers, complex optical systems, particle-beam weapons, and so forth. The deputy commander looked over my syllabus, liked it, and sent it on for ministerial approval, which was granted rapidly—either because I was the general's son-in-law or because they really liked it.

A month later, I received a phone call. "Nikolai Vasilievich here. I'm sorry to hear you're having some trouble at the academy. My sources tell me you're about to be fired. Is there anything I can do for you?"

"No, thank you. I appreciate your interest, though."

Obviously he had heard of the forthcoming staff cuts at the academy, but his informants had apparently failed to apprise him of my new course.

"Well, let me know if things don't work out. Remember, we have a lot of pull. . . ."

"I'm sure they will," I said.

"But if they don't," he insisted, his words tumbling out faster and faster, "please don't hesitate to give me a call."

A month later, I received a letter informing me that because of the ministerial order modifying the curriculum, my services would no longer be required at the Military Tank Academy. That decision also meant that I would no longer be employed either at the Dubna Institute for Nuclear Research or the Kurchatov Institute of Atomic Energy. Both of those jobs had come about as a result of a personal intervention on the part of the president of the academy. I was jolted by all this, and couldn't figure out what was happening. First, my new course had been approved. Second, the policy for firing was "last in first out," and I had seniority in the physics department, where only three teachers were being let go.

All my colleagues interceded in my behalf. But Marshal Losik, the director of the academy, remained noncommittal. "There's nothing I can do," was his pat phrase. And that was that.

To tell the truth, I was not too upset. For a physicist of my experience, finding a job in a laboratory or institute would not present any insurmountable obstacles. Or so I thought.

Someone in a high place must have decided to make me unemployable. I can't remember how many turn-downs I received. Strangely, even all that did not perturb me. From a financial point of view, we were still fairly well off. I was earning royalties from both my books, receiving good fees for scientific articles I was translating from English for Soviet reviews, and still doing some tutoring. Besides, I figured, this was a convenient way of becoming declassified, under the five-year rule. For the first time in several years, I had free time, which I put to good use furthering my knowledge of biology and attending classes in biochemistry at the university. I finished several articles on my theory of electrical discharges. At home, I took over the cooking duties, not to mention the cleaning, since Tatiana was working at the Institute of Biochemistry of the Academy of Sciences. Each morning I took Tania to kindergarten, where she mingled with all the other children of the Moscow elite. In the evening I prepared dinner for the three of us, at which time we all exchanged news of the day's events. To an outsider, we would have seemed the ideal young Soviet family.

Six months went by. I had stopped counting the number of times I had been turned down for various jobs. At one point I was sufficiently exasperated to gather all my documents and send them, together with a letter of appeal, to Nikolai Podgorny, the president of the Soviet Union. A month later, I received a reply. My letter had been duly forwarded to the director of the Military Tank Academy, who telephoned to say how terribly sorry he was that there was nothing he could do to help.

During this time, I also received several phone calls from Nikolai Vasilievich, who wanted to know whether by chance I had changed my mind about the Sunday Scientific Seminars.

"I'm sure your professional problems could be cleared up in a matter of minutes," he would say.

"Thank you," I would respond inevitably, "but I'm afraid my views remain as I expressed them to you last time we met."

Finally, toward the end of 1975, he called again and suggested we meet in a Moscow hotel room.

This time his eyelids did not flutter, his eyes did not dart about incessantly, and no smile graced his lips. With a solemn air he said, "Edward Dmitrievich, we have given the matter much thought and have come to the conclusion that we can now trust you with an important task. I'm not authorized to give you the details, but I can tell you this much: We're talking about an assignment that will take you, your wife, and your daughter to Israel for a period of two to three years."

I tried not to react, but I was sure he could hear my heart pounding. At length I asked, in what I hoped was a normal tone of voice, "Israel? Why would you want to send me there?"

"We'll go into that later," he said. "All we wanted to know at this juncture was whether you might be so disposed. Needless to say, you would leave with a letter from the Presidium of the Supreme Soviet authorizing you to reenter the Soviet Union once your assignment had been accomplished."

"Of course," I murmured, thinking about what I would do with such a letter. "I must confess that your proposal takes me somewhat by surprise. I need to discuss it with my wife. We have to consider what the general's reaction will be. I assume in any event that we'll not be made to leave ignominiously, like ordinary emigrants?"

"Don't worry. We've taken care of everything. General Kozlov will make an announcement disowning his daughter, which will exonerate him. And you should know that the entire operation will be carried out with the knowledge and consent of his superiors."

"So he's already agreed?"

"Not yet, but I think it is safe to say that we can convince him," said Nikolai Vasilievich with a disarming smile. "Let me repeat: You don't have to say yes or no immediately. Take some time to think it over. And do discuss it with your wife."

I went directly from the hotel to Vanya's. Seeing the look on my face, he said, "So they've offered you a job abroad, eh?"

"You guessed it."

"It's a trap. They'll never send you to the West unless they have you sewn up. Wait and see. The next time you meet, they're going to ask you for 'a little favor'—nothing much, mind you—then another, until they have such a string on you that they can blackmail you for the rest of your life. At that point they may send you, because they know you can't betray them. It's a question of pure logic. If you really want to leave, be prepared to submit to what I've just described."

"Then they can all go to hell!"

"In which case, be prepared to spend the next several years in Moscow."

"We'll see," I said bravely.

Two weeks later, I met with Nikolai Vasilievich again. I told him that I had discussed everything with my wife and she had given her assent to proceed. So what exactly were they proposing?

"I'm delighted to know you are so inclined," said Nikolai Vasilievich in his most affable tone, "and you will know the nature of the assignment very soon. Meanwhile, there remains one small formality, what I might term an insignificant detail. Let me be frank with you. Our section is ready to send you abroad. The only thing lacking is the written authorization of our superior. If you want my advice, the only way to get that approval is to demonstrate beyond any shadow of a doubt that you are our man. And the best way to do that is to furnish us with some information about the Sunday Scientific Seminars."

Vanya was right once again. All of a sudden I was terribly depressed—depressed and angry with myself. Here I was, thirty-four years old and allowing myself to be taken in as though I were a schoolchild. I decided they would never let us leave Russia.

Vasilievich saw my reaction and tried to buoy my flagging spirits. "Don't be depressed," he said solicitously. "All we're asking you to do is to tell us about people whose guilt has already been established."

What's so terrible about that?

"I understand," I said. "But I repeat: I'll never agree to be an informer. What's more, I'm not at all sure I want to go to Israel. It all depends on the nature of the assignment. Go back to your bosses and tell them I want to know the specifics before I make up my mind. Otherwise, let's forget it."

That evening I gave Tatiana a detailed report of my meeting. We both agreed that it would be best to break off relations with Vasilievich. It was a depressing thought, but Tatiana, who at first thought the situation might be retrieved, finally came around to my way of thinking.

But suddenly I had a flash of insight that changed everything. "I've got it!" I shouted, so loudly that Tania, who was seated at the table drawing a picture of a house and tree, dropped her crayons. "Forget everything I just said. I know how to work it. In fact, the idea comes from Vasilievich himself."

I picked up Tatiana and swung her around madly. When finally I set her down, she caught her breath and said, "What idea? Don't keep me in suspense."

"It's so simple, so elementary. Listen. What were the obstacles standing in the way of our leaving? First, my security clearance. Second, your father. But the KGB told me that none of that matters. All your father has to do is renounce you, and he'll suffer no negative consequences. Which means that we can apply for exit visas, and if anyone says no, I'll remind them of my conversations with the KGB. It may take some fighting. Are you ready to fight, Tatiana?"

"I'm ready."

"Do you love me?"

"I do. More than ever."

"Are we going to leave this country?"

"We are."

"With you by my side, no one can beat us," I said. "I swear we'll win."

"I know," she whispered.

That evening, I received a phone call from a friend who asked if I could meet him right away. I took a taxi to a deserted street some distance away. After the taxi drove away, my friend appeared, glancing left and right in a way that would have made anyone suspicious. Then he began to whisper, even though there was no one within a block.

"Listen," he said, "today I was visited at work by KGB agents. They took me to Lubyanka and for three hours they tried to convince me to emigrate to Israel, together with my whole family. They promised I'd have no problem getting back into Russia whenever I wanted."

It sounded vaguely familiar.

"Did they mention that you might first have to do a little informing for them?"

"Yes, in fact, they did. Nothing major, though."

"Those guys really lack imagination!" I said. "You aren't the first one they've made that proposition to, and you won't be the last. You want my advice? Tell them to shove it, and go request an exit visa. Otherwise, they'll never let go of you."

My friend followed my advice, and is happy he did. He now lives with his family in Boston. Others did likewise. It was clear that the KGB was using the technique on a fairly massive scale, involving dozens of people.

Whenever I had any significant new information, I passed it on to Vanya, who made meticulous notes, to whatever end. Maybe someday he'll publish the results of his curious investigation.

Before we could make an official request to emigrate, we first had to be "invited" by relatives in Israel. The following Saturday, I made my way to Arkhipov Street, location of the only remaining synagogue in Moscow. As always, there was a crowd of people outside in the street, come less to pray than to exchange information in general and discuss their emigration status in particular. These gatherings irked the police. Arkhipov Street is narrow, with hardly enough room for vehicles to get through. To make things difficult for the congregants, the police closed off the broad boulevard that ran parallel to Arkhipov and diverted traffic down the tiny thoroughfare. It created the desired confusion, causing the crowd to disperse as it dodged the cars and trucks. But the

ultimate purpose, to discourage the Jews from coming, failed
totally. Each Saturday they gathered again, as if nothing had
happened. The young people sang and danced, under the
watchful eye of the police, who sometimes took photographs to
upset them further. There were times when the police went so
far as to provoke violence, at which point they would arrest a
number of Jews at random and charge them with "minor hooliganism."

That Saturday I mingled with the crowd, looking for a familiar
face. At length I spotted a friend, to whom I confided my mission.
"I'm looking for some 'relatives' to invite me to Israel."

He pointed to a short, vivacious man of about thirty, who
was moving rapidly from one little knot of people to the other,
as though he were hawking tickets to a football match.

"Come with me," said my friend. His introduction was short
and accurate. "Edward Lozansky, physicist at Kurchatov. Tolya
Shcharansky. He knows everyone."

Thus did I come to meet a most remarkable man, one who
had dedicated his life to furthering human rights in the Soviet
Union. Emigration, religious persecutions, internment of dissidents in psychiatric wards—he was involved in every aspect
of the vast struggle for freedom in Russia. Not only was he a
staunch advocate of the right to emigrate, he was also one of
the founders of the Moscow Helsinki Watch Group. His innate
charm, together with his uncontestable ability as an organizer,
kept peace and harmony among the various dissident groups.
It was a difficult and demanding job, made all the more so
by the fact that KGB agents had infiltrated most if not all of
the groups. To cite only one example: It turned out that one
of Tolya's closest friends, his roommate Sanya Lipavsky, was a
KGB informer.

But Tolya was stronger, more patient, more intelligent, more
supple than his enemies. He managed to satisfy the needs of
everyone without compromising his principles. Needless to say,
he was detested by the KGB, and eventually they arrested him
and sentenced him to thirteen years in prison, despite the protests of the international community. So hated was he by the
authorities that at one point the Central Committee discussed

whether he should be sentenced to death. Jimmy Carter's administration tried to strike a bargain for his freedom, offering to exchange two Soviet spies, Engel and Chernyaev, but the Kremlin spurned the offer. The Russians considered, and rightly so, that a man such as Shcharansky, one of the highest-minded men in the world and also one of the most efficacious, posed a terrible threat to their regime.*

In May 1976, we finally received an invitation from our "relatives" in Israel. Our next step was to obtain the general's permission to go.

The Soviet Union is the country of legal illegality. The authorities require that parental document, and there is no way around it. The reasoning is as simple as it is duplicitous. "Ours is a humanitarian government," goes the party line, "and therefore must concern itself with the welfare of its citizens. Suppose that, after you have emigrated, your parents retire on a pension insufficient to support them. Under our legal system, it is then the obligation of the children to provide for their parents. This is why we cannot entertain your application to emigrate without your parents formally stating that you are no longer responsible for their well-being."

Reasonable enough, of course, until one remembers that the Communist State had promised from its inception to provide for *all* its citizens, including the elderly. Part of the problem stems from the fact that pensions in Russia are woefully small. Add to that the fact that, given the decline of human relations under Communist rule, children often do fail to come to their parents' support. Indeed, the Soviet Union is perhaps the only country in the world where, each year, tens of thousands of poverty-stricken parents sue their children for support.

My own parents were making plans to emigrate, so getting their consent posed no problem. Now we had to face the tough problem: convincing General Kozlov.

---

*Shcharansky was finally released in February 1986, as part of an exchange between Russia and the West.

We had not seen him for some time, either for personal reasons or perhaps because the KGB had suggested to him that it might be prudent to put a certain distance between us. In any case, he always seemed to have some good reason why he couldn't see us when he came to Moscow. Tatiana was frightened at the very thought of broaching the subject of emigration. She kept putting it off, waiting for "the right moment." Finally, a friend of ours, a woman who was aware of our plans and our predicament, picked up the phone and told the general.

The next day, General Kozlov rang our doorbell. Anna was with him, as was another general. The offensive went off as planned. First Anna launched her attack, leaving both generals in the kitchen. She took me into a bedroom and for an hour subjected me to a devastating tirade. "You're out of your mind!" she said. "The whole thing's unthinkable! What are you trying to do, kill us?" She went on and on, her tone bordering on hysteria. I felt sorry for her. But there was nothing I could do. My decision was irrevocable.

"Anna Ivanonva," I said finally, "my parents have already given their consent. Now we need yours."

"Never!"

She sounded like a banshee. And her timing was terrible, for just as she let out this scream, Tania, who was on her way to school, stuck her head in the door. Tatiana had to leave for work, so I was left alone to deal with the three of them. Anna sighed and cried and pleaded. I had to confess that I did understand her viewpoint. She pointed out that for the general to sign such a document was tantamount to political suicide. But that wasn't my problem. Kozlov had lots of friends who would bail him out. I also remembered what Nikolai Vasilievich had said to me about the general's not suffering any dire consequences as a result of our departure. My goal now was to remain calm and not lose my temper. I didn't want to alienate Anna. I knew that ultimately the general would go along with whatever she decided.

"You'll never get out. You'd better get that into your head," she was saying. "What's more, they'll evict you from this apartment. You'll find yourself in the street, with no job, no place to live, no friends. And don't count on us to bail you out."

She stormed out of the room, slamming the door behind her. A few moments later, she returned, with both generals in her wake. The older general clearly felt out of place. After all, what was he doing here, anyway? Avoiding Anna's steely gaze, he began to rummage in his briefcase, finally extracting a sheaf of papers from which he began reading in a voice as slow-paced as it was boring.

"Edward Lozansky, you cannot emigrate. You are in possession of State secrets. You have worked at the Kurchatov Institute and the Joint Institute for Nuclear Research. You are a member of a prominent military family. On the other hand, for a year you have been out of work. We know, too, that you appealed personally to the president of the Soviet Union. I have had long discussions on the subject with several ranking comrades, and I am authorized to inform you today that very shortly your situation will be normalized."

He coughed and folded his papers. He seemed to be awaiting my response. When he was greeted only by silence, he began looking around the room. His eyes stopped at a point on my bookshelf, and, following his gaze, I saw that he had discovered a copy of Solzhenitsyn's *The Gulag Archipelago*. He started to reach for it, but Anna's withering gaze stopped him, and again he looked imploringly in my direction. I did not want to offend the poor man, so I said, "Why didn't they answer my requests sooner? I sent the Central Committee the full list of all the heads of laboratories and institutes who wanted to hire me but who had orders not to. Where were your comrades then?"

"They are busy people, Edward Dmitrievich," he countered, "but now they want to help you."

"I don't need their help," I said. "Or anyone else's, for that matter. My wife and I want to leave the country. Under Soviet law, as well as international accords, we have every right to do so. That's the end of it. As for the question of security clearance, I never had access to anything of vital importance. The fact that I taught in a military academy, or that my father-in-law is a general, is quite irrelevant. Besides, I didn't ask for your help.

The marriage of Tatiana and Edward in Moscow, 1971. On the left, Edward's mother; on the right, Tatiana's mother Anna Kozlov.

Tatiana, Edward, and Tania in Kiev, 1972.

Edward *(right)* with friends at the Red Square, November 1976.

Tatiana in Moscow, 1981.

The Divided Family Group, 1982. From left: Tatiana Lozansky, Iosif Kiblitsky, Tanya Azure, Yuri Balovlenkov.

May 10, 1982. Marriage by proxy in the rotunda of the Capitol in Washington, D.C. From the left: David Barron, Chairman of Young Republicans, Congressman Jack Kemp, Rabbi Joshua Haberman from the Washington Hebrew Congregation, Senator Robert Dole, Edward Lozansky.

Members of the Divided Family Group on hunger strike: Tanya Azure, Tatiana Lozansky, Iosif Kiblitsky, Yuri Balovlenkov.

Tatiana in her apartment during hunger strike, May 1982.

Press conference in Washington National Airport prior to Tatiana's arrival, December 12, 1982. *Marty Katz/Outline*

Edward and Tatiana's happy reunion, December 12, 1982. *Michael Schwarz*

Tatiana, Edward, and Tania, Washington, D.C., December, 1982.
Marty Katz/Outline

Meeting with Senator Edward Kennedy, December 13, 1982. *United Press International.*

May 19, 1983. President Reagan reads a proclamation declaring May 21 National Andrei Sakharov Day. *Front row:* Nobel laureate Sheldon Lee Glashow; Sakharov representative Efrem Yankelevich; President Reagan; Sakharov's stepdaughter Tatiana Yankelevich; Edward Lozansky. *Back row:* Senator Edward Kennedy; Senator Daniel Patrick Moynihan; Congressman James Courter; Senator Robert Dole; Congressman Gus Yatron; Congressman Jack Kemp; Congressman Thomas Lantos. *Bill Fitz-Patrick/The White House*

In fact, this whole comedy is completely useless. I'm not the one you should be offering to help, but General Kozlov. Why don't you advise him how to conduct himself in this situation with honor. Let him disown his daughter, saying that she has sold out to the capitalists and been deceived by Western propaganda. His superiors will know, if they have any sense, that he had nothing to do with all this. He can sign a certificate saying he has no material claims against us, or if he has any claims, let him state what the amount is and we'll pay. We have no desire to hurt him or his career. I trust he feels the same toward us."

I was proud of my self-control. Despite what I was feeling, I had not once raised my voice. The general looked to his wife for a signal, then shrugged his shoulders in a gesture of hopelessness. She gave him a disdainful look and told him to leave the room. Then she followed him out, slamming the door behind her again.

Act Three. I could hear fragments of conversation emanating from the kitchen, which they had turned into their headquarters. I felt like throwing out all three of them, but I needed that damned piece of paper.

Scene One. The door opened and in stalked General Kozlov, followed by his wife, obviously determined not to let the top brass handle this on their own. I decided that the best defense was a strong offense.

"Pyotr Ivanovich," I said sternly, "I've heard enough insults from your wife for one day. I would like to speak to you alone."

I turned and walked over to the window. In the street below, several cars were parked, with officers either seated inside or lounging against the doors. A real military operation. The general had declared a war alert—as well he might. His career was on the line, and he was determined to take no chances, or let the battle go on for too long. That was my intention as well.

My back was still turned to Anna and the general. I could hear them whispering. Then, finally, there were the sounds of Anna's footsteps, and the door slamming. Later I learned that she had dashed downstairs and had one of the military cars drive her to the Institute of Biochemistry, where she mounted a flank attack against Tatiana.

Scene Two. The general and I were alone. I was slow to turn around. When finally I did, I met his stare, but neither of us said a word for what seemed minutes. Finally, the general began: "We absolutely have to repair this situation before it turns into a disaster."

"I agree. What do you suggest?"

"First of all, get this mad scheme out of your head. You're not going anywhere. I know that you have some reason to feel you have been mistreated. And maybe you have. But to simply pick up and take off would be childish, totally absurd. It's never too late to make amends."

"Pyotr Ivanovich, I want you to understand one thing. My decision is neither irrational nor impulsive. We've thought it over for a long time, and believe me, it has not been an easy decision. But now there's no question of reneging. What we ask is that you take it seriously. Otherwise, we're all heading straight for disaster. I know you have the means at your disposal to prevent our leaving, that you can have me thrown into prison or committed to a psychiatric ward. But I also want you to know that I have foreseen that possibility and taken my own measures. Without going into details, you should know that my friends will not abandon me, and that if ever such a misfortune should befall me, your involvement in it will be known immediately both here and in the West. I don't think that is what you want—which is why I suggest that we work out a solution acceptable to everyone."

I could see the general's face turning bright red as I talked.

"I told you it's out of the question," he said, taking a step toward me, "but I am prepared to discuss your demands. And I'll make every effort to see that you get what you want."

"I want only one thing: that you write down the sum you have in mind as compensation for your material claims on Tatiana."

"If that's the way you're going to act, how do you expect to avoid the unpleasantries you just alluded to?" the general snapped.

"I'm ready for them," I said as calmly as I could. "Go ahead and call the KGB. By the way, did they tell you they tried to recruit me? I had the feeling you were being kept informed all along, and that you would see no objection to our being sent to Israel if we agreed to work for the KGB there."

"I know nothing about all that. That's none of my business."

"Listen. I really believe it would be best if we leave the country without any hint of scandal."

"I said it's out of the question!" he repeated, beginning to pace the floor in front of the window, his arms flailing wildly. "Have you any idea what you're doing to me? I expect my promotion any minute, and a transfer back to Moscow."

"I suggest that you have a little talk on that subject with my pseudo–guardian angel, Nikolai Vasilievich of the KGB. He has assured me that any trouble you might risk could be taken care of quietly. So why don't you go see him?"

Kozlov turned on his heel and left the room. Once again, the poor door slammed shut, this time with such force that a piece of plaster fell from the ceiling. Five minutes later, I heard boots stalking down the hallway, then the sound of the front door banging. I watched from the window as the general climbed into their car and drove away. I called Tatiana at work but was told she had gone out "somewhere." I called again and again throughout the day, to no avail. That night, she arrived home with her face undone, her cheeks streaked with tears.

"Mother told me that she and Father will both kill themselves if we don't change our minds," she sobbed. "I don't know what to do."

I was stricken. I had feared something like this might happen but kept on hoping it wouldn't. I had led Tatiana down a blind alley. But now there was no way of turning back, and I told her as much. "Are you sure? Are you sure?" she kept repeating between sobs. I was torn between my love for Tatiana and my growing hatred for the society that had led us to this precipice. Anywhere else, the fact of leaving one's country would be difficult or agonizing, but not . . . this. Perhaps a problem for the family, and for one's friends, but nothing more. But in the Soviet

Union—and perhaps the Russian character itself plays a role here as well—any private decision produces tragedy: broken lives, ruined careers, suicides. . . .

"Your parents are in a state of shock," I said. "Give them a little time to get used to the idea. Once they can look at it a bit more calmly, things will be different. You'll see."

I was trying to convince myself as much as Tatiana, but nothing I said succeeded in stemming her tears.

The following morning, after a sleepless night, she told me she had decided to go to Kiev to try to talk to her parents in quieter surroundings. I was not overjoyed at the thought, but I made no effort to dissuade her. I simply asked her to leave Tania with me, probably because I sensed that in the very near future, I might be separated from her for some time. I had no idea how long that separation would be!

"Of course," Tatiana said, "of course she'll stay with you."

I took her to kindergarten in the morning, then went home and spent the day doing my best to concentrate on strictly scientific matters. That evening, I went to pick her up. Tania's teacher seemed surprised to see me.

"Tania's not here," she said. "Your mother-in-law came here this afternoon to pick her up. She said she was taking her to Kiev for a few days. I thought you knew."

I went into a rage. The poor teacher didn't know what hit her: insults, threats, shouts. I threatened to have her taken to court. All this happened as I watched children running up to hug their parents or grandparents, who had arrived to take them home. Finally, I got hold of myself and apologized.

"In the future," I said, trying to control my voice, "please let Tania leave only with my wife or me."

So Anna had already struck her first blow, a despicable blow. Just how despicable it was, I learned a week later when Tatiana returned without our daughter. I couldn't believe it—the Kozlovs were holding Tania hostage.

"I'm taking the first plane to Kiev," I said. "I'll bring her back."

"Wait," Tatiana said, clutching my arm, "we have to talk."

I didn't like the tone of her voice. She had left Kiev determined to talk me out of our "mad" plan. Our discussion lasted
the whole day. Her arguments were not new, but I understood
them. She was caught in an inextricable situation: I refused to
remain in the Soviet Union and the general would never allow
his daughter to emigrate to the West.

Finally, when we were both exhausted, I heard her utter
the words I had feared but hoped I would never hear: "Then
you'll have to leave alone."

I could feel the blood drain from my face.

"Then, in a few months, after Father gets his promotion,
Tania and I will follow you to America. That's the only way we
can get him to agree."

I could feel the ground giving way under my feet. My mouth
must have dropped open, and one thought kept running through
my mind: *So she, too, is betraying me, turning her back on me.*
But all I said, in a tone that must have frightened her, was, "So
you're leaving me!"

Her eyes glinted for a minute, then softened again as she
said ruefully, "That's not fair. And you mustn't torment me that
way. You're the one who wanted to emigrate. You alone are
responsible for our problems. You've created them, not me. No
one's betraying you. At most, we'll have to wait a year before joining you. You must understand that we have no other
choice."

I knew she was right. Her next words were like hammer
blows. "Imagine the other scenario. Suppose by some miracle
we did escape. And suppose, as a result, my parents committed
suicide as they threaten. I would never forgive myself, Edward,
and neither would you, whether we were living in America or
on Mars. Our lives would be ruined."

Again she was right.

"Whereas if we opt for the solution I've suggested, everyone
will be happy. My father will have his promotion and we'll be
able to leave this country."

It sounded too good, and too easy, to be true.

"Whose idea was this anyway, your mother's?" I growled.

"Are you crazy? As far as they are concerned, leaving is out
of the question. The idea is mine and mine alone."

"How do I know things will work out the way you pre-
dict?"

"You don't," she said, without hesitation, "but my parents
do love me, and they know I couldn't live without you: They
won't stop me."

"Have you discussed this with them?"

"No. I wanted to work it out between us first. Then I'll go
see them."

I was convinced that the plan would never work. I was sure
that as soon as I was gone, Anna and the general would do their
utmost to make Tatiana forget me and forge another life for
herself. We were digging our own tomb. For a month I tried to
convince Tatiana of that, but she refused to believe it.

"They'll do their best to dissuade me," she said, "but there'll
come a time when they'll have to realize they're wasting their
time. In any case, what other choice do we have?"

"To stand together and fight the authorities with all our
strength," I would respond, "no matter how long it takes. Five
years, seven, ten—until they give in. I'm ready to do it. And if
we do, we'll win, I'm sure of it."

"No, we'll lose," she would reply quietly. "And why should
we put ourselves through all that if we can do it in a friendly
manner? If we become *refuseniks*, we'll ruin Daddy's career as
surely as if we asked for asylum at the American Embassy. Plus
there's no telling what he might do if he gets mad enough.
Mother told me the KGB has been watching you for years, and
without my parents' protection you wouldn't be here discussing
all this with me."

Everything she said struck me as reasonable. The ease with
which she had seemed prepared to live without me for a period
of time had blinded me. In fact, I was still upset by the thought,
and tormented by doubt and suspicion. I couldn't help telling
her. She looked more stricken than I.

"If you think what you've just confessed to me," she said
painfully, "then you have all the more reason to leave alone. It

would show I no longer loved you and that you'd be better off
without me."

I felt miserable. "Please forgive me," I said. "I'm stupid,
that's all."

But my mind was made up. Irrevocably.

One day in July 1976, I went to the OVIR office to fill out an
official request to emigrate. I was shown into a cubicle, where
a heavy-set, almost masculine woman glared at me. She was
wearing the uniform of a militia officer. Before I could open my
mouth, she shouted, "I swear we'll let the functionaries of this
office emigrate before we let you go! You shouldn't be sent to
Israel but to prison. That's where you belong! Parasite! Get out
of here!"

But despite her words, she took my form.

Later, friends told me that I had made an unpardonable
tactical error by going to OVIR alone. My whole family should
have gone with me.

But it was too late to worry about such details.

When I look back on that summer of 1976, I see only one explanation for what happened: I was out of my mind. My hatred
for the Soviet Union had deprived me of my senses. The KGB
had not forgotten; it was only biding its time. Sooner or later,
it would once again reach out its long arm and tap me on the
shoulder. Under such conditions, a normal family life was impossible. Tatiana would never be happy with me in the Soviet
Union. I had only two choices: sell my soul or emigrate. If I
chose the latter, then—once free—I could fight for as long as
it took to free my wife and daughter as well.

It was the latter choice I made, obviously, and one that I
would make again if the occasion ever recurred. I'm sure that
if I had stayed in Moscow, sooner or later Tatiana would have
left me, and she would have been right: It's impossible to live
with a man consumed with hatred for the social system under
which he is living, and filled with guilt over the crimes committed by his country. If I had come across a good psychiatrist

at the time, he probably would have tried to straighten me out with words such as these:

"You don't have such a terrible life. You have a charming wife, a delightful daughter, countless friends who sincerely like you and on whom you can count in times of need. You socialize with the cream of the Moscow intelligentsia, sophisticated people who feel the same as you do about Soviet society yet somehow manage to adjust and live pleasant lives. In the West you'll never find the kind of friends you have here. You'll feel alone and uprooted. So why don't you throw away your television set, your radio too, and stop reading the newspapers? If you do, ninety percent of your problems will disappear overnight. The other ten percent will be easy to put up with. Be smart, tell a few white lies now and then, speak well of the government when you're asked your opinion. When you attend party meetings, sing its praises the way people do who go to church and mouth the words while their minds are on other things. It won't kill you. Once the KGB is convinced you have come to your senses, they'll leave you alone. Forget you. They have plenty of informers. As for the Sunday Scientific Seminars, they don't need you. They have plenty of stool pigeons there every week, believe me. So put all those old notions behind you, keep your political ideas to yourself. You may even come to terms with the general. Live your life, have children, read *samizdat* in the secrecy of your own home, despise the old farts in the Politburo as much as you want. Only don't show it. You'll see. Everything will work out just fine."

But there never was such a psychiatrist, no therapy or therapist to change my thinking. Mine was an obsession, and Soviet propagandists would doubtless have termed it a terminal case of anticommunism. Each time I heard the word *party,* or even Lenin, I was overcome with a feeling of nausea. Yes, I had to leave. It may well have been a mistake. But I had the feeling I'd already paid for it. Little did I know how wrong I was.

Two months went by. I telephoned OVIR regularly, and each time the answer was the same: Be patient.

Tatiana asked me to take her on a trip to Leningrad and the

Baltic states. We did not express it, but we both knew it was a
farewell trip. Farewell to everything we had deeply loved: the
beautiful, serene countryside that had not yet been ruined by
man's baser instincts or works. For three weeks we were happy.
I will never forget our wanderings, our sense of wonder. I will
never forget Leningrad, Tallin, and Riga, the cold perfume of
the Baltic Sea, the silence and calm of those precious but all-
too-brief moments.

On our return I found a letter from OVIR, asking me to
come to the office at my earliest convenience. The same militia
woman with the fishmonger's voice greeted me with all the
femininity she could muster, replete with a smile, as though I
had come to ask for her daughter's hand.

"Please have a seat," she said, "and we'll look over your
application together. We have no basic objection to your leaving.
All we need is a document confirming that you and your wife
are divorced. As soon as we receive that paper, you'll be free
to leave."

"I'm not sure I understood you. Who ever said anything
about a divorce?" I asked.

"No one, my dear comrade, but that is a given. You submitted an application for yourself alone."

"That's because I'm going first," I insisted. "My wife and
daughter will join me later."

"Out of the question, my dear comrade."

"Why?"

"Because it is, that's why. It's not our job to supply you with
reasons."

"But I assure you it is. And I expect you to give them to me
on the spot."

"We cannot let you leave unless you are divorced. That's
the law."

"What law?"

"Soviet law, my dear comrade."

"Show it to me."

"I'm sorry. That is all I have to say."

"Well, it's not all I have to say."

By now we were both shouting. Her courtesy had vanished

and her old voice had returned. There was no point arguing with her. She was only a tiny link in the enormous chain. It wasn't her fault. I went out to the waiting room, sat down, and wrote a letter to Brezhnev, admonishing him for allowing the authorities to interfere in our personal affairs. I personally delivered the letter to the Central Committee headquarters on Old Square (Staraya Ploshchad).

The following day, Tatiana left for Kiev to see if she could clarify the situation with her parents. Two days later, she was back. They had had endless talks, and it seemed to me that they had won her over. What she outlined as a generous concession on their part struck me as an obvious trap. It was simple: I would divorce Tatiana, then leave the country. There would be a short period of relative calm, during which Kozlov would receive his promotion. Then Tatiana and Tania would join me in the West.

"They could have been pigheaded about it," Tatiana argued, "but it seems to me they're doing their best to help us while looking out for their own interests as well."

It was obvious that Tatiana had already adjusted to the idea of a divorce. The green-eyed monster took over once again. I was sure they would never let her out.

"I know what you're thinking," she said, "but you're wrong. I'll never abandon you. My parents could have been intractable. But this way, they're offering you your freedom. Which proves their honesty. Accept it as that."

Accept it? How could she fail to see the trap? Honesty? How could she think her father was being generous? Once he had gotten rid of me, he would concentrate on his daughter. Sure, she might raise a hue and cry at first, but he knew how to muffle that kind of thing, and once he had convinced her that she had everything to lose, she'd come around. Remarry. And live happily ever after.

But how could I convince Tatiana of the accuracy of that script? She had confidence in her parents, loved them dearly. And she was too young, too naive to believe they might be duplicitous.

"If you think that's too dangerous," she said, "withdraw your request and we won't divorce."

Maybe she was right. If we did divorce, there wasn't much of a chance, but at least a slight one, that things might work out.

"You have to do what you feel is right," was her final word.

Two days later, in early September, she filed for divorce. In Russia, divorce proceedings usually take six months, but in our case, it was over in two days. The judge was a pretty woman who was obviously embarrassed by her role in all this. She went through the motions, noting our "incompatibility," which seemed incongruous, since Tatiana and I were holding hands and hugging each other as though we were there to get married, not divorced. Finally, the judge reminded us that we should observe proper decorum. I requested that the record show that I saw no reason for this divorce, that I loved my wife, and that, whatever the decision of the court, I still considered myself her husband and the father of our daughter. It was like talking to a wall. The judge exited with the other officials to consult, then returned a few minutes later to announce that as of this date, the marriage between Edward Lozansky and Tatiana Kozlova was hereby annulled. Tatiana would keep my name. The fee, it was announced further, would be 150 rubles. But before I could pay it, I heard a rustling of money in the next room. Anna, afraid I would cause a scene, or that my modest income would prevent me from paying, was counting out the money to the court clerk. It had all been conducted with military-like precision. At this rate, I assumed I would be out of the country in a matter of days. But Kozlov's influence was not as pervasive as I had thought. He did everything he could to get rid of me as soon as possible. Yet, for reasons not fully clear, the well-oiled machine apparently ground to a complete halt.

A number of strange and sometimes frightening things began to happen. Strangers would come up to me on the street and warn that terrible things would befall me if I didn't leave Moscow immediately. The phone would ring in the middle of the night.

I would pick it up and be greeted by a string of insults and curses. One time, the person on the other end identified himself as a certain Sedov, claiming he was the friend of a friend who had recently emigrated to Israel. He had important revelations he thought I should hear.

We met in a café, and he opened the conversation with a dire warning: "You ought to be very careful. Take my word for it."

He was a strange-looking man, bone-thin with a facial tic that made it difficult to concentrate on his words. His voice also seemed out of control, passing without transition from a whisper to a near-shout.

"The KGB has a constant watch on you," he said. "If your father-in-law wanted to, he could have you eliminated in five minutes."

To buttress his argument, he told me about a Soviet agent that his colleagues suspected wanted to defect. His body was found in a German forest, riddled with a dozen bullets.

This Sedov did not, as they say, inspire confidence. I started to leave, but he grabbed my sleeve and held me back.

"I know your position is highly dangerous," he said. "The KGB has not made up its mind what to do about you, but I know that your file is in the high-priority section. How do I know? Because I have a woman friend who works there. She, by the way, could be very useful to you. I don't have to tell you that the KGB is just as bureaucratic as the rest of the Soviet government. And just as chaotic. She could take certain documents from your file without anyone being the wiser. One of the items that most intrigues the KGB relates to your visit to the British Embassy. One agent has been focusing on that. Well, it so happens that the man is going on vacation. We could arrange for you to leave the country before he gets back."

I was impressed by the range and degree of Sedov's information. But things had become so Kafkaesque that I found myself indifferent, as though I were already on another planet.

"So what do you expect of me in exchange for that little service?" I asked.

"It's always a pleasure to do business with a scientist." Sedov smiled. "They go straight to the heart of the matter. It's very simple. Marry this woman I was referring to, and take her with you to the West. All she dreams about is leaving. But she's Russian. If you marry her, she'll help you. As I said, it's very simple, and straightforward."

"Straightforward? Marry a KGB agent? Sorry, I'm not James Bond."

"Maybe not, but you're in deep trouble. Threatening to tell your story to Western journalists. Blackmailing a Russian general. Those are no laughing matters. This woman hates the Soviet regime as much as you do, so why not help her?"

Sedov was too well informed. I concluded that he was a provocateur. But why had they put him onto me?

"I'll think it over," I said. "Give me your phone number."

"I would prefer if you would write to me in care of General Delivery at the Central Post Office," he said.

"Fine." Again I got to my feet, and this time he did not try to restrain me. I was perplexed. Vanya, to whom I told the story in detail, was as confused as I.

"The only thing I can think of," he offered, "is that they don't like sitting on their hands. For every troublemaker like you, they have a hundred agents. Since they don't know what to do, they start playing detective. My advice is to go home and call all your friends, as many as you can, and repeat the whole episode to them. Then all of Moscow will know what the KGB has been up to, and the KGB will know it too. So then they might leave you alone."

I did just that, calling at least twenty friends, trying to make light of the story and emphasizing the part about marrying a KGB agent and smuggling her out of the country with me. I began embellishing, telling how the plan was to set her up with a McDonald's franchise, which she would then use as a front for Soviet intelligence-gathering.

I never heard from Sedov again.

But that did not mean they had forgotten me. A few nights later, a policeman rang my doorbell and said that if I had not found work within two weeks, I would be arrested for vagrancy.

At that point, I had the impression I was in more of a vaude-
ville show than a Kafka nightmare. Obviously, the KGB could
not figure out what to do with me.

I kept all this from Tatiana, who was too upset and nervous
to have dealt with it. The slightest incident made her cry. On
the surface, nothing was changed. Our mock divorce was just
that. But underneath, something had broken between us. Our
comfort and solace was Tania. I had bought her an alphabet cube
and was teaching her to read. Each time she got a word right,
I'd go to the piano and play one of her favorite tunes, which she
would sing, revealing a precocious talent for music. "As soon as
we're in America," I would tell her, "we'll start you on music
lessons."

But when would that be? And why did I necessarily assume
America? I would have been hard pressed to say. But for some
strange reason, my heart was drawn irresistibly toward that mythic
land, which I knew only through films and books. Without quite
knowing why, I was less drawn to Europe. I was sure that I
would fit into America without any problem, that I would feel
at home there almost immediately. As it turned out, I was right.
But for the moment, I was trying to think about it as little as
possible. I read, I did the cooking, I spent as much time as
possible with Tania.

Early in October, the general called me. "It's still not too
late to work things out," he said. "I guarantee you can get a top
job, move to a better apartment, have a car. . . . Think about
it. To leave your homeland forever is terrible."

I could almost hear the violins in the background.

"It all depends on what your homeland does to you," I said
huffily. "Were you aware, General, that last month when a group
of Jews wanted to place flowers on the monument to the memory
of their brothers assassinated by the Nazis at Babi Yar, the police
broke up the peaceful procession? That they beat and insulted
the participants, arrested them, and interrogated them all night?
Do you know why? Because they had some signs written in
Hebrew. What do you think about that? You who were a hero
of the homeland's fight against fascism?"

"You're missing the point," he said dryly. "I've done as much as possible for you. The rest is up to you."

His threats left me cold. I sat down and wrote a detailed letter describing all the events that had befallen me over the past few weeks. I gave it to a friend, saying that if anything happened to me, he should give it to Alfred Friendly, *Newsweek*'s Moscow correspondent, whom I knew. I also sent a copy of the letter to the general in Kiev.

I needed professional guidance. The following Saturday, I went down to the synagogue looking for Tolya Shcharansky. He introduced me to another man from the Kurchatov, then left us together.

I had heard of Edward Trifonov more than once on the Voice of America broadcasts. He was one of the activists of the emigration movement. When he began to talk to me about the biology section of the Kurchatov Institute, I realized that this was the same Trifonov I had recently been trying to contact for purely scientific reasons. He had published a series of articles on DNA in the magazine *Chemistry and Life,* and I was anxious to talk with him about this subject, which fascinated me even though I knew little about it.

As luck would have it, we only had time to touch on the subject, for Trifonov was getting ready to emigrate to Israel. It was not until two years later that we had a chance to discuss the matter more at length, at the Weizmann Institute in Rehovot, Israel. For now, he was spending all his time and energy crisscrossing the Soviet Union, making contact with various human rights groups. When he was in Moscow, he rarely had a minute to himself. Still, he did find time to introduce me to Aleksander Ginzburg and a number of other dissidents. One day he asked me why I had never attended the Sunday Scientific Seminars held at Mark Azbel's apartment. "Make a point of coming next Sunday. I'm giving a lecture on DNA that you might find interesting."

I had studiously kept away from those seminars, figuring that if the KGB learned I had gone, it would assume I had changed my mind about informing. But I was nonetheless tempted, if only to find out why the authorities hated these meetings so. I also wanted to hear Trifonov on DNA.

The following Sunday I went to Azbel's apartment. There were about forty people there, including Irina and Viktor Brailovsky, Naym Meiman, Alexander Lerner, Veniamin Fein, and Yakov Alpert. Also present was my old professor from the Moscow Physical Engineering Institute, Veniamin Levich, who had been trying for years to emigrate.

Trifonov's lecture was fascinating. It was followed by an animated discussion, which I also enjoyed—so much so that I became a regular at these meetings. Every fourth week, science was put on a back burner in favor of discussions on art, literature, history, psychology, and sociology. I even remember one session devoted to parapsychology. The numbers tended to increase on these fourth Sundays, which sometimes were attended by well-known Western scientists as well. For me it was a breath of fresh air, not only interesting from a scientific viewpoint but also a source of moral support. One Westerner who came was the Nobel laureate Howard Temin of the University of Wisconsin. He had been officially invited to Moscow by the Academy of Sciences, but he gave his first lecture at Mark Azbel's apartment.

After a few weeks, I began to understand why the authorities so disliked these Sunday meetings. Anything discussed here, any theories expounded on, escaped the control of the system. This was unacceptable. Added to that was the fact that opinions were exchanged freely with Westerners. Yet these seminars continued. The only reason I could find for this "liberalism" was the Soviet government's need to keep up a façade of "détente," without which they would not be able to meet their needs in the area of computers and other aspects of high technology. When Ronald Reagan was elected president in 1980, the seminars were stopped. A new era had arrived, and it appeared that the West had decided, as some leaders described it, that it was no longer inclined to sell Russia the rope with which the Kremlin could hang it. In any event, the KGB's thinking apparently went something like this: Since it's clear the present occupant of the

White House is not going to buy our version of détente, why keep up the hypocritical stance?

After Azbel emigrated to Israel, the seminars were taken over between 1977 and 1980 by Viktor Brailovsky, who was subsequently arrested and sent into exile.

In November 1976 my father called me to say that he and the rest of our family had received authorization to emigrate. When he had learned that I had put in my request with OVIR, he had decided to do the same. He, my mother, and one of my sisters were ready to leave.

A scant three weeks later, I received a packet from OVIR, informing me that my application had been approved and I could pick up my visa.

I found it hard to believe. The threats and pressures worsened. Almost every day I would receive a phone call from someone saying that "your number is up" or "they will get you." A huge hulk of a man used to loiter just outside our building, and I constantly had the feeling I was being followed. Things became so bad that I even thought of taking Tatiana and Tania and seeking political asylum at the American Embassy. I admitted as much to Tatiana, who only looked at me sadly and pointed to her head as though I had lost my mind. "Don't worry," she assured, "my father will keep his end of the bargain."

I asked Mark Azbel if I could present a paper the following Sunday, since I expected to be leaving shortly. He agreed and put me on the program. But in the middle of the week, he called to say he had forgotten that he had scheduled Yuri Orlov, a prominent physicist and head of the Moscow Helsinki Watch Group, and would have to reschedule me. Naturally I attended that seminar, where Orlov presented a fascinating paper detailing his theories in the area of quantum physics. It was exciting to see these leading scientists who had come together for a free interchange of ideas and politics. Mark Azbel was continuing his research on DNA, Viktor Brailovsky in computer science, and Veniamin Levich in electrochemistry. We were all in the same boat.

Sometimes we did manage to send the results of our research to Western journals. By ordinary mail, I sent a paper on gaseous discharges to an international congress in Great Britain. Two weeks later, I called London to see if it had been received. It had not. So I sent another copy, then called again two weeks later. No, neither the first nor the second copy had made it. I really wanted that paper read at the meeting, so I decided to resort to an old trick. Tatiana and I went down to the Intourist Hotel, which is reserved solely for foreigners, and tried to find someone who would take my paper and mail it to London from some Western country. Several listened to my proposal, smiled embarrassedly, and walked away. Finally, a Canadian agreed to take it. Tatiana was sure he'd throw it into the first trash basket he found, but in fact, not only did he take the paper but he made a special stop in London to hand it directly to the organizers of the congress. Unfortunately, I never got the man's name, so if by chance he reads these lines, I hope he will contact me so that I can thank him properly.

Orlov's paper turned out to be too long for one session, which meant that I never was able to present mine, a fact I have always regretted. For those Sunday get-togethers were an oasis in the desert of dictatorship, an island of freedom in the midst of the most gigantic prison in the world, and I would have liked to have been a part of them.

December 2—my scheduled departure date—was fast approaching. On November 30 I threw a big farewell party to which I invited all my friends, some seventy people. Roughly fifty came, which touched me deeply, for they all knew that the apartment was being watched by the KGB, and their names would be reported the following morning. My old friend Sasha Polyakov sent a typewritten note signed only with his initials:

> *Please forgive me for not showing, but I cannot afford to take the slightest risk. I'm sure you will understand. If I keep my nose clean for a while, chances are I'll be able to join you abroad. Best luck.*
>
> *Yours, S.P.*

Other friends called, disguising their voices so that the tapped line would not identify them. It would have been funny if it had not been so tragic. Those who came drank more than they should have, and I confess I did too, but somehow I remained cold sober. Doubtless the pain I was feeling at the idea of leaving Tatiana and Tania was responsible. But I did my best to smile and sing with the others, until I would catch sight of my wife or daughter, which would bring me up short. Only then would I remember the enormity of my act.

What on earth have I done? I kept thinking. *I'll never see them again. If I had an ounce of sense, I would tear up my exit visa and throw it in the garbage. Then I would take them outside, in the snowy streets, and breathe the fresh, freezing air. I'd make a snowman for Tania. Then we'd come home, our cheeks red, and put Tania to bed before we'd sit down to a cup of tea and hours of talk, laying plans for the future. And now, what future? O God! Was I making some horrible mistake?*

But it was too late. The die had been cast. In my mind I was saying good-by to each of my friends. Forever. There was Sergei, my old college friend, a mathematician working on problems applicable to sociology, psychology, and economics. He also played the guitar professionally and was well known for his renditions of all the *samizdat* songs. He was making a real name for himself in Moscow. At one point he saw the shadow cross my face and flashed a sign of encouragement to me. I knew he was aware of what I was feeling and that I could always count on his support. And I was right. During the following years, he proved a constant source of help for Tatiana—advising her, helping her write letters to the authorities, keeping up her morale.

And then there was Sveta, one of the most remarkable women I have ever met. A talented artist, she was also a fount of wisdom—clear, precise, and logical in her thinking. Her paintings were a fine reflection of that mind—mature, concise, conceived like mathematical formulas. I found her titles as intriguing as they were poetic: *Blue Axion, A Broken Plane, Light/Static Space.* Abstract paintings, therefore forbidden. But that did not discourage her. When I tried to persuade her to emigrate, to go to a country where her paintings could be properly shown and appreciated, her answer was, in Bulat Okudzhava's words: "Mozart did not choose his country, yet he still composed throughout his life."

Grisha was also an artist, of a very different sort. He used biblical themes, ancient Hebrew symbolism, as his inspiration. By some miracle he had been authorized to exhibit in one of the major Moscow galleries. The show lasted only three hours, and only a select few, with special passes, were allowed in. It was as though his admirers belonged to some monstrous, secret sect. Subsequently his paintings were declared "harmful," "contrary to the spirit of Soviet reality." He wrote a letter of protest to the Central Committee, who called him in and strongly urged him to spend some time in Siberia soaking up the real artistic needs of the people, focusing especially on several huge construction projects. At the time, Grisha still hoped that he would be able to lead a normal life in Russia. Some American tourists who saw him recently in Moscow brought me news of him, along with slides of his latest work. It is called *Illusions*.

I have shown slides of Sveta's and Grisha's works to several American art critics, all of whom have assured me that they would have good careers in the West. I pray to God that one day they will make it here.

I made my rounds at the farewell party, exchanging good-bys with all of them.

"I'm sure we'll meet again."

"Who knows? Let's hope so."

"I'm not so sure," another said, shaking his head. "These are hard times."

"Come, come," said another, "hard times pass. In any case, Edward, don't forget us. We'll never forget you."

"Yes," chimed in another, "you'll be with us in spirit wherever you are."

I felt like walking over to my desk, taking out the visa, and ripping it up on the spot—then *really* celebrating. *Back to reality, Edward*, I thought.

One by one, they said goodnight and quietly left. Sergei was the last, and his parting words were very special.

"May you and Tatiana grow old on the same pillow," he said.

This made Tatiana burst into tears.

And then we were alone, alone at last. It was one of the worst moments of my life.

"You really will come to the West?" I asked for the thousandth time.

"Of course I will, silly. Why do you doubt?"

"Because I do, that's all."

We were like children, playing games, but they were terribly important games.

"But *when* will you come?"

"Soon, very soon."

"I feel sick."

"You can always stay."

"If I knew that would make you happy, I would."

"I know. So leave. You'll hardly have time to get settled when Tania and I will be on the plane winging our way to meet you in America."

"One thing . . ."

"What?"

"I want you to promise: Don't take Aeroflot. Promise me you'll take Pan Am or Air France."

"What's the difference?"

"You'll be in enemy territory for all those extra hours."

"All right, I promise."

"Tell me, are you sorry I got you into this whole mess?"

"Don't be silly. Besides, we have been happy together."

"What do you mean, *have been?*"

"We still will be, I swear it."

The next two days were spent packing, sorting papers, reiterating instructions. Days of anxiety and doubt. Endless days.

Then the grim moment came, a sad winter evening when we left for the station. A dozen friends came to see me off. Someone had brought a bottle of champagne, another a guitar. We drank and sang. Two minutes to departure. I hugged everyone. Then Tatiana was in my arms, warm and tender and vulnerable.

"Do you love me?" I asked her.

"Yes."

"Will you always love me?"

"Yes."

"I'll be waiting for you."

"I won't be long."

I turned away to hide my tears. *Good-by. Good-by, my love. Good-by, the maple trees of Kiev. Good-by, Moscow. Good-by, the country of my birth. Good-by, my friends. Good-by, my youth.*

The train moved away from the platform and gathered speed. Tatiana was receding, until I could no longer see her. I moved from the window and buried my face in my hands. There, I could see her once again.

3
The Fight

Americans are not naive. Even though, unlike the Soviets, they do not consider suspicion and distrust basic factors of civilization, and even though they are naturally generous and hospitable, they nonetheless have to take their precautions. Not just anyone can enter the United States from a foreign country, especially to become a permanent resident—and above all, straight out of the Soviet Union.

I was required to spend three months in Rome, which is where the American immigration authorities assemble candidates for immigration to the United States from Eastern bloc countries. I was overwhelmed by the exuberance of the Italian capital, and one of my first experiences was to down a whole bottle of Chianti.

American intelligence agents questioned me long and hard, as well they might. It was not every day that a Soviet physicist left his country, especially one who was the son-in-law of a ranking Russian general. I answered all their questions honestly and candidly, and they seemed to believe me. What a pleasure to be *able* to be open and candid, to feel that doublespeak was not a daily necessity for survival!

They were apparently convinced, after it was all over, that

I was who I said I was, and that they were not dealing with a future double agent or a KGB mole. I was authorized to enter the United States, and advised to go to Rochester, New York, where the university had a laser fusion laboratory. I arrived there in the spring of 1977.

I took to America immediately, and, had the images of Tatiana and Tania not been constantly with me, I would have been a happy man. Within weeks, I had the impression that I had lived in the United States all my life.

My English at that time was not very good, but America is used to having scientists with foreign accents. In two weeks I got a job at the laser fusion laboratory, but my decision to switch to biophysics was firm.

I had the good fortune to find at the University of Rochester a man named Henry Sobell, the director of the biophysics laboratory. Despite my lack of basic preparation in the field, he took me in and added me to his team. Henry's specialty was the X-ray analysis of the structure of DNA, whereas I was interested in the mechanism by which chemical substances interact with DNA. Experiments carried out in laboratories throughout the world had led us to believe that the structure of DNA differs somewhat from the classic double-helix structure. One school of scientists believed that individual sections of DNA could, under certain conditions, be located in a slightly modified form. Sobell asked me to focus my research on the physical basis of these modifications.

This problem interested me for a very specific reason: According to the existing literature on the subject, scientists still did not fully understand all the aspects of the mechanism by which the start of a gene is recognized by the RNA molecule during the data processing by the DNA. The fact is, it is vital for the RNA molecule to know the exact location of the gene's beginning, because even the slightest miscalculation means that all the data from the DNA molecule will be transferred incorrectly, just as the meaning of a word is lost if you only start reading it from the third or fourth letter on. In the case of living cells, this kind of error is disastrous, which is why the mechanism for recognizing the beginning of a gene is one of the most important aspects of the life process. The simplest and most obvious explanation for this mechanism would be a change in the structure of the DNA at the point where the gene begins, as compared with the rest of the molecule.

All of this I found utterly fascinating. After having studied this question for about a year, Henry and I came up with a physical explanation of the possible existence of DNA sections in which the structure is different from the double helix. To reach that point, we had had long and controversial discussions with physicists and biologists not only from the University of Rochester but also from other parts of the United States.

Henry and I became inseparable. We began our discussions early in the morning and were often still at it late into the evening, over delicious dinners prepared by Henry's wife, Lourdes. We published two articles about our findings, and later Henry sent me off to meet with other specialists in the field. I visited a number of American universities, as well as Cambridge in England and the Weizmann Institute in Rehovot, Israel, where I met my old friend Edward Trifonov. I also participated in an international scientific conference in Liverpool, England. It was the first time that I had attended an international scientific congress without seeking government permission! I still had trouble believing that all you had to do to go abroad was visit a travel bureau and buy your ticket, with no questions asked.

In Liverpool, the Soviet Union was represented, but when it came time for the Soviet delegate to read his paper, the president of the conference went to the podium and said, "We regret to announce that our Soviet colleague will not be present. Unfortunately, his paper has not arrived either, so we will be unable to read it to you today."

A few knowing glances and smiles. Everyone understood. After I had delivered my paper, I remarked to the audience that I was attending the conference for the first time, having emigrated to the United States from the Soviet Union. Many of the participants came up and congratulated me afterward on my newfound freedom. True, I was free. But I still had the job of making certain my wife and daughter would find freedom as well.

Tatiana wrote me regularly. I telephoned her virtually every day, and she always tried to be reassuring. "Yes, yes, everything's fine. Daddy should have his promotion and new post very soon, and then we'll be free to come. Just be patient a little longer."

In mid-1977 the general did indeed receive his promotion. Now a three-star general, he was appointed Chief of Staff of Soviet Civil Defense. I wrote him several letters congratulating him and thanking him for the help he had given me at the time I had emigrated. I also asked him to do everything in his power to help Tatiana and Tania join me as soon as possible. I promised that we would be completely discreet once they were in the West; we would avoid any political activity and confine ourselves to pure scientific research. I also swore that neither Tatiana nor I would give any interviews to the press and we would do all we could to keep out of the limelight. It was in all of our best interests, I added, that Tatiana and Tania come to the West with as little publicity as possible.

Everything seemed to be going more or less according to plan, but before we knew it, a year had passed since my departure. Tatiana kept counseling patience. After all, she would remind me, the emigration of a three-star general's daughter was not an everyday matter. In fact, it was probably unique in the annals of Soviet history.

I began to imagine the worst: Tatiana had given up the whole idea of emigrating; she had decided to make a new life for herself in Russia. There were the old fears and suspicions, which were dispelled constantly by the beauty and fidelity of her letters. All she was doing, she kept telling me, was to try to cause as little trouble as possible. She loved her parents. I shouldn't blame her for trying to spare them.

Then one day she called to say that she was preparing her documents for OVIR, and that the general had promised to give her written authorization to leave within the next two weeks.

I was so excited at the prospect of their arrival that I went straight out and bought a house in Rochester. I also submitted a curriculum vitae for Tatiana to the chemistry department of the university, where I was assured that she would have no trouble getting a job as a researcher. Our dream was about to come true—to work together in the same university in a free country. I kept pinching myself: Could it be true? I continued to call Tatiana almost daily, as we went over her travel plans and discussed what she should bring and what she should give away to friends. I asked her to buy several books I wanted, and some Russian records.

Then one day her phone was dead. I kept calling her Moscow number—261-87-04. The Moscow operator said that there was trouble on the line. I called friends in Moscow and asked them to try, too, but they had no better results.

Two weeks went by—two agonizing weeks, which I spent pacing the floor of my new house like a trapped animal. Then, at last, a letter from Tatiana arrived. I tore it open and began to read:

Darling:
Something terrible has happened. My parents have let me down. Yesterday I went as we had agreed to pick up the written permission that they had promised me. Before I had opened my mouth, they began to attack me, cursing and threatening. I didn't recognize them. You have no idea what I was forced to hear. Worse yet: We even came to blows! Real blows. I fainted, and apparently was in a coma for several hours. When I came to, this morning, they told me that our "case" had been examined at the highest levels. My father had been summoned to the Ministry of Defense, where he was shown copies of our letters and made to listen to our phone calls. It is hard for me today, as I write this, to refer to the terms mother and father. In their eyes, our fate is sealed. They made their decision on the basis of purely political motives. My father is an eminent Soviet general, a member of the Supreme Soviet. It is unthinkable that his daughter be allowed to emigrate. It would be, to use their expression, "a serious blow to the prestige of the State." As for me, I had better get used to the idea, I

should forget you and remake my life. That is what they told me.

My pleas fell on deaf ears. They continued to threaten me and heaped the worst kind of abuse on you. But maybe they were frightened by my reaction. Maybe, when I passed out, they had an ounce of pity for me. They left me with one glimmer of hope. Since it's out of the question, they said, that I'll ever leave the Soviet Union, you ought to return. They swore that they would arrange it, that they would help you find work when you did. I know you'll never accept. And yet that is my only hope. And without that hope, I don't believe I can go on living. Think about it. Are you really happy in America? After all, you've had a chance to see the rest of the world, to have a taste of the freedom you so longed for. But, on the other hand, remember that back here in Moscow there are two people who love you and suffer from your absence. Think about it. But don't linger. My life is unbearable. Each day is a living hell. Come back. Please come home.

There was more. At the end of the letter, Tatiana threatened to kill herself. I knew that that had been written while she had been in a state of shock, but I also knew that she was a person of her word, and capable of doing what she said.

Her letter plunged me into a state of despair. And I too lost my bearings. I vacillated hour by hour from the absolute conviction that I should pack my bags and return on the next plane, to the certainty that I should banish the idea from my mind. Then, in a flash, it came to me, the perfect middle ground. I would go back, but not on a permanent basis. I would return as a tourist. I would talk to the general. I would request an audience with the authorities to plead our case. They would listen to me. They could not keep harassing an innocent woman and child. Surely they would listen to reason.

I called the Soviet Embassy in Washington and inquired about the regulations for a tourist visa. I gave my name to the operator, who asked me to hold on for a moment. Then she came back on the line to suggest that I come to Washington at my earliest convenience to meet with the consul. "We're glad you called," she ended. "The consul was trying to reach you. Can we set a date?"

I tried calling Tatiana again, and, by some miracle, her line was once again in working order. I talked with her for over an hour. She was so happy at the idea of seeing me in Moscow that I thought she had not understood that I was only coming for a few days. I kept telling her that over and over, but she seemed not to hear, simply repeating, "Oh, Edward, it will be wonderful to see you. You'll see, it will all work out in the end."

I went to Washington at the end of that week. As an insurance policy, I called the FBI and told them of my impending visit and asked them to take all the necessary precautions in the event something happened to me once I was inside the Soviet Embassy. They were very reassuring, telling me that no one had ever been harmed inside the Russian Embassy in Washington.

I was received not by the consul—who I was told had been "called away" only half an hour earlier on urgent business—but by a man named Evgeny Ponomarev, a colorless functionary who struck me as totally mechanical, even in his speech. He said that he was sorry that he had not had time to acquaint himself with the particulars of my case, and he handed me a document that turned out to be an official invitation to return to the USSR.

"You should not hesitate to accept the invitation," he said. "You should go home. You've seen how these Zionists over here conduct themselves. And you've had time to see that all these dissidents and so-called human rights activists are nothing but a no-good lot of Jews and Israeli agents. You don't belong with people like that."

It dawned on me as he spoke that, indeed, he had not looked into my file, that he took me simply as a member of General Kozlov's family and had no idea of my Jewish background. I wondered if he was so mechanical that he was even incapable of noticing the non-Russian shape of my nose. I almost burst out laughing at his prepared anti-Zionist tirade. But instead I said, "Zionists? Jews all? What about Solzhenitsyn? Rostropovich?

Bukovsky? What about Maximov and Sakharov? They're not Jews."

"That's precisely what I'm saying," he went on. "Either they're Jews or under the influence of Jews. About Sakharov, you're right. He was one of us, a true Soviet devoted to the ideals of the party, until he married the Jew Bonner. That's when all the trouble began. She completely dominated him and turned him into a Zionist agent."

Trying for once to control myself, I patiently explained to Ponomarev that I had no intention of returning permanently but only for a week or two as a tourist. That took him aback, but he gave me the forms to fill out. As I left, he said, "If you change your mind, call me right away and I'll send you the other forms."

Back in Rochester, I began to wonder what in the hell I was doing. What could I hope to achieve in Moscow? It was a miracle that I had gotten out in the first place. And besides, I had to assume that the FBI and the CIA were keeping a wary eye on me, as well they might. After all, I had had access to Soviet documents of a scientific nature; I had taught at a military school—all of which must have struck the American authorities as pretty odd. If indeed I did go back, would I not be doing myself in with the American authorities? On the other hand, what made me think the KGB would let me out a second time? Did miracles ever repeat themselves?

I called a Russian émigré friend in New York to see what he thought, since I no longer trusted my own judgment.

He heard me out. Then he said, "Edward, I think you're crazy even to think about going back. Anyway, do me a favor. Meet with a man I know here in New York. I can't tell you his name or give you his telephone number. All I can say is that he's an ex-KGB agent who defected. He generally refuses to see any Russian émigrés, but if I ask him, I'm sure he'll agree to meet you. It won't commit you to anything. But before you make up your mind, at least hear what he has to say."

I agreed, and the next weekend I flew to New York and met the ex-KGB agent at my friend's apartment. I agreed never to reveal his name or to describe him. In essence, here is what he told me:

"Here's your situation as I see it. I know from experience that no Soviet citizen who emigrates is ever allowed to return to the USSR—except, of course, if they have been sent abroad on a mission. As for you, I see two possible explanations. First: The general realized that he made a basic mistake in letting you leave in the first place. He hoped that your wife would forget you, that she'd meet another man and all would work out fine in the end . . . from his viewpoint. In that he was wrong. So now he wants to get rid of you, which explains why he wants you to come back. Don't think you'll get to see your wife and daughter. My guess is that you'll be met at Sheremetyevo Airport and sent directly to Siberia. Nobody will ever hear of you again. There is no way the Kremlin will ever tolerate the fact that the Chief of Staff of Civil Defense has an émigré for a son-in-law. A traitor. If that is true, then you're dead and gone as far as they're concerned. And since you're not a citizen of the United States, there's no way the Americans can help you.

"There's another possibility. It may be that the Kremlin has decided to get rid of General Kozlov. In that case, the reason they want you back is to use you as part of a huge propaganda operation. The KGB specialists would not send you to Siberia but take you and grill you for whatever time it takes to break you—three days is my best guess—until you're ready to go on television and tell the Soviet people what a terrible place America is, and how sorry you are ever to have left. After that they would do away with you, as in the earlier scenario. It's only a question of sooner or later, of that you can be sure."

At that point, my friend cut in. "I want you to tell him," he said, nodding at me, "that I didn't rehearse you, that everything you're saying comes from you, not me."

The ex-agent simply shrugged his shoulders and refused to comment.

What he had said came as no great surprise, and it struck me as totally plausible. I had seen on Moscow television a number of "penitents" humbly asking for forgiveness and thanking the party for having showed them the error of their ways. To make sure the lowliest peasant and the illiterate worker understood the message, these performers inevitably spoke with a heavy Jewish accent. Most of the time, the penitent-traitors were actually KGB agents who had been sent to the West on missions and returned as if by choice. Some, however, were Soviet citizens who had actually returned and been brainwashed. I did not want that to happen to me. Yet I knew it could. Tatiana's letter had upset me so that I had forgotten what the real possibilities were if I did return. To go back would be suicidal.

I called Tatiana and talked with her for over an hour. I couldn't tell whether I had persuaded her that my return would destroy the one tiny ray of hope we still had left, but I did think that at least I had convinced her to do nothing rash, to opt for patience.

For the hundredth time, I shouted into the phone, "Our only hope is to convince your father to let you leave. Everything depends on him, and on him alone."

"Then it's hopeless," she said.

"In that case," I said, "we'll start a press campaign. Newspapers, television, radio. I'll contact senators and congressmen."

"They don't care," Tatiana shouted into the phone. "Why should they care?"

"Maybe Brezhnev and Ustinov* don't care," I shouted back, "but they don't want to see your father's name all over the American press. And I'm sure he wouldn't want to see his picture in all the American newspapers, or have the story beamed all over the world via the Voice of America."

Tatiana admitted that I had a point. She promised to try one last time to convince him.

Back in Rochester, I immediately contacted Senator Jacob Javits and Congressman Frank Horton, both of whom agreed to help me. Horton wrote to the United States Ambassador to the USSR and also to the State Department, which added the names of my wife and daughter to the list of divided families that it regularly sent to the Soviet government, requesting that they be reunited. Some of the people on that list had been separated for ten and even twenty years.

Senator Javits invited me to New York. After listening to my

*Dmitri Ustinov was then the Soviet Minister of Defense.

story, he promised to help me. A month later, he was one of several senators who visited the Soviet Union, where he made a point of mentioning my case to Andrei Gromyko.

I also wrote to the general, trying to make him understand that he was making a major mistake in keeping his daughter and grandchild from leaving. I begged him to have pity on those two innocent creatures, and not make himself responsible for the tragic end that our story might have. I ended my letter by saying, "If you refuse to change your position, you leave Tatiana and me no choice but to use every means at our disposal to make sure that we are reunited."

Three months went by. The State Department had still not received a reply, and Senator Javits's request had been greeted by stony silence. Tatiana began talking about suicide again. I called all my friends in Moscow and asked them to take care of her, not to leave her alone if at all possible. Without exception, they responded. I will never be able to thank them enough for what they did, especially since they were all well aware that the KGB was taking careful note of anyone who became involved in this affair.

One day I opened my mailbox to find a letter from Moscow. I did not recognize the handwriting, but the return address was Tatiana's. I tore it open and glanced down at the signature. It was from General Kozlov.

Eagerly I began to read, but by the end of the first page, I wanted to throw up. There is only one word to express what I was feeling at that point: *disgust*. In sentence after sentence, he dragged Tatiana through the mud, accusing her of every foul deed imaginable. "I can't imagine," he concluded, "why you'd want to waste your time trying to save such a creature."

I swear that had he been present as I read those lines, and had I been armed, I would have blown his head off on the spot. How could a man descend so low, be so base as to denigrate his own daughter?

I could only conclude that my threat to resort to the Voice of America had sent him into a panic. It would, he was sure, put a swift end to his still-blossoming career. But how could a man put his career ahead of his own family?

The next day Tatiana told me on the phone that she, too, had received a letter from her father, claiming that I was un-employed in the United States and reduced to a state of misery; that I was managing to subsist only through handouts from the CIA. Without quite thinking it through, he also told her that I was remarried . . . to a wealthy widow!

I made several copies of the general's letter and sent them to Brezhnev and Ustinov, and to Ambassador Anatoly Dobrynin in Washington to show them to what depths their esteemed general had sunk.

Normally, the men in the Kremlin would have tried to avoid the threat of scandal by suggesting to Kozlov that he retire quietly. But the general had a lot of solid support at the top, and he remained in his post.

Tatiana and I decided that there was nothing to hope for on that end.

It was time to open the media campaign.

I started by phoning Ponomarev in Washington to tell him that my patience had run out, and I had no choice but to stir up world opinion.

"The capitalist press has been waging war on us for sixty years," he replied in a bantering tone. "It hasn't bothered us to date, nor has it ever made us alter the direction of our policies."

Maybe so, but that was no reason not to give it a try. I wrote to several newspapers, relating our story in all its detail up to that point. The first to respond was the local Rochester paper. Don Colburn, a reporter from the *Times Union,* interviewed me and wrote a long article. The day after it appeared, the American journalists in Moscow learned of it, and Jim Gallagher, of the *Chicago Tribune,* went to see Tatiana in her apartment, together with UPI correspondent Roland Tyrell. That interview appeared in more than a hundred European and American papers. Then Craig Whitney, a *New York Times* correspondent in Moscow, interviewed Tatiana, and on April 26, 1979, the *Times* carried a long story describing how she had fallen into a trap laid by her own father. The Voice of America translated the piece into Russian and read it almost in its entirety.

We had struck the first blow, with results better than expected. The day after the Voice of America broadcast, the general called Tatiana and asked her to desist, that he would sign a document consenting to her departure, "to your damned America," as he put it.

Once again there was euphoria, the illusion of victory. Tatiana sold her furniture and packed her bags. The spring semester was finished, and I made plans to fly to Vienna to meet my wife and daughter.

But May came and went, and still no document. Despite repeated phone calls from Tatiana, the general kept procrastinating. Finally he told her that, due to circumstances beyond his control, she would not be able to leave before July. Why July? I decided it was a trap. Jimmy Carter and Brezhnev were due to meet in Vienna in June to sign the SALT agreement. If the Soviets planned to release Tatiana as a gesture of goodwill they would do it prior to the meeting. By promising to release her in July they were trying to persuade her not to make any trouble prior to and during the summit.

Tatiana and I agreed that now was the time to step up the media campaign. James Wieghart of the *New York Daily News* and Daniel Southerland of the *Christian Science Monitor* wrote articles about us, and, just before the summit, Bernard Redmont of CBS News interviewed Tatiana in Moscow.

I flew to Vienna and remained there throughout the SALT talks. I managed to see presidential aide Hamilton Jordan, who promised that President Carter would include Tatiana's name on the list he was submitting to Brezhnev. Redmont also interviewed me in Vienna, and segments from both the Moscow and Vienna interviews were shown on CBS News.

None of this had any effect on the Russians.

Brezhnev had no intention of trying to please Jimmy Carter. As far as I can tell, no person on that presidential list was released. Why? Because Carter had already given Brezhnev more than he ever expected to get without demanding anything in exchange. He had drastically cut the military budget, given the order to stop work on the B-1 bomber, and canceled an agree-

ment with the Western allies to place neutron bombs on their
territories. Meanwhile, the Kremlin was forging ahead with an
unprecedented military buildup.

The SALT II agreement was meant to strengthen the strategic advantage of the USSR militarily. Brezhnev knew that
Carter would sign it and do everything in his power to have it
ratified. So why should he release any hostages? Better to save
them for some future time when they could be used to good
advantage in negotiations.

Depressed and dismayed, I flew back to the United States.
My depression only deepened when I saw, on the American
television screen, my beloved Tatiana's face: She looked drawn
and defeated.

One thing was now clear: We had lost the first round. It
would be a long and difficult fight, years and years perhaps. And
we had to face up to that disconcerting fact.

From that day on, I was a man possessed. Not a day passed
without my taking some positive action. I gathered all the newspaper articles I could find and printed up a leaflet, in thousands
of copies, detailing our story, under a picture of Tatiana and
Tania. I mailed them to any organization or individual I thought
might be even remotely interested. The replies began to flow
in, first in the tens, then hundreds, then thousands, many including copies of letters people had written to the Kremlin.
Senator Daniel Patrick Moynihan got twenty-one of his Senate
colleagues to sign a petition on our behalf, and this was sent to
Brezhnev. Countless religious and human rights organizations
told me that we had their full support.

In the summer of 1979, I attended an international biochemistry congress in Toronto, where Henry Sobell was slated
to read a paper outlining the results of his and my research. I
went to the meeting solely for scientific reasons, but when I
arrived and realized for the first time that there were more than
6,000 delegates from 60 countries, I decided to seize the opportunity. With the express consent of the congress organizers,
I put up posters featuring a picture of Tatiana, asking the del-

egates to sign a petition that would be sent to Brezhnev. In two days, 4,000 delegates had signed it, and it went off to Moscow with a separate telegram from Professor Kaplan, the Canadian president of the congress. The large Soviet delegation at the conference was embarrassed by the unexpected groundswell and had trouble fielding the questions the Western delegates posed about the Soviet government's "barbaric" conduct in the field of human rights. In all fairness, I must mention that several Soviet delegates did come up to me and tell me how much they sympathized with my plight. The well-known Soviet academician Severin, who had been Tatiana's teacher at Moscow University, said that as soon as he got back, he would take up the matter with Anatoly Aleksandrov, the president of the Soviet Academy of Sciences. I thanked him, but I also told him that many scientists, including the Nobel laureates Hans Bethe, Francis Crick, Linus Pauling, and Mark Perutz, had already written Aleksandrov, without result.

"But I intend to speak to him personally," Severin said.

I am sure he did, but he too produced no results. Normally, Aleksandrov did not respond to letters from his Western counterparts attempting to intercede on behalf of some victim or other, but he did reply to Mark Perutz. I must say I was appalled by his response; I had thought him a more decent human being. He said simply that I was an imposter whose case had no merit, and I should be totally disregarded.

At the Kurchatov Institute of Atomic Energy, when Aleksandrov was the director, we used to refer to him as "an almost decent fellow," which is about the highest compliment one can pay a member of the Central Committee. Most Soviet scientists were pleased when he was named president of the Academy of Sciences. I even owed him a personal debt, for it was he who had interceded on my behalf and helped me get into the Institute of Atomic Energy. I had already written him a long letter appealing for his help, on the grounds that he had been not only my director but also Tatiana's immediate superior when she had worked for the Institute of Organic Chemistry.

My appeal, of course, went unanswered.

Aleksandrov's behavior came as no surprise, however. The president of the Academy of Sciences is a creature of the party, someone who has to be ready and willing to say and write what the party dictates. Aleksandrov, that "almost decent fellow," had been named to the post under that specific condition. In that, he was only following in his predecessors' footsteps. Thirty years earlier, the then-president of the Royal Society in London, a man named Dayle, had written to Sergei Vavilov, the then-president of the Academy of Sciences, asking what had happened to his brother, Nikolai Vavilov, a famous geneticist and noted academic, who had been reported as having died in a concentration camp. Faithful to tradition, Sergei Vavilov vehemently denied the allegation, terming it "imperialist propaganda." Dayle, a foreign member of the Academy of Sciences, resigned in protest, but to no avail. Other presidents have done the same—that is, lie through their teeth to the world, as though it were part of their job . . . which, unfortunately, it is.

At Rochester, a new academic year was beginning. It was already September. I resumed my work, while at the same time renewing my efforts on all fronts to free Tatiana. I bombarded the State Department, senators, and human rights organizations with letters. I received replies that were full of sympathy and understanding, a number of promises, and quite a few condolences. But it was becoming clearer and clearer that my campaign was running out of steam, that no single person or organization could make a significant impact on the Soviet monolith. As for the newspapers, they had already told our story. For them the question was: What's new or sensational? I couldn't blame them. They had other, more pressing stories to tell. True, the struggle of a young woman against the Kremlin had its fascination, especially the story of the daughter of a ranking general. But they needed some new angle.

I had an idea. I went to the library and plowed through piles of Soviet journals and magazines published over the previous several years, looking for the names of well-known Americans the Russians thought of as "progressive." There weren't all that many: Jane Fonda, Sargent Shriver, Muhammad Ali, Armand

Hammer, Averell Harriman. I wrote each one a letter, attaching a full range of press clippings on our case.

Not one replied.

I didn't really expect they would. In the first place, if Moscow labels them as "progressive," it is either because they are associated with liberal causes and therefore do not want to get involved with people like me, or because they have business or diplomatic ties with Russia that they do not want to jeopardize. Further, they probably receive hundreds, if not thousands, of letters like mine and couldn't reply if they wanted to. My only question is: How, after reading all those heart-rending pleas and appeals, can they remain "progressive"?

I had to try something new. Anything. One morning I got up at four o'clock and drove to Washington. At nine I was in front of the Russian Embassy, handing out leaflets to passersby. Some people took them, others looked the other way. A pair of Soviet guards kept a wary eye on me from behind the iron grillwork, and at one point when the street was deserted one of them came up to me and said, in English, "Why don't you get lost?"

To which I replied, in Russian, "This isn't Moscow. Why don't you stuff it."

The first guard waved to his pal to join us. Together they must have felt real tough.

"Listen," the first one said menacingly, "if you don't leave, you'll be in deep trouble."

A policeman was standing twenty feet away. I called him over, and the two guards retreated behind the embassy gate. I told the policeman that the Soviet guards had threatened me. "There's nothing I can do," the cop said, "there weren't any witnesses." We chatted for half an hour, and he told me all sorts of stories about goings-on at the Soviet Embassy to which he'd been witness: People running out of the place seeking asylum; people almost making it to the gate and being dragged back inside by guards.

"The fact is," he said, "there are so many people who demonstrate outside the Soviet Embassy that nobody pays any attention anymore."

I had to try another tack. Something sensational. Otherwise, I would begin to be taken for a misfit or a freak.

In Moscow, Tatiana's position was becoming tenser every day. Despite the success of her scientific research, she had made up her mind to quit. Her presence at the Institute of Organic Chemistry was becoming a liability, and her scientific adviser, though saying nothing, was put in an increasingly tricky situation.

In addition, Tatiana was shortly scheduled to take an examination in Marxist-Leninist philosophy. In her case, that test was tantamount to a provocation. The course had nothing to do with philosophy. As everyone openly admitted, it consisted of a series of incantations extolling the virtues of socialism on the one hand and the brilliant works of the current party leaders on the other. While no one took the exam seriously, it was an essential step to a successful scientific career. Those who found themselves intellectually incapable of facing up to the inanities of the test, or simply too bored to open a book on the subject, could always find an understanding and sympathetic soul within the system who, for a few rubles, would give them a passing grade. It used to take fifty rubles for a top grade, forty rubles for a passing grade. It is possible, with inflation, that those rates have escalated since my day. Tatiana's problem was that however diligently she might strive to pass the exam, there was no way she would be allowed to pass it, since everyone knew she was trying to emigrate to the United States, which was a total contradiction of Marxist-Leninist theory.

After she had quit her job, Tatiana was totally dependent on the packages I sent her. That posed a whole new problem, for packages tend to disappear from the Soviet postal system, or, if they arrive, the recipient is obliged to pay exorbitant duties. As a result, I tried as often as possible to send things to her via people going to Moscow on business or on vacation.

Tatiana's letters were so full of despair that I spent my sleepless nights trying to dream up wild schemes to get her out. When day broke, my activities returned to reality: letters, telephone calls, meetings. I must have been impossible to live with in those days. No matter what the subject of conversation, I kept bringing it back to my obsession: Tatiana. Some of my new American friends, obviously afraid that I was going off the deep end, warned me that I ought to try to pull myself together. But how could I do that when each day I learned of some new humiliation to which Tatiana had been subjected by OVIR or some other source, or the sorrow she was feeling at seeing Tania arrive home from school white as a sheet, retreat to a corner of the room, and burst into tears for no apparent reason? Tatiana wrote me that the militia had begun to persecute her for "parasitism" and threaten her with exile, how the KGB had insinuated that it might be obliged to take her daughter away from her because she was being raised in an unhealthy, anti-Soviet environment. She sent me copies of letters she had written to Brezhnev, Andropov, and Ustinov, none of which had brought any replies. How did she find the strength to keep on fighting?

At times I was overcome with despair. I would tell myself that I ought to write Tatiana and tell her she should give up the struggle, which was hopeless, and not ruin her life any longer. She was still young. At twenty-seven she should own up to the fact she had married the wrong person, find herself a new, "normal" husband, get a job and try to be happy. Her father would help her, and this nightmare she was living would be over. My mind was filled with such thoughts every time I returned from a fruitless trip to Washington or New York, where it would be made clear to me once again that no one could help us. Then these moments of total depression would give way to euphoria, as I concocted more schemes.

What if I collected a million signatures on a petition demanding Tatiana's release?

Forget it. The Russians don't give a damn about petitions.

What if I brought a bed to the Soviet Embassy, crawled in, and refused to leave until they gave in?

Ridiculous.

What if I got in contact with the Mafia? I was told they could pull off anything.

Maybe in the West. Not behind the iron curtain. There it would have to deal with a much tougher gang than the one portrayed in *The Godfather*.

What about finding a woman and a child about Tatiana's and Tania's ages and paying their way to Moscow? There they would "lose" their passports, having given them to my family, and simply have to wait for the American Embassy to issue a new one, by which time Tatiana and Tania would be safely in the West.

Fine, except I remembered that each time Tatiana and I had gone to the Intourist Hotel looking for Western contacts, she would be shaking like a leaf.

Mark that one off, too.

Then one day I opened the paper and read that the Nobel Prize for chemistry had gone to Herbert Brown of Purdue and the physics prize to Sheldon Lee Glashow of Harvard. I knew of both men, and had in fact translated an article of Glashow's that had appeared in *Scientific American* for the Soviet journal *Achievements in the Physical Sciences.* Why not ask both of them to make a statement at some point during the Stockholm ceremonies?

As luck would have it, I learned that Herbert Brown would be giving a lecture in Rochester before his departure for Sweden. After the lecture, friends introduced me to Brown, who not only agreed to my request but also suggested that he try to get other Nobel laureates to sign the petition. He noted that the only laureate he would not be able to ask was Mother Teresa, who would be receiving the Nobel Peace Prize not in Stockholm but in Oslo. Here again, luck was with me, for Father William Shannon of Nazareth College in Rochester was a friend of the bishop of Oslo, to whom he wrote to set up a meeting between Mother Teresa and me.

I flew to Stockholm on December 10 and went to see Brown at the Grand Hotel. He handed me a petition, signed by no fewer than seven Nobel laureates, addressed to Brezhnev. That same evening I was scheduled to take the train to Oslo, but in the intervening few hours I managed to get signatures from two more laureates.

The bishop of Oslo received me graciously and said that he would do his best to set up a meeting with Mother Teresa. I attended the award ceremonies, but the crowds were so huge and the number of people pressing forward to see her or talk to her so large that I despaired of ever meeting her. I left the hall convinced that I would have to forgo that pleasure. But the bishop was as good as his word. Early the next day, he took me to the monastery where she was staying, and introduced me. I towered over the tiny woman in her simple, white garments. But as soon as she began talking, I was amazed by her vitality and precision. She heard me out, taking notes from time to time in her little notebook. Then she said, simply, "The Soviet rulers are governed by fear. Everything they do reveals how afraid they are of their own people. It is that fear that keeps them from freeing your wife. Even granting people a little freedom terrifies them."

We talked for an hour, during which she spoke at length about her work in Calcutta and in the South Bronx. Not only did she add her signature to my petition, she also promised to write Brezhnev personally. Then, as I took my leave, she said, "You should pray. It's coming up to Christmas. And I'll pray for you."

I had the sudden, unforgettable image of this tiny, wrinkled woman praying for a woman she had never seen, while at the same time that woman's parents were saying to her that what they hoped most in the world was to be rid of her, to see her gone from their lives.

I have often thought of Mother Teresa's words about fear and the Soviet leaders, and I know that she was absolutely right. I did pray, as she had suggested, but in my heart of hearts, I knew that the only thing that would move the Kremlin to action was a fist aimed at their faces.

I went straight from the monastery to the American Embassy in Oslo, where I met with one of the staff members. After having related my story, I suggested that he might ask the ambassador to inform his Soviet counterpart that virtually all the Nobel laureates had signed a petition that would be sent to Brezhnev. That petition would be made public at a press conference in Stockholm on December 13. If Tatiana were released before then, the press conference would be canceled.

In effect, I was asking the American ambassador to issue

what amounted to an ultimatum to his Soviet counterpart. The ambassador would need State Department approval, and it was highly unlikely that they would get tough over such a minor issue. Nonetheless, the embassy did call Washington, which responded that what I was doing could not be supported officially, but the government unofficially wished me well.

I should not have expected more.

I called the Soviet Embassy in Oslo to inform them of the press conference, to be held at 5 P.M. on December 13 at the Grand Hotel in Stockholm, to discuss the whole question of human rights in the Soviet Union. If Tatiana and Tania Lozansky were sent to another country outside the Soviet bloc within the next twenty-four hours, the press conference would be canceled. I even mentioned that China would be considered an acceptable country.

I half expected that the person on the other end of the line would hang up on me, but to my surprise he said, "What are you getting so worked up about? Why don't you come over to the embassy and we'll discuss this over a cup of tea, the way civilized people should."

"Thanks very much," I said, "but I've already had such a discussion with your colleague Ponomarev in Washington. The only thing I learned was that the Jews and Zionists are responsible for everything. Obviously you people are all acting under the same set of instructions. So please simply pass on my conditions to the proper party."

I returned to Stockholm the night of December 12 and set about preparing the press conference. All the press agencies had been informed by Telex, and I phoned not only the Swedish press, radio, and television but also most of the rest of the Western press, simply giving them a rough idea of the nature of the conference.

Professor Brown had agreed to read the text of the petition, and then the list of signees.

At three o'clock on the afternoon of December 13, I met in the lobby of the Grand Hotel with the one laureate who had not signed my petition, Abdus Salam, a Pakistani physicist.

"I am in complete agreement with what is written here," he

said, "but if I sign it, the Soviet Union might take reprisals and cease cooperating with us in the scientific area."

It was a line of reasoning that I had heard before from other scientists I had approached, and it showed to what degree the Soviets had instilled fear not only among their own people but abroad as well. If anyone from a country in any way dependent upon them so much as raised an eyebrow against Russia or Russian policies, it could and would cancel contracts and refuse permission for student, cultural, and intellectual exchanges, and business deals.

I asked Abdus Salam which Soviet scientists were working with the Pakistanis. He mentioned several names, including Kadomtsev and Vedenov.

"I'll put in a call right away to Kadomtsev in Moscow and ask him point-blank whether your signing this petition will have any negative consequences."

I was not bluffing. I knew the academician Boris Kadomtsev very well, and I was sure he wouldn't hesitate to give me a forthright answer. He was now the head of the Department of Plasma, where I had worked, having replaced the academician Artsimovich shortly after Artsimovich's recent death. Kadomtsev was the only director of an important department at the institute who was not a party member. He had also been one of the first to sign our petition in favor of Leontovich. And, what was more, he knew my story inside and out.

Salam saw that I was serious, and, with a wave of his hand, added his name to my petition, at the same time wishing me luck.

Later I had to change my mind about Kadomtsev. Sakharov appealed to him for help from his Gorky exile, and received no response. Others who scorned Sakharov's appeals were the academicians Velikhov and Kapitsa. The former did not surprise me, for even in my day he was known as a party boot-licker, and many respected Soviet scientists refused to shake his hand. Kapitsa, however, was another story: He was a man who had not hesitated to speak out during the days of Stalinist terror against the arrest of the physicist Lev Landau. But times change. And so, alas, do people.

I lacked only one signature, that of the economist from the University of Chicago, Theodore Schultz. I called him in his hotel room, and he patiently heard me out before saying that he never signed collective letters. This said, he added that he knew about our case and would be happy to write personally to Brezhnev, which he did, via Anatoly Dobrynin, the Soviet ambassador in Washington. Whether or not he received a reply, I never learned.

I had everything I needed. Still a little giddy from all the excitement and lack of sleep, I went out in search of some food and fresh air. It was a crisp day, and I walked down to the port looking for a restaurant. A car drove up beside me and slowed down. Two men emerged, and one glance at their faces told me who they were. I broke into a run, and they ran after me. The car speeded up and was gaining on me. I heard one of the men behind me call out, "Just a minute! All we want is a word with you!"

I ran even faster, without looking back. I lunged into the doorway of a dark building, flashed past some kind of security guard, and rushed up the stairs to find myself on a balcony. Looking around, I broke into uncontrollable laughter.

I had ended up in the Stockholm synagogue.

I did not speak a word of Swedish, so I asked the guard in English if there was a telephone I could use. I called the American Embassy and asked for the political section. They gave me the number of a special Swedish police department set up to protect foreigners.

"And keep me informed about what happens," the man at the embassy said.

The man at the police station spoke no English, so I asked if anyone there did. I began cursing in my mother tongue, which evoked a "minute, minute," and, after a several-minute wait, someone came on the line, asking, in English, "What can I do for you?"

"I want you to send two men to the synagogue near the Grand Hotel. I'm here from America and I'm being followed by two Soviet agents."

"Who is following you, please? Could you say that again?"

"Soviet agents!"

"What does that have to do with us?"

I began cursing again in Russian, then got control of myself and said, "I believe your office protects foreign nationals. I am a foreigner and I need protection."

"Oh, so that's what you want. I'm sorry, but the service you're referring to no longer exists. You are speaking to the city police."

Half an hour to the press conference. No matter what, I intended to be there.

"Listen," I said, very slowly, "please listen to me very carefully. I am not far from the Grand Hotel. I must be there at all cost at five o'clock. Can you send a police car to take me there? I repeat: Soviet agents are waiting for me outside the synagogue."

A long pause. I could hear a muffled consultation taking place on the other end of the line. Then, finally: "All right. But how do we know this isn't a hoax? We get dozens of calls like this, you know."

I gritted my teeth, then said, "How can I prove to you that I'm serious?"

The policeman reflected for a moment, then said, "Give me your phone number and we'll call you right back."

I gave him the number, hung up, and waited. Five minutes. Ten minutes. Again I called the police station, but the phone rang for several minutes without a response. Finally, a voice answered in Swedish. To identify myself, I began swearing in Russian, to which I received a hurried reply of "minute, minute!" Then silence.

It was a few minutes before five. I went down to the synagogue door, braced myself, pushed it open, and raced toward the Grand Hotel. I thought I heard footsteps behind me, but how much was imagination and how much reality, I'll never know. In any event, sweating like a pig and looking at best disheveled, I found myself in the lobby, surrounded by journalists and television crews. I raced up to Professor Brown's room; he was clearly upset that I was so late and started to scold me. I told him there was no time to explain, that they were waiting for us downstairs.

We led the reporters to a press room, where, after a brief explanation of why we were there, Professor Brown read the petition in the name of the Nobel laureates. Afterward, the reporters bombarded us with questions, mostly focusing on the most sensational aspect of the case—namely, the involvement of General Kozlov. Then a Swedish woman reporter, Disa Hastad, who said she had worked in Moscow for several years, stood up and asked a question I kept thinking about for months afterward.

"Naturally I can't criticize what you are doing, Mr. Lozansky," she said, "but why are you only referring to your personal tragedy today? Why not mention the other victims of the Soviet system as well? It's all well and good for you to call this press conference, with so many eminent Nobel laureates present, but why aren't you also talking about Tolya Shcharansky, Yuri Orlov, Sergei Kovalev, and the other scientists in Soviet prisons? After this press conference, the newspapers will be filled only with the name of Tatiana Lozansky, as if the others did not exist. With all your energy and organizing skill, you could help the others, too."

At the time I felt that the question was somewhat unfair, for I was only one person fighting for his own family. But later, when I had time to reflect, I knew she was right. Turning that knowledge into action, however, was a whole different matter. It would mean leaving the university, stopping my scientific research, putting all my energies into that endeavor, and changing my entire life, my philosophical outlook. Was I capable of such a change? Was I ready to make a decision of that importance? And even if I were, would I really be able to do it?

After the publicity with the Nobel laureates in Stockholm, the campaign in favor of Tatiana grew more heated. During December recess from the University of Rochester, I toured Western Europe, promoting our case with every newspaper, radio, and television station I could contact. Tatiana sent me a letter containing an appeal to all the governments of Western Europe, and I also circulated that widely.

At the end of that year, 1979, I went to Geneva at the invitation of Professor George Sharpak, to read a scientific paper at a seminar given by the European Center for Nuclear Research (CERN). At the end of the meeting, I gave a talk about my family, showing slides of Tatiana and Tania and asking the delegates to write Brezhnev and Aleksandrov in their favor. One of the delegates stood up and said, "Why don't you try to get help from Roger Dafflon, the mayor of Geneva? He's a Communist. Maybe the Kremlin would listen to an appeal from him."

I wasn't wild about the idea, basically because the Western Communist leaders never answered any of my letters. There was a naive belief fostered in Moscow among many intellectuals and relatively sophisticated people that Western Communist parties had greater respect for democratic institutions than did the Moscow party. Many Soviet émigrés did their best to open the eyes of Western Communist leaders to the repressions taking place within the Soviet Union, but their appeals fell on deaf ears.

Nonetheless, I decided to try to see Dafflon. I took a letter to the Town Hall. In it I said that I realized how busy he was, that it was almost Christmas, and that if he could not see me on this trip, I would come back at his convenience.

A few days later, I called his office, and a surly secretary informed me coldly that the mayor had no intention of seeing me. Not that I really expected he would. But I had other plans for the good mayor.

I called all the Geneva papers and related how their mayor had shut the door in my face. My timing could not have been better, for *Pravda* had just run a long article praising Dafflon to the skies and citing him as one of the Soviet Union's staunchest friends, a man who, through sheer will and talent, had risen to become, despite his Communist affiliation, mayor of one of the citadels of Western capitalism. The Geneva papers ran long segments of this dithyrambic piece, alongside my story about Dafflon's giving the cold shoulder to someone who was being persecuted by his friends in the Kremlin. The mayor received a flood of mail protesting his stance, and the switchboard was jammed. By that time I was back in Paris, totally unaware of the furor I had caused. A week later, I received a phone call from Dafflon's secretary, saying that the mayor would be delighted to see me, and suggesting a date. How they had found my phone number, since I was staying with friends and not at a hotel, I'll never know.

When we did meet, the mayor proved less than cordial. "What the hell are you doing to me?" he demanded. "You've turned the whole city against me. Even the children are calling. Aren't you ashamed of yourself?"

I told him I wasn't, and that I couldn't be blamed if his refusal to see me coincided with the *Pravda* article. I still thought he might do something for me and that I should profit from his presumed direct line to Brezhnev, so I laid out my story for him in full detail. He promised to do his best, and I, in turn, promised to tell the press how warm and generous he had been.

I returned to Rochester for the start of the spring semester. I wrote Dafflon several times, without receiving a reply. Finally, Professor Sharpak saw him and learned that he had indeed written Brezhnev, who wrote back immediately . . . telling him to mind his own business.

Later I had occasion to lock horns with a far more influential Communist party leader in the West, Georges Marchais, head of the French party. Marchais was afraid of neither irate letters nor phone calls, all of which he had received in profusion over the years. I should know: All my letters and petitions to the French Communist party apparently went straight into the dead-letter box.

In any event, on January 22, 1980, France's Antenne 2 television channel invited me to appear on its program "Dossiers de l'Ecran" ("Television White Papers"), dealing with human rights in the Soviet Union. Others invited included Arthur Goldberg, former member of the United States Supreme Court; Jean Poperen, national secretary of the Socialist party in France; a

Lithuanian sailor, Simas Kudirka, who had defected from a Soviet ship; members of the Bolshoi Ballet who had defected and sought political asylum in the United States; the Soviet Ambassador to France, Stepan Chervonenko; and Georges Marchais. At the last minute, these last two pulled out, to no one's great surprise.

I suggested to the program's producer, Anne-Marie Lamory, that during the course of the show we try to contact Tatiana by telephone in Moscow. She doubted it would succeed, given the normal problems of calling Moscow and the fact that the KGB would react and cut the lines as soon as they learned of the plan, but she agreed to give it a try.

Then, during the afternoon of the day the program was due to be shown, the bombshell news came through: Andrei Sakharov had been arrested in Moscow. Once again, we had underestimated the Soviet leaders, who were clearly demonstrating by that act how little they cared about world public opinion. We had thought that Sakharov, because of his worldwide fame, was safe from the Kremlin's thugs. What we had failed to take into account was the fact that the Moscow Olympic Games were fast approaching, and the Russian leaders had no intention of letting someone like Sakharov undermine the propaganda value of the games by his eternal pronouncements. For the Kremlin, the games were as important to them as they had been to the Nazi leaders in 1936.

The report was that Sakharov had been accosted in the street, shoved into an automobile, and driven to police headquarters. Then, about four o'clock, there was a news report that he was being expelled and sent to France. Hundreds of reporters raced out to Roissy Airport to await his arrival. The Antenne 2 people decided they should try to have him brought directly to the studios to take part in our program. Then, around seven, the news came that he was not being expelled from the country but exiled to Gorky, an industrial city on the Volga that was off limits to all foreigners.

That evening, the program led off with the Sakharov story, on which each of us was asked to comment. My turn came, and

I was starting to give my reaction when suddenly I heard Tatiana's voice. The "crazy plan" had worked after all. As she spoke, her photograph was projected onto the screen, too.

She spoke in Russian, but there was a simultaneous and very good translation. Tatiana told the millions of French viewers that she had received only a few days before a reply to a letter she had written to French President Valéry Giscard d'Estaing. He had expressed his sympathy for her plight but said that he could do nothing, since any positive action on his part would be construed by the Russian leaders as interference in their internal affairs. This, of course, was precisely the reply the Russians wanted. Giscard, however, could have taken the viewpoint that since the Soviet Union had signed the 1975 Helsinki Accords, it was bound to respect basic human rights, including the right of divided families to be reunited.

When Tatiana had finished, I picked up the thread. "The violation of human rights is hardly an internal affair in the Soviet Union. Any country, especially a superpower, that disregards the Helsinki Accords represents a danger for the international community. The ruthless repression of any belief, the lack of respect for international agreements, and the passive attitude of the West have allowed the Soviet government to continue its policy of international piracy. Hungary in 1956, Czechoslovakia in 1968, Afghanistan in 1979. Who will be its next victim? Poland? Yugoslavia? Why not France? What makes you think you'll not one day see Soviet tanks rumbling through the streets of Paris?"

I had said all that in a rush, and when I had finished, I heard Tatiana's tearful voice, still on the line by some miracle, begging the French to stand up for her. "Love," she said, "that is what we need. And after all, is France not the country of love?"

During the next few weeks, hundreds of viewers wrote to me, saying that they had lived her drama as they saw Tatiana on the screen and had wept with her that night.

The following morning, the program made front-page news, and Tatiana's picture graced the pages of most of the newspapers and magazines. Even the French Communist daily, *l'Humanité*, carried the story, but it had a typical, somewhat special, viewpoint: It lambasted Giscard d'Estaing for having orchestrated, on French television, more anti-Soviet propaganda, at the same time castigating me for having tried to frighten the French with my image of Soviet tanks.

In Russia, the news agency Tass and the newspaper *Izvestia* simply accused all the participants on the program of taking part in a "grandiose provocation" against the Soviet Union. Not once did they mention Tatiana by name, or attack me with the usual epithets of "turncoat" or "traitor." A French journalist asked me why.

I told him that I suspected the reason was that when I had come to the West I had come well armed. When he seemed puzzled by my reply, I smiled and said, "For one thing, I brought a letter of high recommendation from the top man at the Military Tank Academy, Marshal Oleg Losik. It said that I was a peerless professor and that I had conducted my lectures 'with the highest degree of scientific thoroughness.' It also said that I was held in the highest esteem by my fellow professors and by my students as well."

I explained to the reporter that I had sent copies of this panegyric to both Brezhnev and Dobrynin, with covering letters saying that if the Russian press accused me of the usual ignominious acts—from raping my grandmother to stealing from the local store—I would make public this letter from the renowned marshal. This warning seemed to have had an effect! To date, the Soviet press had carefully refrained from attacking me personally, despite all the furor surrounding my case—unless, of course, it was sensitive to the possible involvement of General Kozlov, who preferred to remain out of the news.

After the "Dossiers de l'Ecran," my name, and especially Tatiana's, became so well known that the Communist party resigned itself to the necessity of addressing the issue. Letters asking that Tatiana be freed piled up on the desk of Georges Marchais. Instead of tossing them in the wastebasket, Marchais went on record as saying that he was in favor of reuniting divided families. That was already a step in the right direction. But I was especially touched by the French people, in all walks of life, who came forward and asked what they could do to help Tatiana.

They are too numerous to mention, but I would like to single out Nicole Dolfi, from Paris, Anne and Raphael Chailleux of St.-André-des-Eaux, and Madame Jacqueline Peron of the village of Ustaritz. Not only did Madame Peron send countless packages to Tatiana in Moscow, she also wrote endless letters to Giscard d'Estaing, Marchais, and Jacques Chaban-Delmas, the speaker of the French National Assembly. Thanks to these people and the pressure they created, Marchais did speak out for Tatiana when he went to Moscow for the Olympics.

By this time I had made friends in virtually every Western country. They gave me food and lodging and, above all, moral support. Wherever I went, I always felt at home. After the "Dossiers de l'Ecran," strangers in France, Belgium, and Switzerland would come up to me in the street and ask what they could do to help. Most of them I do not know by name. Without their daily encouragement, I could not have carried on all those years and accomplished what I did.

The Winter Olympics were due to be held in early 1980 at Lake Placid, not far from Rochester. I decided to take advantage of the event to get the signatures of as many gold medalists as possible on my interminable petitions. But I had to keep sending them. I started by getting the president and executive director of the United States Olympic Committee to sign, and then as many medalists and distinguished guests as I could reach. Local activist Frank Shatz was an enormous help in all ways, and it was he who made the contact with the hero of those Olympics, Eric Heiden, winner of five gold medals. The members of the French Olympic team, who knew me through the "Dossiers de l'Ecran," were particularly helpful, not only in signing my petition but also in promising that the French would do their best to speak up in my favor at the summer games in Moscow. They invited me to dinner one night and served me a sumptuous meal, with more wine than I was used to. When I headed back toward Rochester that night, I ran into one of the worst snowstorms I had ever seen. I arrived home in the wee hours, barely in time to shower and shave and take a plane for Washington, where I was to appear on an NBC program. A friend, a doctor for the American Olympic team, had told me to come to the White House gate after my television appearance, for President Carter was receiving the American medalists for lunch, and the doctor promised he would make sure that most of them signed my petition either at the lunch itself or with me outside afterward.

The next day, the world learned that the majority of the Olympic champions had signed a request to Leonid Brezhnev to let Tatiana and Tania Lozansky leave the Soviet Union. Tatiana learned of the petition from the Voice of America, as well as from several Western journalists in Moscow.

My various campaigns were, it seemed, bearing fruit. By now millions of men and women around the world knew of our story. But the sad fact was that nothing had really changed. After three years of steady and vigorous effort, Tatiana and Tania were still prisoners in their Moscow apartment.

I returned to Rochester and resumed my courses. Yet the words of the woman reporter in Stockholm kept nagging me. The question was very simple: Was I going to give up my scientific career and devote myself not partially but wholly to the matter of human rights? Or was I doing what I should, concentrating on getting my wife and daughter out of bondage so that I could get on with my scientific research, which had been the core of my working life to date? My constant campaigning had already taken its toll. How could I concentrate on science when every letter, every one of Tatiana's appeals, went straight to my heart like the thrust of a knife?

Despair, recovery, struggle, silence, despair: Such was the continuing and not always self-renewing circle of my life. My nerves were strained, perhaps to the breaking point, and I knew that my friends and colleagues were worried about my physical and mental health. Maybe I was waging a hopeless fight. Maybe I should throw in the towel. Maybe Tatiana and I would both be better off going our separate ways, rebuilding our lives.

No, I could not accept that. I loved Tatiana and I was sure that she still loved me.

My friends took a different view, assuring me that theirs was more realistic than mine. "Face up to it," they would say, "the Soviets will never let a general's daughter leave. It would be too humiliating for them. You've done your best, tried the impossible. But the results are clear: You're no further ahead than when you started three years ago. The KGB is making fun of you. It's delighted at your suffering and setbacks. It's killing two birds with one stone: punishing you on the one hand and dissuading others who might be tempted from going over to the West if they have to leave their families behind."

I listened to what they said, which indeed was the voice of reason, and decided they were wrong. I was being unreasonable, that I knew. But I also knew it was the only course, the only method—not just for Tatiana, but for all the other divided families behind the iron curtain, all the others deprived of their rights as human beings. And I would fight on against all odds until we had attained victory.

Sakharov's exile had also opened my eyes. That superb human being, who embodied all that was noblest in the Russian character, who had been labeled by many within the Soviet Union as "the conscience of Russia," was a symbol of repression. Shortly after he had been sent to Gorky, his wife, Yelena Bonner, had made an appeal to the outside world. "Our only protection," she said, "is the spotlight of public attention on our fate by friends around the world. International public opinion is all that stands between us and disaster." Her stirring words had a profound effect on the world, and indeed on me—to such a degree that I decided to change the focus of my whole life.

My friends from Rochester, businessman Sanford Gradinger, attorney Tom Fink, Rabbi Judea Miller, and several scientists from the University of Rochester, helped me to found a new organization, the Andrei Sakharov Institute. We contacted Sakharov's son-in-law, Efrem Yankelevich, his official representative in the West, who gave us his support. The institute's beginnings were modest. Our initial objective was to acquaint the American people with Sakharov himself, his work and his importance, for it soon became apparent that not even American scientists fully understood the scope and nature of his research, beyond recalling that he had been one of the creators of the hydrogen bomb. This was due in part to the fact that so much of his work had been done in complete secrecy. Even his famous Tokamak project was little known. When research on controlled thermonuclear reactions had been declassified, one of Sakharov's articles on Tokamak had been published by Leontovich in the collection *Problems in the Theory of Plasma,* but that had had only a limited distribution and was read by a handful of specialists.

In April 1980, the institute held its first conference, the goal of which was to better acquaint the American public with Sakharov. Melvin Gottlieb, director of the Princeton Plasma Physics Laboratory, and Nobel laureate Sheldon Lee Glashow of Harvard gave a rundown of Sakharov's work, while Herman Feshbach of MIT, president of the American Physical Society, spoke of the efforts being made by the scientific community on Sakharov's behalf. At the end of the conference, the 700 participants sent a telegram to Sakharov in Gorky, the text of which was later broadcast by the Voice of America.

This conference was followed by a series of other public events, which received good coverage in the media.

We were on the right road. Lectures by prominent people, gala performances, scientific conferences, and other public events in support of Sakharov and other victims of Soviet oppression proved to be a powerful tool in generating wide publicity. I had to curtail my own scientific work, but I felt nonetheless that my efforts were still closely related to my basic interests, art and science.

In July 1980, at the time of the Moscow Olympics, Tatiana and I both undertook hunger strikes, she in Moscow and I in Paris. I had chosen Paris partly because our case was so well known there but also because, unlike the United States, France had decided to take part in the Moscow Olympics. I took up my station at the Trocadero, where I spent my days during the Olympics sitting surrounded by posters of my wife and daughter, soliciting passersby to sign petitions on their behalf. Although most of the press coverage was on the games themselves, both French and American television covered our protest. The Associated Press disseminated a picture of Tatiana taken during her hunger strike in our Moscow apartment: She looked thin and drawn and feverish. The picture was picked up by papers around the world. In Moscow, the French athletes descended on Georges Marchais and urged him to bring up the matter with Brezhnev when they met. Finally, the French party's Human Rights Committee took the cases of Tatiana Lozansky and Anatoly Shcharansky under their protection. It was a first for the French Communist party, but also a last: Tatiana and Shcharansky were the only two Soviet citizens to benefit from their "support."

Things finally seemed to be going our way. And then the KGB called on Tatiana and said that if she stopped her hunger strike during the Olympics, the government would in all likelihood grant her an exit visa as soon as the games were over. The Associated Press disseminated that story, which a friend brought to me at my post at the Trocadero. I was so overjoyed that I jumped to my feet and began hugging everyone who happened by. "We've won!" I shouted. "We've won!"

We both stopped our hunger strikes. I called Tatiana almost every day, congratulating her and making plans to meet her. Then one day when she answered the phone, she was distraught. Through her sobs, she told me that she had just heard from OVIR, and that her exit visa had been refused.

Once again we had been had. The Soviets had made their empty promise because they were afraid we might have a negative effect on the games. Now that the games were over. . . .

Tatiana called her father and asked when she would no longer be the victim of the KGB's little maneuvers. "As soon as you get this foolishness out of your head," he said, "and not one minute before."

November 1980. In Madrid, a conference on security and cooperation in Europe was due to be held. The invitees were all the countries that had signed the Helsinki Accords, to reaffirm the specifics of those accords, especially the human rights aspects, which the Communist countries had knowingly tossed into the wastebasket as soon as they had signed them.

The Sakharov Institute decided to organize a gala performance on November 10, the day of the opening of the conference. It was an ambitious—and expensive—project. When we approached a number of European and American organizations with a view toward raising funds, our reception was always enthusiastic—until we asked for money. In all fairness, most organizations involved in human rights are not very wealthy, and our project was beyond their limited budgets. In addition, no one on our committee—least of all me—had any experience in fund-raising. In desperation, I put all my own money into the project, including the proceeds from the sale of my Rochester house, which I had bought in anticipation of Tatiana's arrival. But since I had gone off the University of Rochester's payroll, the amount I could personally contribute was limited. Friends told me I was crazy to put all my money into a pro-Sakharov demonstration in Madrid, but I had no qualms about it. It struck me as a sound investment. And I also hoped that in Madrid I would meet organizations and people who would keep me from financial disaster. It was a crucial period, filled with anxiety and concerns, and even tragedy. The Russian dissident historian Andrei Amalrik, the author of *Will the Soviet Union Survive in 1984?*, was scheduled to take part in the Madrid conference. He left Marseilles and was killed en route in an automobile accident. The death of this brilliant and dedicated human rights advocate cast a pall over the city and those of us awaiting his arrival.

But the fight had to go on, and the demonstration had to take place. Our plans were to give a concert tribute to Soviet dissidents in Madrid's 2,800-seat Teatro Real. The musicians from several countries were donating their services, but we still had to pay for their travel to and from the Spanish capital.

In Madrid I made the acquaintance of a Spanish journalist, Gabriel Amiama, who turned out to be a pillar of strength and perseverance. As a child, during the harsh and confusing events of the Spanish Civil War, Gabriel had been sent to the Soviet Union. He grew up there but later wanted to return home to Spain. The Soviet authorities refused to let him leave. On several occasions he tried to sneak across the Russian border, but he was always caught and sent back. Finally, thanks to the intervention of the French socialists, Gabriel was allowed to leave.

For the better part of two months, Gabriel and I battled to obtain permission to hold our concert. As hosts for the conference, the Spaniards were concerned about embarrassing the Soviet delegation. Finally, however, we did get permission to use the Teatro Real. Phone bills, posters and programs, hotels and taxis—all were already adding to our costs in frightening dimensions. We ordered the tickets, but for some strange reason they arrived only five days before the concert, leaving us virtually no time for what is normally referred to as advance sales. We called a hasty press conference to announce our plans and advertise as best we could the event and its purpose.

At that point, I received an urgent phone call from Pierre Juquin, secretary of the French Communist party's Human Rights Committee, asking that I meet him as soon as possible "about my family." With so little time left before the concert, the last thing I needed was a trip to Paris, especially because I had come down with a bad case of flu and was running a fever. But Gabriel convinced me there was little more I could do in Madrid, and since Tatiana had started a new hunger strike in Moscow, I did not want to pass up this opportunity, however slim, in case the Russians had really decided to let her go.

I also suspected I knew why Juquin wanted to see me. In connection with Tatiana's hunger strike, my French friends had decided to demonstrate in Lyon during an upcoming conference of the Franco-Soviet Friendship Society.

Juquin received me in his office in Paris, on Place Colonel-Fabien. His glasses perched at the end of his nose, his eternal young-man smile fixed as if in concrete, he bypassed any amenities and came straight to the point. "You've picked the wrong weapons for your fight," he said. "You're wasting your time."

He had called me all the way to Paris to tell me that? He pretended he couldn't care less, but in fact I knew he was scared stiff, since a large Soviet delegation, headed by Ambassador Chervonenko, was scheduled to attend the Lyon meeting.

"All right," I said, "let's assume we'll call off this demonstration in Lyon. But only if you pick up the phone right now and tell Comrade Brezhnev to let my family emigrate."

Juquin shook his head sadly. "I'm afraid that's impossible."

"Why? Isn't he a friend of yours? Isn't that a small favor to ask between friends?"

His smile was still there, but slightly faded, it seemed to me. "The bourgeois press and television are giving you plenty of attention," he said, "but they don't give a damn about you or your wife and daughter. All they want is a sensational story and a chance to stir up a little more anti-Communist hysteria. We— and I speak for the French Communist party—are ready to help you. But only if you cease feeding anti-Soviet propaganda to the press."

I was furious at having wasted my time, and I brought the meeting to a brusque end. I was tired of hearing the same old stories from the world's "comrades," while an innocent woman and child continued to suffer. The demonstration in Lyon was quite impressive. Publicity was so strong that the French members of the Franco-Soviet Society's executive committee were forced to see me, and ultimately they agreed to sign a petition requesting the release of Tatiana and Tania. At least that is what Roland Leroy of the Communist paper *l'Humanité* announced to the press.

On November 9 I returned to Madrid to find Gabriel in a state of near-despair. It appeared that my meager bank account was already overdrawn. When we had paid the fee for the theater weeks before, there had been money in the account, but by the time the theater management got around to cashing my check, we had already paid so many other bills that the theater check bounced. So we had to come up with a replacement $3,000 within twenty-four hours. Rumors began to circulate in the capital that the gala would not be held because the Sakharov Institute not only was insolvent but also was writing bad checks. On Sunday, Gabriel called the theater director at his home to request an extension, but he was turned down. On Monday, I called my bank and explained the situation to them, asking them to honor the theater's check, which had bounced for a mere overdraft of thirty dollars, and they agreed. Now we had the theater, but virtually no tickets had been sold. I took to the street and tried to sell tickets to passersby. Finally I gave up trying to sell them and stood near a subway entrance holding a sign that read:

GRANDE CONCIERTO FOR SAKHAROV
MUSICA RUSSO
GUITARRA NARCISSO YEPEZ
ENTRATA LIBRE

When people learned about the cause, some took tickets and helped me distribute them. The event might end up a financial disaster, but at least the hall wouldn't be empty.

The night of the concert came, bringing with it further problems. The Spanish guitarist and the master of ceremonies failed to show up—"for political reasons," we were informed. I tried to get Gabriel to present the program in Spanish, but he blanched, saying he had never spoken in public in his life, and there was no way he was going out on that stage. At seven-thirty a burly theater manager appeared and said that if we didn't start at once, he would go out himself and announce that the Russians were fighting in the wings and everybody should go home. As he was telling me that, a young Spaniard came up to me. I was ready to bite his head off. "What the hell do you want?" I said in my most surly tone.

"Sir," he said, "you make announcements in English, I will translate into Spanish."

So out we went, arm in arm. The whole thing would have been pure Marx Brothers had it not been so filled with drama and stress. But the gala did go on, and the next day the influential Madrid daily *ABC* headlined its review with:

NOBLE IDEAS, WONDERFUL PERFORMERS
WOEFUL ORGANIZATION

Which was a pretty adequate description. But the fact was, we had pulled it off. The theater was about two-thirds full, the musicians were all first-class, and press coverage was wide and good.

I flew back across the Atlantic with mixed feelings about the whole event. I was jobless, homeless, and penniless. But the bills had been paid.

I had reached rock bottom. Had he known, General Kozlov would have been happy that all his predictions had come true.

Meanwhile, back in Moscow, Tatiana was the object of a full-scale psychological attack by the KGB. Agents in felt hats lurked outside her apartment house day and night. Sometimes they came into the lobby, or planted themselves on the landing of one floor or another. At times they actually barged into her apartment and engaged her in interminable "conversations," the tenor of which was that I was "washed up." Not only was I broke—which was true—but my political reputation in the West was completely compromised.

"Just wait, Tatiana," they would tell her, "one day your husband will come crawling home to you, pleading to be taken back. So why persist? All you need to do is be patient and avoid causing any further scandal."

I used my last few dollars to call Tatiana to try to reassure her, but she was in such a state that my call hardly helped. She was in tears, in such obvious distress that I ended up shouting into the phone: "Gestapo! Fascists! I hate their guts. O God, why don't You destroy the monsters?"

The KGB wiretappers must have been having a ball listening to us.

When next I tried to call a few weeks later, Tatiana's line had gone dead, and it stayed dead for the next six months. It was just as well: On the one hand I had no money, and on the other our exchanges were proving both frustrating and debilitating.

Give up? Never. I decided that the time had come to move my operation, if you could call it that, to the only city where I might make it effective: Washington, D.C.

The director of the Federation of American Scientists was a man named Jeremy Stone, a staunch advocate of Sakharov's. He offered me the use of a tiny basement, where I set up a cot. I had to be up early, since it was used during the day as an office.

But for my purposes, the site was great—right on Capitol Hill. Each morning I would venture out to meet with as many senators and congressmen as I could collar, especially those who had anything to do with the Soviet Union. I became one of the thousands of lobbyists who represent the interests of hundreds of causes and organizations—except that, unlike my fellow lobbyists, I had no financial backing. To pay for my food, I taught a few courses at American University. I was lobbying for "human rights in totalitarian countries." One day I was finishing a twenty-minute conversation on the subject with several people, including a congressional staff member, when one of my listeners came up to me and invited me to lunch. At last, I thought, I've found an interested party. At lunch, however, he wasn't offering me support for human rights but a job.

"I was impressed by your persuasiveness," he said. The head of a large computer company, he offered me $50,000 a year to represent him as an official lobbyist. I thanked him and declined politely.

My day usually began at 7 A.M. and ended at midnight, when I would crawl into my cot and look over the letters I had sent to various organizations. I slept badly, partly because the basement was both noisy and damp, but my insomnia gave me the chance to plot further ways to win my war against the Soviet dinosaur. That term might seem hyperbolic, but I remain convinced that a single, dedicated individual, however alone and powerless except for his or her convictions and the resources of the mind, can wage war effectively against a totalitarian state. Especially with the help of such experienced fighters as Vladimir Bukovsky, Vladimir Maximov, Edward Kuznetsov, and Aleksander Ginzburg, who by that time had joined the Sakharov Institute. They had all fought the monster from within. My situation was more comfortable, for I had the luxury of fighting it from without. And I was still convinced I would win.

Tatiana's letters continued to arrive, often provoking me once again to the thought of insane violence that I had to force from my mind. One of her letters during this period read:

*Every morning I look into the mirror and wonder about
my life, about those five years that have already been
stolen from me. Some of the best years of my life, too.
Why? Who is interested in breaking my heart, in leaving
my family in shambles? Whose ideals, whose principles
are furthered by all this? Who will punish those responsible for such acts of barbarity?*

When I had rid myself of my mad projects for violent retri-
bution—ranging from kidnapping a Soviet diplomat, which Tatiana had suggested, to returning to Russia clandestinely and
spiriting my family out across the border—I knew that propaganda was a far stronger weapon. In fact, the Soviet leaders
themselves have long been convinced that the battle between
their political system and that of the West will be decided not
by missiles and tanks but by the conquest of people's minds.
The tremendous Soviet military buildup is meant solely to blackmail the West into paralysis, while tens of billions of dollars are
spent on psychological warfare. The free world needs no similar
counterpropaganda; it needs only to preserve its institutions and
to counter with the truth.

In my case, I knew our cause was just, and truth was our
ultimate weapon. So back to work. Our next large project was
a concert-tribute at the Kennedy Center in Washington to celebrate Sakharov's sixtieth birthday. We asked former Soviet musicians to perform, and a number of dignitaries to speak. It was
a major undertaking, once again done on a shoestring. I approached a wide array of scientific, religious, ethnic, and human
rights organizations. Most of them agreed to help. For two months,
I went door to door, handing out information about the Sakharov
Institute and trying to sell tickets. Unlike Madrid, we had a full
house for this event. Speakers included members of Sakharov's
family, Senator Edward Kennedy, Nobel laureate Sheldon Lee
Glashow, who had agreed to be president of the Sakharov Institute, Congresswoman Millicent Fenwick, and several other
prominent individuals.

Not only did the event exceed our wildest hopes and expectations, but it was so successful that we decided to make it an annual event, which it has become, on May 21, Sakharov's birthday. More important, it has brought attention to and support for the Sakharov Institute from a wide variety of organizations, which, however disparate, are united on the issues of human dignity, peace, and freedom.

It was especially heartening to see the participation of several Jewish organizations in this project. There is a justifiable concern among most of them that if they come out strongly in support of the dissidents, the two million Jews still living in Russia might suffer for it. Their view is that if they focus on the problem of the Jews themselves, whom they look on as hostages within Russia, they would be more effective. My feeling is that this is the wrong strategy, that the fate of Soviet Jews is and will be determined solely on the basis of the Kremlin's domestic and international political interests. For the Kremlin—and obviously this changes to some degree from leader to leader—the Jews are a dangerous minority, a rebel tribe that might well, in some foreseeable future, trigger a revolution among the docile Russians—whence the desire to get rid of them.

In 1973 I had had a lengthy talk with a high-ranking Soviet official who told me, in confidence, "The problem is, the Jews have always been a foreign body in the Soviet organism . . . except perhaps in the early years after the Revolution. Because of their many contacts abroad, they generally lack any feeling of real patriotism. We'll only feel comfortable after we've expelled the last Jew from the country. We've started by eliminating them from all key posts—not brutally, mind you, but by a process of attrition. And the number of Jews being admitted to the universities has been curtailed severely. In the not-too-distant future, most Jews will be allowed to emigrate."

Unfortunately, however, the Soviets have discovered that this "humanitarian" policy can be made to pay off, in the form of credit, technology, grain, and advantageous international treaties. This principle of paying the ransom to the Soviets is not only odious but also, in my opinion, suicidal in the long run. Keeping pressure on the Soviets, both internally and externally, will be the only effective way to get them to allow the remaining

Jews to leave the country. Support of Sakharov and other dissidents fighting for the democratization of Soviet society is the best way to maintain this pressure.

In Moscow events were moving swiftly. In her messages to me, Tatiana made it clear that she was coming around more and more to my opinion that tears and pleas, whether to the authorities or her parents, were useless. As a result, in 1980 she helped set up what they called the Divided Family Group: Any Soviet citizen who was married to a foreign national or to a Soviet émigré and prevented from joining a spouse by the authorities could in principle be a member. Any such unauthorized group in Russia tends to be crushed by the regime, and Tatiana was well aware of that, but she and those involved with her were by now beyond the fear of threats or intimidation. They felt that at this point they had nothing to lose. They wrote hundreds of letters—to the United Nations, to presidents and prime ministers, to the Madrid conference, to Communist party secretaries, and of course to members of the Politburo, as well as to the major Soviet magazines and newspapers. Then they wrote to artists and scientists, to workers and peasants. They held press conferences and exhibited paintings and documents relating to their case, inviting Western reporters and visitors to their apartments. My job was to make sure the Western press was kept constantly aware of all of the group's activities, and that the Voice of America broadcast the news to the USSR. In November 1980, for example, the group sent a telegram to the Helsinki Review Conference in Madrid. I ran off 500 copies of it and made sure it was in every delegate's mailbox—including those of the Soviet delegates—the next morning.

No one knew how long the regime would tolerate the group's existence, but then by chance the Soviet media inadvertently gave the group a great, though dangerous, idea. In 1981, several members of the Irish Republican Army imprisoned in Northern Ireland decided to undertake a hunger strike in order to force the British government to recognize their status as political prisoners. The Soviet press, eager to discredit Prime Minister Margaret Thatcher, launched a massive campaign in support of the hunger

strikers, depicting them as martyrs and heroes in the great struggle against the forces of capitalism. For weeks the campaign
continued. The Divided Family Group decided to adopt the idea
and use it for their own purposes.

Hunger strikes were not original—in fact, as noted, both
Tatiana and I had used it as a weapon in the past to try to free
her. But those had been limited strikes. Now the plan was to
go all the way. Of the group members, only Tatiana and four of
her friends were prepared to carry it through to the end: Yuri
Balovlenkov, who was married to a nurse in Baltimore; Tanya
Azure, a doctor, who was married to a French engineer; Maria
Yurgutis, wife of a Lithuanian defector; and Iosif Kiblitsky, who
was married to a West German teacher. All five had agreed that
if there was no change in their status by the spring of 1982, they
would begin their strike together.

Then, suddenly, the news broke that Andrei Sakharov and
his wife, Yelena Bonner, had begun a hunger strike in an effort
to obtain an exit visa for their son's fiancée. The strike was front-
page news around the world and resulted in a storm of protest
from governments, the scientific community, and thousands of
people from dozens of countries. After seventeen days, the pressure was such that the Soviet authorities gave in. It was a major
victory for the Sakharovs, but also for Tatiana and her friends.
In a message smuggled out to me, Tatiana urged me not to join
the strike itself, but to bend my efforts to getting as much press
coverage as possible in the West. She also asked me to arrange
for our remarriage by proxy—something we had been discussing
for some time. We set the date for May 10, 1982, the day the
hunger strike was due to begin.

From that point on, I worked almost around the clock, av-
eraging no more than three hours of sleep a night. I scoured all
my old files, notebooks, reports, all the thousands of business
cards I had collected. I drew up a master mailing list and sent
out full details of the forthcoming hunger strike. After summarizing the history of the previous six years, I confirmed the
starting date of May 10.

In April I returned from a meeting of Young Republicans—
the purpose of which was to support the British in the Falkland

Islands crisis—with the promise of support from the group's two leaders, Kathy Royce and David Barron. They put their resources at my disposal, and we produced mailings, contacted the press, organized meetings and rallies outside the Soviet Embassy, and met with members of Congress and spokesmen at the State Department and the White House.

Meanwhile, preparations for the remarriage went ahead. Rabbi Joshua Haberman of the Washington Hebrew Congregation agreed to perform the wedding ceremony, and the Young Republicans arranged for it to be held in a room in the Capitol. Senator Robert Dole and Congressman Jack Kemp agreed to act as best man and witness, respectively.

I felt both elation and despair at the turn of events. I knew the risks were enormous. Tatiana would indeed go all the way. There was no turning back. She had more than once spoken of suicide. Her latest letter told of her determination:

> *I want to marry you under American law. If I die, I will have no regrets. I will be your lawful wedded wife in the eyes of God, and our daughter will have a better chance of being reunited with you. My companions in the group and I have all made our last will and testament, according to which we ask that all our material possessions be turned over to Amnesty International. In my will I have added a clause requesting that I be buried in Washington. If the hunger strike ends in my death, I want you to avenge me. You know what I have in mind. . . .*

Reason should have made me try to stop her at that point while there was still time, but I knew she would not listen, that there was nothing I could do to dissuade her. And although I could not even dare to think of the pain and suffering she would have to endure, I also knew that she was master of her own fate, that her decision was the only course. The moment was well chosen, the organization to utilize all our resources was in place. And for some reason I remained confident. "Those who take no risks," goes a Russian proverb, "never drink champagne." Unfortunately, the risks were being taken not by me but by Tatiana and her group.

I was also counting on General Kozlov, which may seem strange. To be sure, he was loyal to the party. True, he would take orders from the party to attack and if necessary kill Czechs or Afghans, or even Russian workers who might dare to protest or revolt. But his own flesh and blood? His own daughter? Surely there was no ideology on the face of the earth strong enough to force a man to commit such a crime. One would have to be a robot to do that. Was Kozlov a robot? Wouldn't his heart prevail over his fidelity to country and party? I knew him fairly well. Despite everything I held against him, I was convinced that the man in him would win out over the Kremlin ideologue. But could I be sure?

On May 10 the hunger strike began. On that same day, Tatiana and I were reunited in marriage, by proxy, in the Rotunda of the United States Capitol. Senator Dole and Congressman Kemp made an attempt to telephone Tatiana in Moscow, to offer their congratulations, but to no avail. Her line had been disconnected—permanently, this time. I also learned that she had been placed under house arrest.

A UPI dispatch received shortly after the ceremony in the Rotunda announced that the hunger strike had begun and that Western reporters who had tried to gain access to Tatiana's apartment had been turned back. The same dispatch noted that two more people had joined the group, which meant that now a total of seven people had decided dying was preferable to the inhuman life they were leading. The two were Andrei Frolov, a free-lance journalist married to a Chicago woman, Lois Becker, and Vitaly Volobuyev, who had a French fiancée.

In Washington there were daily demonstrations outside the Soviet Embassy. There were candlelight vigils and freedom songs. Tracts were distributed to passersby. All of this drew the attention of the American press. *The New York Times*, the *Washington Post*, the *Chicago Tribune*, and many other American newspapers carried daily stories about the strike. ABC's "Nightline" somehow managed to interview the strikers, graphically bringing their plight before millions of viewers. In France, the indefatigable Jacqueline Peron bombarded President François Mitterrand with letters and telegrams. Other journalists lent their voices, and friends their support. In Germany, a similar campaign was waged, led by Mrs. Kiblitsky.

Ten days passed. The Kremlin remained unbending. For the Soviet authorities, these seven people simply did not exist.

Vice-President George Bush met with the American spouses of the hunger strikers. He assured us that the American government, together with several Western allies, was trying to negotiate with the Soviets. Congress passed a resolution, introduced by Senator Dole and Congressman Kemp, demanding the release of the strikers. Even the State Department, which is generally slow to act, joined in. The American consul in Moscow, together with a French doctor, visited the strikers almost daily, to monitor their health. The KGB agents stationed at the building tried to keep them out, using threats and intimidation. On one occasion there was physical violence between Tatiana's self-appointed guards and the American consul. But even that did not deter the visits.

Three weeks went by. Still not a word from the Kremlin.

Then, suddenly, came an initial victory: The oldest of the seven, the journalist and photographer Andrei Frolov, was summoned to OVIR and informed that he could leave the country. We judged that victory to be due, at least in part, to the fact that Frolov's wife, Chicagoan Lois Becker, had filed a lawsuit against the Soviet government, demanding a million dollars restitution from the Russians for every day her husband had been detained illegally.

Shortly thereafter, the KGB burst into Tanya Azure's apartment and informed her that her exit visa had been granted. We assumed that that second "victory" had been won through French President Mitterand's personal intervention.

In a few days, another victory. Biophysicist Vitaly Volobuyev from Novosibirsk was told that he could go to France. Then a terrible thing happened to a Lithuanian woman, Maria Yurgutis, who was staying with Tatiana. She was taken from the apartment and escorted to Vilnius, where she was put under house arrest.

Tatiana was also warned that she might be prosecuted for allowing Maria to stay in Moscow without permission from the authorities. Maria has very little chance of ever getting out. Soviets
never allow defectors to reunite with their families. As far as I
know the only time they allowed the family of a defector to leave
Russia was in the case of grandmaster Victor Korchnoi and film-
maker Andrei Tarkovsky.

As for Tatiana, she grew weaker day by day.

Twenty-five days without food. Twenty-six. Twenty-seven.
I was beginning to panic. We had played all our cards, and only
three out of seven had won their freedom. What about the
others? I was on the verge of sending a desperate note to Tatiana, via diplomatic pouch, pleading with her to stop. Later she
told me she would not have listened. She had already reached
the point where she was fully prepared to die. Nothing, nobody—not even I—could have dissuaded her.

I had one last hope. Contact General Kozlov and beg him
to save his daughter's life.

I knew this, too, was a long shot, for I was fully aware that
Tatiana had called her father late in May and told him she was
dying.

"As far as I'm concerned," he had replied, "you're already
dead."

Still, I hoped to move him. Perhaps he had thought his
daughter was bluffing. I had to try. The problem was, his telephone number was classified. Tatiana had always refused to give
it to me, for fear that I would hound her parents with my appeals.
And in the Soviet Union, revealing a classified phone number
is an act of treason and punishable as such. Since the start of
her hunger strike, I had badgered Tatiana to give it to me, but
she had steadfastly refused.

On the thirtieth day of the strike, I called one of my friends
in Moscow. Fortunately, the automatic dialing system installed
by the French at the time of the Moscow Olympics was still
working. Three weeks later, the Russians shut it down, "for
technical reasons."

I explained the urgency of the situation and begged my friend

to go to Tatiana's apartment and, one way or another, get that
telephone number from her.

Three hours later, I called him again and he confirmed my
worst fears. Tatiana was now bedridden, incapable of taking even
a few steps. She was deathly pale, and her emaciated arms were
hideously ringed with bulging black veins. But he had managed
to get the number.

I dialed the general immediately. At the first ring, he picked
it up. He must have been expecting a call, but not this one.

"Hello, Pyotr Ivanovich," I said, trying to control my voice.
"This is Edward. Please don't hang up. Hear me out. I'm calling
to tell you that your daughter is dying. Did you know that? I
swear it's true. I beg of you to take a few hours out of your
schedule and go see for yourself. Go see her. With your own
eyes."

I realized that tears were streaming down my cheeks. My
voice was cracking. *Don't hang up. Please don't hang up. For
God's sake, don't hang up. Please. Please.*

"Please don't hang up," I said, in a voice now more or less
under control.

"Yes," the general replied. "Yes, I understand. I didn't really
think it was that serious. I thought Tatiana was simply trying to
pressure me."

"I swear she's not. This is dead serious. Please go see her
right away, before it's too late. The doctors tell me that in a day
or two at most, there will be irreversible brain damage."

That medical information, which had been given to me by
an American doctor, had been transmitted to the State Department from Moscow.

Then, to my consternation and horror, the general's tone
suddenly shifted. "She's crazy," he shouted. "How can she ever
have gotten mixed up in these anti-Soviet activities? She, of all
people! Our country gave her everything: studies, a job, happiness. And this is how she pays it back? Antisocial groups.
Capitalist journalists, the Voice of America! It's unforgivable!
She's been duped by our enemies, people who don't give a damn
about her. Or you either, for that matter. All they're after is

propaganda. All they want is to discredit our country, make people hate the only peace-loving country in the world. . . ."

He raved on in this way for several minutes. I sensed that I should let him go on and not interrupt, either because he didn't realize what he was saying or, on the contrary, that he knew very well what he was doing and was aiming his speech at the KGB operatives who were undoubtedly tapping his line.

Finally, his voice resumed its normal tone. "I understand your concern," he said, "I really do. Call me tomorrow at this same time."

Slowly I put the receiver back on the hook. And then I blacked out. My nerves, my brain, my body had reached their limit. When I came to, I crawled to my bed and threw myself on it. I slept for twenty hours straight. During the four hours remaining before my call to Moscow, I spent most of the time praying. On my knees. Anyone who saw me during that time would have thought I had lost my mind. But I did not feel ashamed. My fate, the rest of my life, was to be decided during the next few hours. Nothing else mattered.

Precisely twenty-four hours after my first call, I dialed the general's number again. No answer. I let ten minutes elapse and tried again. Still no answer.

What could be wrong? My fevered imagination projected the worst possibilities on the screen of my mind: Tatiana had been arrested for having revealed her father's secret phone number. She was being force-fed by the KGB. The general himself had been placed under house arrest. His phone had been cut off. The dreaded black cars of the KGB were parked in front of his building.

Over the next six hours, I dialed that same number every fifteen minutes. Between calls I prayed. I felt, once again, close to the breaking point.

Then, at long last, the general answered. His voice was quiet and sounded weary. "I did go to see her," he said. "I can't describe to you how she looks. It's horrible. Yes, she is dying. I begged her to stop fasting, but she wouldn't listen. She said, 'First show me my exit visa.' How could I? That takes time. A week, maybe two. I beg you to call her. Call her this minute and tell her to stop this terrible thing she's doing. Tell her I've already made all arrangements for her. The decision's been made at the top. She can leave. But she won't listen to me. She wants her visa. This is insane. Call her immediately and try to talk some sense into her."

We've won! My God, we've won! It was all I could think of.

This time, I knew, the general was not lying. Now I had to reach her. Get her to take some food. "I *can't* call her," I shouted into the phone. "Her line's been disconnected. I'm sure I can convince her, if only I can reach her."

"Of course. I forgot. Damned incompetent technicians! I'll give the order immediately to fix the line. Call her in one hour."

Poor General Kozlov. He didn't realize that from then on no one would obey his orders. He had contacted the ranking members of the Politburo and asked them to leave his daughter alone. He asked them to let her leave Russia. Clearly, the Soviets were fed up with the whole story. They had replied that as far as they were concerned Tatiana could go anywhere she wanted— preferably to hell. But there was a price to pay. The Red Army could not tolerate the presence of a leading general whose daughter had emigrated and whose son-in-law was an enemy of the State. "Resign," was their order to him.

Kozlov, of course, had anticipated their reaction. He knew very well that in asking for his daughter's freedom he was sacrificing the career for which he had worked so long and fought so hard. Maybe he hoped that his case would be different, that they would forgive and forget. But no, he did not really believe that. Still, at the end of our conversation, he reverted to the tone and style of our previous day's conversation.

"Listen, Edward, let me ask you one thing. Don't let the CIA use this story as anti-Soviet propaganda. You know how they are. They'll start screaming about human rights, about how we heartless creatures separate families. . . . You know it's not true. Our government is only in search of coexistence and peace. . . ."

Once again, I knew, he was covering himself.

"Of course," I reassured him, "but the important thing now is to save Tatiana. Go with Anna and see her. I'll try to get a message to her through the American Embassy."

Later I learned that the general and his wife had gone to Tatiana's. The foreign press corps heard about it and rushed over to check out the story. When they arrived, they ran into the American consul and Yelena Bonner, Sakharov's wife, who had come to give Tatiana a copy of the letter she and her husband had written to Brezhnev on her behalf. As it turned out, Yelena was the first person to congratulate Tatiana on her freedom—a symbolism that was not lost on us.

The Kozlovs arrived at this point, and the KGB agents, who had no precise orders on how to handle this disparate group, simply stood by and scowled.

The general went into his daughter's room. What happened between them is not for me to say. It is their secret. If Tatiana cares to reveal it, that is up to her. All I know is that at that point Tatiana agreed to take a little fruit juice. The pain it caused her was almost intolerable. Her only words were, "Now there are only two left."

Her reference was to the two who still fasted and who had not been freed: Iosif Kiblitsky and Yuri Balovlenkov. Subsequently, Kiblitsky, too, was granted an exit visa. The only one of the seven who, as of this writing, is still trying to get out of the Soviet Union is Balovlenkov, whom the KGB regarded as the leader of the Divided Family Group and chose as a scapegoat. His wife and daughters are still waiting for him in Baltimore.

Six months more, six months of anguish and torture on both sides. Papers had to be obtained. The general's resignation had to become official. Tatiana had to regain her strength and health. A painful time, yet one of reconciliation between Tatiana and her parents.

My main concern during those months was that something might happen to worsen relations between the USSR and the United States. I seized the newspaper each morning with trepidation, and sighed with relief when I saw that nothing momentous had occurred between the two countries. Then one morning

I walked into my class at American University, where I was teaching physics and math, to learn from my students that word had just come of Leonid Brezhnev's death. I almost fainted, for I knew that the deal to release Tatiana had been struck with Brezhnev. Would his successor reverse the decision? I was probably the only person in the West who was truly devastated by Brezhnev's death.

When Yuri Andropov was named to his post, I learned that Vitaly Fedorchuk would remain head of the KGB. I was reassured, for Fedorchuk was an old friend of the Kozlovs.

The day finally came when Tatiana was summoned to the OVIR offices to receive her passport, good for travel abroad, and exit visas for her and Tania.

Remembering what I had told Tatiana at the Moscow train station six years earlier, I bought tickets for her and Tania on Air France. There was no way the Lozanskys were flying on Aeroflot. The Soviets did not appreciate that final slap in the face. They took their revenge by preventing Tatiana and Tania from boarding the Air France plane at the last minute. Some French friends went to the airport to meet them in Paris, and one of them called me and announced in a frantic voice that the plane from Moscow had arrived safely but that my wife and daughter were not on board.

I immediately called the State Department. Poor people! For six long years I had been hounding them, and I could well imagine the looks on their faces when they heard that a call was coming through from me. Nonetheless, once again they performed. An hour later they called back to tell me that Soviet customs officials had simply asked Tatiana and Tania to take the Aeroflot plane that left a few hours after the Air France flight. Tatiana had turned them down flat. "Nyet," she had said, "my husband booked us on Air France, and I intend to do whatever my husband asks."

As stubborn as ever. But without it, where would we be today?

Finally, the next day, she left Moscow forever.

At two o'clock in the afternoon of December 11, 1982, I received a call from Peggy Palk, a UPI correspondent who had been following our story for years. "I'd like to read you a dispatch just filed by our Paris correspondent. Have you got a minute?"

"Yes, go ahead."

"All right. Here it is: 'Tatiana Lozansky, wife of Washington professor Edward Lozansky and daughter of a high-ranking Soviet general, arrived today at Roissy Airport, together with their daughter, Tania, en route for the United States. During her stopover in Paris, Mrs. Lozansky declared to the journalists who had been waiting for her arrival for over twenty-four hours that she fervently wished that all divided families everywhere in the world could be reunited.' "

With tears streaming down my cheeks, I started to scream "Freedom, freeeedom, freeeeeeedom . . ." and then asked Peggy to join me. She did, and the two of us kept repeating this blessed word.

Our six-year calvary was over. I thought of all the people—journalists, statesmen, friends, militants—who had in various ways contributed to making this moment possible, and wished I could thank them all.

Without doubt, it was the happiest moment in my life.

4
Tatiana's Story
by Tatiana Lozansky

Sheremetyevo Airport was built by the West Germans. It was the first time that I had ever seen it. Despite the mixed emotions I was experiencing, I could not refrain from admiring its cleanliness and ultramodern look. At the old airport, the customs officials had performed their rituals behind barred windows. Today the travelers, and those who come to see them off, can marvel at modern electronic gadgetry from Japan or West Germany that makes baggage control efficient and rapid.

Three hours to takeoff. All the time in the world to say goodby, to laugh and smile through our tears. Everyone is there, even one of Tania's classmates who got the day off from school to come and bid farewell to her friend. Here we are, with our two suitcases, making small talk, and every now and then glancing nervously at the customs man who is checking some unknown passenger's baggage with his X-ray machine. We have heard that the passengers leaving Russia forever are subjected to the most meticulous checks. But Tania and I have nothing to fear; all we have are our clothes, a few gifts, and the traditional caviar and vodka.

Sheremetyevo is virtually empty. Now and then a group of hatchet-faced men in civilian clothes strolls past our happy little group. I feel good. Not a shadow of apprehension. Homesickness will come later. For now, it's the dizzying thought of leaving, the sudden realization that freedom is truly here. How many years has it taken to reach this point? To leave, to leave behind the country of my birth, the country that has formed me and made me what I am, to head for a new world and a new life. . . .

To leave? *Escape* would be a better word. After six years, I should know the difference. Those who have been waiting forever for their exit visas swear that they feel a strange kind of gratitude for the bureaucrats and their tricks, their about-faces and chicanery, for they mitigate the feeling of homesickness that besets all Russians who for one reason or another are forced into exile.

For the umpteenth time since the day began, I rummage in my handbag. Yes, it's still there: my brand-new passport, bright red with a gold crest. Stapled to my passport is a piece of paper that says: "Permitted to leave for the United States of America. Purpose of visit: Permanent resident." How simple it all seems. Who, looking at that little purple stamp, could imagine what it took to obtain it? All the sweat and tears, the fear and trembling, the long periods of utter despair.

Three months ago, a postcard had ordered me to report to the OVIR office, together with the sum of 200 rubles and a mountain of documents. I had spent weeks running from one end of Moscow to the other to gather all the required documents, proving that I was leaving no debts behind me. Finally, I went to the OVIR office, to the ugly, well-scrubbed room dominated by a graph showing all the various branch offices, each indicated by a light bulb. I noted that half of the lights were out. There were, as always, a couple of dozen *refuseniks* in the waiting room with me. I could tell what they were feeling from the frowns and anxious looks on their faces. "Good luck, good luck to you all," I whispered as I crossed the room to the office—or, rather, cubbyhole—where they handed out the passports. That morning the cubbyhole was empty.

I went from door to door, knocking, until finally I came upon one occupied by a short, dour bureaucrat, who took my papers and checked them closely, as if to find fault, before adding them to a file he had fished from a drawer: employment record, birth certificate, diplomas. One could only take from the country copies of the original documents. "Sign here," he ordered. I signed. "Internal passport," he said. I handed him my internal passport. Finally—oh blessed moment!—he handed me the external passport, similar but slightly smaller than the one I had just turned in. I opened it and read the magic words: "The bearer Lozanskaya Tatiana is departing for abroad." Was that possible? Ten years ago, if a soothsayer had predicted what was going to happen to me, I would have laughed in his face. And if he had said how my last six years in Moscow would have been spent, I would have laughed even louder.

Yura Balovlenkov, my dear friend and comrade-in-arms, put his hand on my shoulder. I could barely feel the pressure of his hand, which was little more than skin and bones after his two-month fast. A tall man, he leaned down and smiled at me through his beard. He had a sense of the true values of life, which gave him the strength and purpose to overcome the constant stresses and pressures to which he was subjected. I knew that he was happy for me, and for the others of the Divided Family Group who had already left. Yura and Maria Yurgutis were the only two who had been denied an exit visa. Two months later, we would learn, Yura was summoned to the Attorney General's office and issued a warning that his activities were viewed as being anti-Soviet. Nonetheless, the following year he formally reapplied to OVIR and again was turned down.

But all that was in the future. At the airport, Yura was all smiles, as was everyone else who had come to see us off. We took out our address books and made sure we all had one another's proper address and phone number. In truth, we were trying to cover up our real feelings with idle small talk. Some, though, could not hold back their tears. Departure time was fast approaching. I wished my father were present, but he was not well—hospitalized, in fact. "Age," people would say, shaking their heads. But it is not really that: He feels he is a ruined man. His life is shattered. A victim of this whole sordid business. If only Edward

could put himself in Father's place, just for one brief moment. . . .

*Freedom. Only a three-hour flight to Paris and I will be free.
Tania and I. Impossible to believe.*

I was trembling like a leaf. The deep-rooted fear of leaving,
of taking something forbidden with me that the authorities would
uncover and, at the last minute, use as an excuse to keep me
from leaving. Stone faces of all the airport officials: cashier, passport control, customs itself. Not the trace of a smile anywhere.
Only the foreigners were treated with a modicum of civility.
Why? Were foreigners first-class citizens? What about me? What
about Tania? Weren't we simply a mother and daughter going
abroad, to rejoin our husband and father? Why was that such a
crime? It wasn't, I kept telling myself. Then why was I still
plagued with this deep sense of guilt?

At a party, someone once told me that the basic difference
between bourgeois democracy and Communist society was that
in the West you could do anything that was not expressly forbidden by law *(licitum est omne non explicitur prohibitur)*, whereas
in the Soviet Union you could not do anything unless the law
specifically allowed it. You can go through Soviet law with a
fine-toothed comb without finding any reference to restrictions
on travel. Which does not mean such restrictions do not exist.
One cannot, for example, travel from some remote Russian prov-
ince to Moscow without authorization. There are some "free-
doms": You can, for instance, swap your apartment in Sverdlovsk
for one in Moscow; if you are a construction worker or truck
driver in the provinces, you can get a job in Moscow and lodge
in a workers' dormitory without express authorization to make
the move, doubtless because the jobs are in high demand. You
can even marry a Moscow girl and thus obtain a Moscow resi-
dence permit. But that is the only kind of "freedom" anyone
has.

Moving abroad is not mentioned in the Soviet Constitution,
while failure to return from abroad—"defecting"—is "a particularly serious crime against the State." If, for example, you cross
the border illegally—say, to join a relative abroad—provided
there is no "intent to undermine Soviet power," you are *only*

subject to a three-year prison sentence. In any case, the older generation in Russia finds it hard to understand why anyone would want to leave the country today. They still have vivid memories of the Stalinist era, when defectors were tracked down in the West and harassed or even assassinated. They also remember the times when marrying a foreigner was the fastest route to the *gulag*.

Our generation was brought up in a more liberal atmosphere. We could listen to Western radio programs with relative ease. In the 1970s, we were accustomed to seeing friends or even relatives pack their bags and leave for the West, especially for Israel and the United States. To be sure, these would-be emigrants were ill-treated in the months before they left, held up to ridicule at party and trade union meetings as well as in the press, but they were not jailed or killed.

How did all this affect me? What did I care about the West? All I wanted, after six endless years, was to be back with my husband. Yet I was afraid. Would time have made strangers of us? And what about Tania? Would she get along with a father she barely remembered? What were we going to say to each other when we met? Would we really be able to adapt to this new country? Could we really be happy there?

I heard them announce the Paris flight. I was surprised at how few people there were at the airport, but I thought that might make the customs formalities proceed more quickly.

In the Bible it says something to the effect that a man shall "leave his father and his mother, and shall cleave unto his wife, and they shall be one flesh." The same goes for a woman. My fidelity to Edward threw my once-quiet life completely out of kilter. I wrote hundreds of letters, went on a hunger strike, gave interviews and press conferences, made countless transatlantic calls to Edward, had the KGB camping on my doorstep. . . . And now it was almost over.

Why was I so worried about the border guards here at Sheremetyevo? In all my letters and public statements, I stressed over and over again that I was an ordinary woman, that the man I married was an up-and-coming Soviet physicist, the man my parents hired to tutor me in math and physics many long years ago. We were two ordinary people, who only wanted to be left alone to live their own lives. But the system made us larger than life, the object of constant attention, constantly followed and watched.

Today, the watchdogs were still here, though they paraded under the guise of "border guards." Why? Why did I worry them so? I was neither a malcontent nor a dissident, only an "ordinary woman." In how many thousands of letters and messages had I used that simple term? And it was true. I had never dreamed of marrying a foreigner, much less an American. I had married a Soviet physicist. The future looked rosy for us: We had an apartment, a dacha, a car—everything one could hope for in Moscow. The West should have remained for us what it was for most of our compatriots: a never-never land, a world of dreams.

And yet . . . Edward did leave. Edward did become an American citizen. After our trumped-up divorce, our marriage was recelebrated by proxy across the Atlantic, according to proper procedures, as Edward has already related. All I would like to add is that, after the phony divorce, I often wondered why I ever agreed to submit to that farce. What ever possessed me to walk into that court and tear up the piece of paper so that the emigration process could begin? Perhaps we should have avoided the humiliating procedure all spouses have to go through—namely, the waiving of material claims. If we had, maybe Edward would have changed his mind, found a better job, and settled down. When the strain of our separation grew too intense, I often used to think that that would have been the better course, the saner route. But I would have been wrong. While it might have kept the marriage intact, it would have torn our souls asunder. The end would have been not a mock but a real divorce. When a man has to leave, he has to leave. If we had given in, especially at that initial stage, Edward would have regretted it for the rest of his life, would have felt that he had missed the chance of a lifetime.

I have always been an optimist. The "divorce," a "temporary separation," always struck me as a reasonable solution. After all, if the Soviet government was acting humanely, letting people leave, why should we be so superior? Edward would emigrate, go to the United States, find a job, and prepare the terrain for us. All very simple. I even dreamed that I would be able to leave on a Soviet passport, which would enable me to return from time to time to see my parents. The Jews who left had to give up their Soviet citizenship, leave the land of their birth forever. *Forever* is a frightening word, at least for me.

Yes, that original decision we had made had seemed like a wise one. And yet between it and today lay six long years, 2,200 days, or about the same length of time Jacob had to wait for Rachel. Yet we paid dearly for that "wise" decision, both my parents and I. My father's career is ruined, and he is a broken man. All he has to look forward to is puttering in the garden of his dacha. How did we ever manage to hurt each other so, cursing and screaming at each other, and even coming to blows? Who is to blame? Not them, certainly. I bear them no grudge. We spent my last five months in Moscow under the same roof, together again, and happy. In all fairness, it was a happiness tinged with sadness, a sadness I still felt here at the airport. I knew I would keep in contact with them, write them often. And I knew even my headstrong husband would write them, too.

Time. It was time. In a few hours I would no longer be a *refusenik,* "the foreigner's wife." I would go back to being the "ordinary woman" I used to be and wanted to be again. Without cameras and flashbulbs. Without newspapermen forcing their way through the guardian angels outside my apartment. No more lonely nights, either. How wonderful to love and be loved! O God, let it be like it was! Let neither of us be changed. Just Edward and Tatiana together, the way it used to be, with Tania to show for it and others who will come after! Let's start a new life in a new world, and put the past six years behind us. Forget, yes, forget!

Reunited. A reunited family. I could not get the words out of my mind. What did Soviet law have to say on the subject? Not much. Only a couple of lines in the Helsinki Accords. "The Soviet Government pledges to consider petitions for reuniting families, and to consider them in a humanitarian spirit. It also agrees to reduce the exit tax." To give the Kremlin credit, it actually did lower the tax, from 400 to 300 rubles, and then to 200. But it took seven years to do it. What it gave with one hand, however, it took away with the other: Emigrating Jews still had to pay a "supplementary tax" of 500 rubles. That was the price exacted for allowing them to renounce Soviet citizenship. What about the humanitarian spirit mentioned in the Helsinki Accords? We all know that one unfortunate case garners far more attention than a hundred happy ones.

The Soviet authorities claim that most requests to emigrate are granted. Novosti, the news agency that provides background material for periodicals, claims that 98.6 percent of Jews who apply are allowed to emigrate. The 1978 edition of a publication called *A Hundred Questions and Answers,* issued mainly for foreign consumption, states that: (1) 9,000 Soviet citizens married foreigners "in the past few years," and (2) have been authorized to join their spouses in over a hundred countries around the world. The only thing is, the statistics are vague about just how many of the first category were able to reach the second. What is more, it has become increasingly difficult even to make a request to emigrate, a fact that is completely absent from the official statistics.

But even if most requests to reunite divided families supposedly are granted, there is little comfort in that knowledge for those who are made to wait for six endless years, or forced to go on a hunger strike before being granted an exit visa. When a group of miners is trapped in the mines, the world's attention is focused on them, while the millions of miners who go about their daily work without incident are completely ignored. The only thing that matters is that team of trapped miners, and rightly so. In my own case, I am grateful that so many people around the world took notice of our plight.

It is strange to have to justify what is an inalienable, God-given right: the pursuit of happiness, the right to live with the person you love. And that is what our group has had to do incessantly over the past several years.

I looked at Yura Balovlenkov and thought of the gifts I was carrying in my luggage for his daughter, the messages I was bearing for his wife, Lena, in Baltimore. I could feel the tears welling. I was leaving Yura behind, alone with his courage and his undying loyalty to his friends. He smiled at me, just as he had smiled earlier at Inna Lavrova when she left, at Tanya Azure, Andrei Frolov, Vitaly Volobuyev, and Iosif Kiblitsky. He was a born optimist, Yura was, and despite his precarious health, I knew his spirits were still high. The special food that Lena brought him last summer from Baltimore arrived too late to help him regain his health following his hunger strike, which was the longest on record!

I could go on talking about my group forever. Without it, I would never have made it. When I was fighting on my own in the beginning, I got absolutely nowhere. But over the next two years, even though our letters, petitions, and protests produced no tangible results, I felt so much better, simply because I was no longer alone.

I could still vividly remember my first hunger strike, in July 1980, during the Moscow Olympics—that feeling of desperate isolation, alone in my apartment, with, once in a rare while, a friend stopping by to check on me. The press sent only two journalists to see me, and two television crews—one French, the other American. The Olympics themselves, and the Western boycott, were the big story. I was too small a fry to get worked up over. But I did have the authorities worried; they kept promising me the moon, and gave me . . . nothing.

But all that was in the past. Now it was time for last good-bys. I hugged my relatives and friends. Kisses mingled with sobs. Finally, I broke away, picked up my suitcase, took Tania by the hand, and headed toward the customs gate. A woman customs official checked my papers. "You're not going anywhere today," she said dryly.

"What do you mean?" My heart was pounding so loud I was sure she could hear it. Now what did they have up their sleeves?

"Just what I said. You won't make it in time. It's too late."

"How could it be too late? The plane doesn't leave for more than two hours."

"You don't understand. You're leaving the country, and going to America to boot. You should have come to the airport yesterday."

My friends couldn't believe what they were hearing. I was so devastated I didn't know what to do or say. What if tomorrow's flights were all full? Worse yet: My visa would expire in a week. What if all the flights for the next week were fully booked? And what if people in high places had changed their minds about letting me go? I voiced some of these concerns.

"I wouldn't put it past them," I heard Yura mutter. "But don't worry," he hastened to add, "they won't succeed," and he ran into the customs office.

I left our luggage with my friends and hurried over to the Air France reservation counter to see if there was room on the flight the next day. If there was, we would stay at Sheremetyevo overnight, going through customs at night and leaving the next morning. All the joy and excitement I had been feeling were gone. I felt my knees shaking as I approached the ticket counter. I felt sick and frightened, so frightened I was afraid I might throw up. It was a feeling I had experienced so many times before that I recognized all the symptoms. For years that deep-rooted fear lay within me. I couldn't get rid of it, couldn't forget the anger and bitterness one feels whenever one does battle with that immovable force, the stubborn resistance of Soviet authority.

Each day, I had burned more and more bridges behind me. Each month, it had become clearer and clearer that I was fighting the major battle of my life. That conviction overwhelmed everything else, especially after our group was founded. We went through every possible stage: strength, vacillation, anger, depression. But because of our conviction, we prevailed. Without it, I wouldn't be here this morning, at the Air France counter, my stomach filled with a tight little knot of cold anger.

It all began thanks to Irina McClellan, the veteran among us. It was her idea that we should band together and join forces. It was in her apartment that I met Yura Balovlenkov for the first time. Irina had been fighting for five years. Her name was well known to the Western press. In her struggle to join her husband, an American professor, she was the first Soviet citizen to chain herself to the gates of the American Embassy. She had staged countless protests, marching in the streets of Moscow with signs pleading her case. American statesmen had intervened on her behalf with Andrei Gromyko and even Brezhnev. Rumor has it that in the course of a reception for American diplomats, Brezhnev is reported to have said, "All right. You can have your McClellan. Good riddance as far as I'm concerned." But rumors are only that. The fact was, Irina was still in Moscow, no further along than she had been a decade earlier. Like clockwork, she went regularly to the OVIR offices and officially requested an exit visa. Like clockwork, OVIR responded in the negative. I would have much more to say about Irina if our paths had not diverged relatively early on. She wanted to enlarge the group, let in everyone, anyone with close relatives abroad, even spouses of defectors. Either she was braver or nobler than we, or perhaps simply more desperate, because of the time she had already spent fighting and because for years her husband had not been allowed into Russia to visit her. In any event, we felt too precarious, too afraid, too close to the edge of illegality. It terrified us to consider crossing that fine line between what was allowed but frowned upon and what was forbidden and illegal. We were still naive enough to believe that if we were good little boys and girls, *they* would be reasonable and yield to what they would realize were legitimate demands. Hence our slogan: "We shall do nothing against the State. Never will we break the law." Under Soviet law, defectors were considered traitors. The families had no hope of ever seeing them again. That was the stand we took with Irina, and we stuck to it. The only exception was made for Maria Yurgutis, and only because she was my close friend and often stayed with me in Moscow. Time showed how wrong we were. Our attitude—that if we were nice to *them,* *they* would be nice to us—was hopelessly naive. On the contrary, experience proved that the more timid and submissive we were, the more brutal, aggressive, and pitiless they were with us.

Irina was also against hunger strikes, which she found pointless. "Nobody cares," she said. "Nobody pays any attention to them anymore." So she and several others dropped out of the group she had founded. Despite this, however, I am eternally grateful to her, and I pray that one day she will succeed in rejoining her husband.*

In April 1981 we were still optimistic. I wrote to Brezhnev, "As a mother and as a human being, I believe in one's right to happiness. Once again I ask for your help. Help me reunite my family. We love each other. It's as simple as that."

I wrote to every other leader in the same vein. How silly I was to expect results, especially from Brezhnev. I had simply forgotten that every day he received hundreds of letters from Soviet citizens, letters ranging from someone wanting reinstatement in a job to someone begging for an apartment or seeking to have a leaky roof repaired. Officially, the Central Committee of the party has no executive or legislative power, but it is the final court of appeal for those seeking justice or a redress of grievances on whatever level. There is also the Party Congress, which meets every five years, and I appealed to it as well—not about my exit visa but about my telephone, which had been mysteriously and summarily cut off after I had received what they must have considered a disquieting number of calls from abroad. That poor little black telephone, it always rang too loudly. It did its bit for freedom, as, thousands of miles beyond the iron curtain, Edward moved heaven and earth to have Tania and me set free. After I appeared on the French TV program "Dossiers de l'Ecran," where I broke down and began to sob hysterically in front of millions of French viewers, that little phone worked heroically, as French people responded by calling me directly to voice their support. *They* had somehow allowed me to appear on French television, had let me express the pain and anguish of a whole people. But *they* still had kept me prisoner in Moscow, on the eighth floor of the massive gray building that Stalin's uninspired architects had designed.

When we first formed our group, we were five, then seven. After five years of struggle, two hunger strikes, and my hundreds of letters, I was considered a veteran. Of all of our spouses, Edward was the only former Soviet citizen, and abroad his voice was raised louder than the others. He proved more stubborn

*Irina was reunited with her husband in January 1986.

and unyielding. But the time came when the actions of my friends and colleagues gave plenty of sleepless nights to the authorities as well. Looking back, I remember our first letter, sent to a friend. We complained about the incompetence of certain OVIR officials, but carefully went on to praise the wisdom of our Great Party and Admirable Government. We had the foresight to sleep on that first letter, and fortunately consigned it to the wastebasket before it went out and made fools of us.

I saw Yura run toward me. "Hurry up," he said, "I've arranged everything. They'll check your papers immediately. Get your luggage and go through customs before they change their minds."

Poor Yura. He looked so awful. But I was sure I was no pinup myself at that point.

Once again I said good-by, picked up my luggage, took Tania's hand, and headed toward customs. The minute I entered the customs area, I was surrounded by half a dozen officials and border guards. My blood turned to ice. Now what? We were carrying no diamonds, no works of art, no icons, no anti-Soviet manuscripts, not even any current books (a recent Soviet law forbade taking *any* Soviet book abroad except children's books, official political brochures, and works purchased with hard currency in stores reserved for foreigners). So why were *they* turning our suitcases upside down, examining each piece of clothing, each seam, each photograph? Why read through each line of each page of my address book? I bit my lip and tried to control my anger. *I'm not your enemy*, I said to myself. *Why do you treat me this way?* Beyond the customs barrier, my friends were watching silently, their expressions meant to be encouraging. Ten minutes. Half an hour. An hour. And still they squinted and searched and looked. *Patience, Tatiana, patience. What is an hour compared to six years?*

My mind flashed back to the beginning of our group. We spent our first five months, from November 1980 to March 1981, writing letters. Hundreds and hundreds of letters—not as childish as our first attempt, but nonetheless nonthreatening. Letters from decent Soviet citizens. Here again, my past experience was useful, or so I thought. For five years I had avoided politics like the plague. At first I tried to inculcate that attitude in other members of the group. We were still going hat in hand, making requests humbly, as in the case of a letter I sent to the minister of justice in January 1981. I asked him to verify the legality of some responses I had received, such as: "Your husband has emigrated to Israel. You indicate that you want to join him there, but at the same time say that you are leaving for the United States. Under the circumstances, there is nothing we can do for you." How could I know in those days that the good minister would not even entertain the idea of responding?

But we did learn, however slowly. And we did change our tactics. We no longer begged. We protested. Together. One group, indivisible.

Inna Lavrova deserves a book to herself. When I met her for the first time, I was struck by her good looks and slim figure. She and her two daughters lived in a prestigious wedding-cake building on the Kotelnichesky Embankment. Her hallway was filled with fine, well-thumbed books, her kitchen bright with flowers both fresh and dried. The impression was that she had been born in that apartment and would die there, after having spent her life penning millions of letters of appeal and protest. I remember her gentle but sad smile, which never left her lips. And her courage. Inna's first husband had been a Soviet diplomat who was posted to Paris. There she had met Guy. Her husband was both decent and civilized, and bowed to the inevitable. But he asked her to return to Moscow so that they could be divorced properly, after which she could return to France. To save her husband's career, Inna acquiesced. He kept his word and they were divorced. Guy, an engineer, came to Moscow to marry her and take her "home." They duly applied for a marriage license at the town hall on Griboyedov Street reserved for foreigners. Its name is symbolic: Griboyedov was a famous playwright, a contemporary of Pushkin, who married a non-Russian, the Georgian Princess Tchavtchavdze, and was stoned to death by a crowd in Teheran.

Once the formalities had been accomplished, there was a three-month wait before the ceremony itself. Guy returned to

Paris, and three months later, he applied for a visa to return to Moscow. His request was refused. He reapplied twenty-seven times, and each time he was turned down. Finally, he went to work in Africa, from where he phoned Inna daily for three years. Inna was a familiar sight at the French Embassy, where she was both known and loved. Thanks to her, and her friends at the French Embassy, our group was able for a long period to correspond with our loved ones without the watchful eye of the Russian censor monitoring our every thought and word. Ultimately, *they* let her go. But I knew I would not see her when I got to Paris, for she had gone to join Guy in Africa.

Paris. Will I be there in three hours as I had hoped? Will I ever get there?

The customs officials were still sifting, still exploring every nook and cranny of my luggage as though they thought they might find a gold ingot, a stash of hard drugs, or perhaps a manuscript that could turn out to be the new *Doctor Zhivago.* What do *they* have against Tania and me? Why can't they treat us as they do the French tourists, whose passports are stamped smartly and suitcases not even opened? *They* had discovered my jar of caviar, my amber necklace, the Faulkner novel I had planned to read during the flight. Our belongings, stacking up in a makeshift pile on the counter, were eyed suspiciously by a fat customs woman with a toadlike face who was bursting out of her navy blue uniform. Meanwhile, a plainclothesman, who seemed to be in charge, went from one official to the other, whispering instructions.

I could see that my mother was getting nervous. Two of my friends were making signs that they had to leave. They waved good-by, and as I waved back, the sight of the separated hands reminded me of our group's symbol, the outstretched, not-quite-touching hands of divided families.

That symbol had been Iosif Kiblitsky's idea. Two hands—one male, one female—stretched to reach each other. It came from Michelangelo's famous painting in the Sistine Chapel. Kiblitsky was the painter in our group, and we had a show of his paintings in my apartment as part of our "cultural program."

The idea of having Michelangelo as the godfather of our group pleased us all. We transferred our symbol onto buttons, which were circulated widely. Buttons sporting images of cartoon characters were available at various newspaper kiosks, so we bought them there, removed the cartoon images, and replaced them with the outstretched hands.

Iosif's wife, Renata, and his son, Mark, lived in West Germany. For months he had been knocking at countless doors, and he had achieved only one minor victory. He had gotten Renata to sue him through a Soviet court for child support, and thus he was "obliged" to send his family a quarter of his monthly earnings in hard currency. Iosif earned his living by going from *kolkhoz* to *kolkhoz*, immortalizing their war heroes, decorating their buildings with portraits of milkmaids and tractor drivers. What he could send to West Germany was a relative pittance, but at least he knew that his wife and child were receiving something.

Then there was Tanya Azure, who was a medical doctor. She married a French engineer who was hired by a construction company to work on a project for the Moscow Olympic Games. Tanya was from the town of Vladimir, and she would arrive at our meetings worn out from her five-hour trip to Moscow. Whenever she stayed at my apartment, we spent hours drinking tea and talking, about anything and everything, as though the world were not out of whack. We talked of our husbands, our feelings, our hopes and fears, about clothes. Those sessions helped relieve the drama and anxiety of our everyday existence.

The last person to join the group was Andrei Frolov. He participated in our second hunger strike, after OVIR had turned him down twice in a row. He was the first to be granted an exit visa, and the first to go, while Yura and I and the others had nothing but vague promises to show for our efforts. A bearlike man, over fifty, Frolov had been a journalist and had traveled widely throughout the Soviet Union, doing free-lance work for a magazine called *Around the World*. He had met and married a young American student, a history major who was in Russia on an exchange program. After she returned to America, she got a job as a barmaid, where she earned more than she could

get teaching history. She needed the money to pay her astro-
nomical phone bills to Moscow, and to save up for a trip
there, since *they* would not let her husband out. Every patron
of the bar where she worked knew her story, and the quantity,
if not the quality, of the advice she received apparently was
impressive.

So the battlelines were drawn: seven powerless souls filled
with utter conviction on one side and a huge, tentacular bureaucratic machine on the other.

Our only weapons were pen and paper, which we used incessantly if not always effectively. The head of OVIR was blus-
tering, bemedaled General Zotov, whom we petitioned endlessly,
to no avail. We also petitioned the Minister of the Interior,
General Nikolai Shcholokov, and from the United States Edward
wrote to the president of the Academy of Sciences, complaining
about the incompetence of "negligent OVIR officials." We also
wrote to the Helsinki Review Conference in Madrid, arguing
our cause. As a result of one of these steps, or perhaps all of
them, we were notified that we would be received at OVIR—
not by General Zotov, of course, but by one of his lackeys.

We were received politely, but the official who spoke with
us, after reviewing each of our cases, informed us, much as he
might do with a group of naughty children, that our departure
would "contravene the interests of the Soviet State." He went
on to say, with an indulgent smile, that of course we had every
right, "as instituted by law," to reapply for permission to leave
"every six months." Then his smile froze, as did his tone, as he
warned us that such group efforts would be fruitless and that,
in the future, we would have to submit our cases individually.*

Sadly, the five of us found ourselves back out on the rain-
swept Moscow streets, a rather bedraggled and sorry-looking
group.

What kind of government were we dealing with? One that,

---

*It is worth noting that, even before our struggle was over, General Zotov was
ousted from his post and sent to jail for taking huge bribes. As for Shcholokov, he,
too, was ousted within a year of Brezhnev's death, and for the same reason. Such
were the qualities of our opponents, those who held our fragile destinies in their
hands.

in peacetime, talked about our "contravening the interests of the Soviet State," when all we wanted was to unite our broken families. One that liked to boast that "the only privileged class in our society is the children," while keeping children away from one of their parents. One that termed any group action as criminal, whereas the Constitution formally recognized the right of workers to band together in order to defend their interests.

So we were being treated as criminals. Up until March 1981, we continued to act as private citizens dealing with a private complaint. While our spouses abroad may have attacked the Soviet Union and blasted its policies, we dissociated ourselves from their declarations. We stayed within the appointed procedures. We wrote twice to the Twenty-sixth Party Congress in 1981, once in my name alone and once collectively. In my letter, requesting the restoration of my telephone, I noted that I was "a powerless woman who does not know what to do next, nor where to turn, and so have decided to write to the Party Congress, the finest representatives of the Soviet people." Our joint letter begged the Party Congress to decide our fate. My letter went unanswered; the group letter produced minimal but tangible results. From then until May 1982, I had periodic telephone service. Then it went dead forever.

At the time of the Twenty-sixth Party Congress, I wrote to Dolores Ibarruri, the woman who after thirty years of exile in the Soviet Union had made a triumphant return to Spain in 1980, and who had been dubbed by the Western press as "La Pasionaria."

> *For four years, I have been trying to obtain permission to join my husband, to leave the country to which you gave thirty years of your life. I know of your ideals and am fully aware of the courage, honesty, and candor with which you have defended them. The letters I write to the government end up on the desks of the KGB. I myself have become "a person dangerous to the State." But our tragedy has no reason for being. It is due solely to the whims of some high-ranking authorities.*

Edward personally delivered the letter to Dolores in Madrid. "La Pasionaria" judged it unworthy of a reply. Edward was right: the Communist parties in the West were as useful to our struggle as a snowball in hell. I failed to understand their reticence. They had to realize that our case was tarnishing the name of communism locally and would hurt them in the elections. But doubtless there are more important considerations than the ballot box. After I appeared on "Dossiers de l'Ecran" in France, my mailbox was inundated with letters and postcards from ordinary French citizens, but there was not a word from any ranking member of the French Communist party.

We did everything we could to avoid political confrontation. After all, we told ourselves, Russia doesn't have a monopoly on divided families. We read in Soviet papers of cases similar to ours involving citizens of Canada and the United States, as well as another where a young Chinese artist was sent to a concentration camp for two years for wanting to marry a French diplomat. But patience has its limits.

On March 24, 1981, we sent a telegram to the Helsinki Review Conference in Madrid protesting that we "have been denied the most inviolable, the most elementary human right: the right to have a family and to live under one roof with that family. This is not only contrary to all humanitarian principles but is in violation of Soviet law and the agreements made in the Helsinki Accords."

That same day, we wrote to Aleksander Ginzburg, who had been imprisoned for handling Solzhenitsyn's fund for political prisoners' families. Another "political" act that would be held against us.

On April 21 we requested that the Presidium of the Supreme Soviet of the USSR "intervene with the Ministry of the Interior to take immediate steps to reunite divided families."

On April 22 we wrote to the Andrei Sakharov Institute in Washington, D.C.: "We earnestly request that you ask the Soviet government to take immediate steps to reunite divided families."

All these messages had some effect, both inside and outside

Russia, expanding the circle of those aware of our plight. But on a practical level, we had made no progress.

On June 22 we took the further step of thanking all those who had given us their support. We sent them letters in which we called the Soviet Union a country governed not by law but by the arbitrary whim of a few. We declared that the way we were being treated by the authorities was cruel and barbaric.

It is fascinating to see how totally apolitical people can be brought to such a point. And, unhappily, that is where we were.

The time for petitions and letters was over. Our OVIR turndown had depressed all of us. We all gathered in the kitchen of my apartment for what amounted to a silent meeting. None of us was quite sure what to do next. Only Inna had some bright news to report. A young Englishman had fallen in love with Inna's daughter Masha. This meant that Masha, once she was married, would be able to leave the country, presumably without trouble, since there was no reason for the authorities to stop her. The marriage ceremony would probably go off without a hitch and Masha would leave for England. Inna's logic told her that then *they* would let her go too, assuming that the only reason she had not been allowed to leave earlier was that she and Guy were not married.

But it turned out that Inna's logic and that of the authorities were poles apart.

The toadfaced woman awoke me from my daydreams. She motioned to Tania and me to go into a cubicle, presumably for a body search.

I unbuttoned my blouse. The toad's fingers probed the seams, then delved into my bra. Then she checked Tania's dress, and told us to remove our shoes.

"Come this way."

I assumed we were going to be X-rayed. Then, all of a sudden, my blood froze. *My God,* I thought, *don't tell me they're going to do a gynecological exam! On me. And on little Tania. I won't allow it. I'll spit in their faces. I'll. . . .*

Before I had a chance to protest, the toad told us to get dressed and return to the customs desk. The metallic voice over the loudspeaker was intoning, "The flight to Paris has finished boarding. . . ." I could see that Yura and my mother were still there. All the others had already left. I began to grab my belongings and stuff them into the luggage. I threw the caviar, the amber necklace, and the Faulkner novel into my mother's arms. At least the customs officials have the decency to let you give your family or friends the objects they won't let you take away with you—unless, of course, it's something they prefer to keep for themselves.

The bastards! They could see we were in a panic. You'd think they might at least help us close our suitcases. I grabbed them, half-closed as they were, and, with Tania in tow, rushed toward the boarding gate. In my haste, I ran into an official and almost knocked him off his feet. He recovered, straightened up, and yelled, "You're too late! The plane's already left. You're not going anywhere today."

Yes, back in the autumn of 1981 we were close to surrender. We were ill and exhausted by all our appeals, all our futile protests. A handful of idealists in the West, and a number of friends in Moscow, were rooting for us. But on a practical level, what could they do? They offered great psychological support and comfort, and sometimes more, but our elusive goal was still as distant as ever.

Renata Kiblitsky flew in and visited Iosif. Two months earlier, she had written to the Central Committee, requesting an audience. In doing so, she had had only one fear: that her tourist visa would be refused. For some strange reason, it was not. I had a moment of jealousy, knowing that at least the couple had been able to see each other. They would never have let Edward visit me in Moscow, even for a minute! But my jealousy soon turned to pity. Renata had overestimated her status as a German national. For three days, she and Iosif sat in the waiting room of the complaint section of the Central Committee, hoping for the audience that would solve all their problems. But no one in the section had ever heard of Mrs. Iosif Kiblitsky. No one remembered ever having received her letter. No one came to speak with them officially. Day after day, knots of bureaucrats came and went. None even acknowledged their presence. No one had the guts to tell her to her face that Iosif could not leave Russia, because it was contrary to the interests of the State.

Renata went home empty-handed.

Our gloomy gathering continued in my kitchen, as we tried to figure out why the government was so adamant. Why was it so opposed to reuniting divided families whose only desire was to be back together? None of us, singly or collectively, was intent on harming the State. We all sifted through our pasts, trying to unearth things we might have done, and to which the party might be privy, that would perhaps explain the situation.

First hypothesis: Inna Lavrova was being "punished" for having divorced a Soviet diplomat. Second hypothesis: Iosif Kiblitsky had spent seventeen years in the Red Army and was vaguely knowledgeable about Soviet missiles, therefore he had to wait out his five-year cooling-off period. That, in fact, was what the OVIR functionaries led him to believe, in so many words. Of course, none of us ever received official notices detailing why we had been refused, only vague indications. My own feeling was that the bureaucrats with whom we dealt were themselves ashamed of what they had to do, or rather what they were made to do. How else could I explain the fact that none of them could ever look us in the eye? How else could I explain the look of abject terror that seemed to flit across their faces whenever we met?

As for Yura Balovlenkov, apparently he had worked in some ultrasecret institute, so he, too, had to wait out the obligatory five years. But at that point it had been more than five years since he had left that institute—seven, in fact. How many more years will he have to wait before being allowed to join his wife, his daughter Katya, and his second daughter, whom he has never seen? Yura swore a dozen times to all of us that the pretext was totally false that he had had access to top-secret information.

Maria Yurgutis was the wife of a defector—the most difficult case.

Tanya Azure thought that she was "guilty" of having lived

for a long time in Arzamas, where nuclear arms were manufactured.

As for Andrei Frolov, he was at a loss to understand what his "reasons" were. He had never been privy to any State secret, and he had no parents to hold him back.

Iosif said that we should not look at our pasts to find the "reasons." His theory was that we should serve as a warning to all the others who might be inclined to think as we—a warning to all the avant-garde artists, the free-thinkers, the would-be rebels, the small-town girls who dreamed of freedom and the West. According to Iosif, we had drawn the losing tickets in a sickeningly grim lottery.

Since most of us did finally manage to emigrate, one has to conclude that all these surmises were wrong. We were not a threat to the State. The "reasons" were much more simple. As everyone knows, the Soviet Union has a planned system: the economy, the election results, the number of artists who can go abroad each year—everything. Why should OVIR not be subject to a five-year plan? Why did it not have its quota, fixed according to the state of relations with the West at any given time? But after we had argued the pros and cons of the system, the whys and wherefores of the turn-downs, we always reached the same conclusion: We were to serve as a warning to the "others." Who were the "others"? Everyone else in the Soviet Union who might harbor ideas such as ours. So, little by little, we came to the conviction that Iosif was right: We were not guilty of anything. We were simply the unwitting pawns in a Soviet campaign to discourage similar rebels.

What to do next? A hunger strike? We kept coming back to it, and the more we discussed other possibilities, the more we thought it was a good idea. It was apolitical; it was active rather than passive; it was dignified. But if we were to proceed, we wanted to generate as much publicity as possible about it, both at home and abroad. We would do what our spouses had been doing abroad: make our campaign public.

Passport control. The "border guard" is seated inside his glass booth. If one were to judge by his expression, he holds the fate of the world in his hands. A number of foreign friends had described to me in gory detail the painful agony of passport control. But I didn't care. All that mattered to me was making sure I didn't miss the plane. The customs man took my passport. He looked at the picture inside, raised his eyes to see if the person in front of him matched that photograph, lowered his eyes again, raised them. Then again. I could see him rummaging through my papers. Slowly. Painfully. Then he handed me my passport, without a smile. He pressed a hidden button, releasing the turnstile. Was it possible that we could still make it after all? In any case, I derived some comfort from knowing that even if I didn't land in Paris that day, my baggage would. It had already been checked onto that Air France plane.

We decided to resort to Edward's measures: the scientific community, the artists, public opinion. We would involve the whole world. *Publicity.* That would be our motto.

Edward wrote of his problems with the fundraising concert in Madrid. He had sold tickets on the street and, even after all his efforts, the concert hall was only two-thirds full. In other letters he wrote of the difficulties he was having in getting people to sign his petitions. Don't misunderstand me: I was infinitely grateful for all his heroic efforts on my behalf. But there were times when we could not keep from smiling at what struck us as his wilder and more desperate schemes.

Could we have tried similar tactics here inside Russia? Hardly. No Russian citizen in his right mind would even think of signing a petition in our favor . . . with the exception of Sakharov himself. Who could blame them? Anyone who did sign would have to be judged insane. And in the Soviet Union, mental patients are sent to psychiatric wards. A very simple equation.

Nonetheless, we continued to hope that someone out there might hear our cries and complaints and respond—which perhaps shows how insane, or desperate, we had become.

There was also the press. The problem there was that Russian newspapers and periodicals do not have the right to focus on individual stories. Want ads, exchanges of apartments, the sale or exchange of goods or appliances from one person to another—

that is the extent of it. As for our press conferences, to which Tass, *Pravda*, and the English-language *Moscow News* had been invited, the only people who showed up were a handful of foreign journalists and a bevy of plainclothesmen.

"We have to write," Inna said, "a flood of letters." But to whom? To the workers, the unions, to every official organization we could think of. To celebrities—artists, novelists, poets. We wanted to make sure that we had explored every possibility before resorting to a hunger strike. Not everyone in the Soviet Union could be deaf to our plight. All those heroes of the Soviet Union, those scientists and intellectuals and cosmonauts. Yet of all the hundreds of letters we mailed, we received only two replies. One, from the Committee on Fitness and Sports, was a decent letter filled with compassion and understanding. It stated that while it was not in a position to judge our case, it had forwarded our letter to the proper authority—namely, OVIR. "We hope," it closed, "that your problems will be solved in accordance with the law."

The second letter was from the official Soviet poet, Nikolai Gribachev.

It is a well-known fact that when marriages with foreign citizens are contracted in the Soviet Union in confor-mance with the relative laws, there is never any problem for the two spouses to leave the country. This being so, why did you form a group made up of citizens from different cities, with requests to emigrate to various countries? Why in the world do you go about writing these incredible collective letters? Moderation should be your keynote, and good faith. Only if you approach the matter with the proper attitude can you hope for success, which I sincerely wish you.

Not a great letter, with its tone of righteousness, but anything was better than silence. We immediately sent him a reply:

Dear Comrade Gribachev:
We have no desire or intent to be anything but straight-

forward. And our problem is really quite simple: We are separated against our will from those we love.

We received no further word from the good poet. Nor did we hear from the Committee for the Defense of Peace. Nor from the Committee of Soviet Women. Nor from Moscow University. Silence from the workers at the Likhachev automobile works, the Moscow Municipal Council, the Leningrad Municipal Council. No sign of life from *Pravda, Izvestia, Country Life,* or *Water Transport.* Nor from the mechanical and construction industries, the Academy of Agronomical Sciences, the Academy of Medicine, the Academy of Pedagogical Sciences. The wall of silence was as solid as the Berlin Wall. At best, our letters had landed in the wastebasket. At worst, they had ended up on the desks of the KGB.

It was at this point that Inna learned, to her surprise and dismay, that her daughter Masha's exit visa had also been refused. Without explanation. "I'd rather die than go on this way," Inna said. So in December 1981, she began her own hunger strike. That meant she had to leave the group, for we were not yet ready for such a step. None of us tried to dissuade her, but we doubted that she would succeed. After all, Sakharov and his wife had gone on a hunger strike, to no avail, so why would anyone pay attention to Inna? Besides, martial law had just been declared in Poland, so the Soviet authorities were not in a conciliatory mood, to say the least.

But then everything changed. On the seventeenth day of their strike, the Sakharovs emerged victorious: Lisa Alexeyeva was allowed to leave the Soviet Union to join her husband—Yelena Bonner's son—in the United States. That gave Inna the courage to go on.

We visited her regularly, and took her flowers. What else could we take her? In Moscow, when you visit a friend who is ill, you take fruit—apples, oranges, bananas—and, sometimes, if the patient is well enough, a bottle of wine. For Inna it was flowers. The French Embassy sent its doctor to check the state of her health, and it was rumored that the French government was negotiating in high places for her release. But by the twentieth day of her strike, we could see that her situation was deteriorating. We would leave her apartment and burst into tears outside.

Then, all of a sudden, the authorities gave in. Either they took pity on her, or, more likely, decided she was not worth the possible impairment of relations with France. In any case, Guy was summoned to the Soviet Embassy where he was working in Africa and issued a visa. Rumor had it that he was told: "Take this woman off our hands, and make it fast."

In January of 1982 Guy went to Moscow, where he and Inna were married. She then requested official permission to emigrate, which was granted. After a few weeks of convalescence, she and her two daughters left for Paris.

That unexpected victory rekindled our hopes.

Tania and I raced toward the departure gate. Closed. Noses against the glass, we saw our plane moving down the runway. I was furious at the pilot. He was the captain, and responsible for his passengers. Why couldn't he have waited, knowing the unusual circumstances? I knew that in the past, some Air France pilots had refused to take off until all their passengers were safely on board, being fully aware of the sadistic games the customs people sometimes played. This was another reason we had chosen Air France rather than Aeroflot.

And then I broke down, first laughing hysterically, then sobbing uncontrollably. So near and yet so far. All the frustrations and humiliations for naught—to be endured all over again.

Dragging Tania behind me, I headed for the chief of the "border guards" and planted myself squarely in front of him. I gave him a tongue-lashing that I suspect he will never forget, ending by saying that I intended to spend the night at the airport, not leave the place until the next day's flight was called.

"I don't know where you can stay," he said. "In any case, not in this part of the airport."

He ushered us back through customs, past passport control, and into the main waiting room.

"There's an Aeroflot plane leaving for Paris in a few hours," a customs official said slyly. "Why don't you take that?"

"Nyet," was my only reply.

So we had to take a taxi back to Moscow. I was still seething. The whole episode was totally absurd. I kept fishing for something to calm me down, something positive on which to focus. At least I would see my mother again. We had no money, but I didn't care. Mother would pay for it on the other end. We sped down the Leningrad Highway, across the Moskva River, past the sign announcing:

YOU ARE ENTERING MOSCOW
THE MODEL COMMUNIST CITY

All I could think of was how frantic Edward would be when he learned that we were not on the plane.

At the risk of repeating myself, I want to reiterate that we were not militants—neither heroes nor political activists. If we were obliged to raise our voices, to solicit the world's help, whose fault was it? Why the regime did not simply let us go, and avoid all the poor publicity it ultimately engendered, I have never been able to figure out. *They* kept talking about *prestige*, saying that our actions would hurt Soviet prestige abroad. It was a term both General Zotov and General Shcholokov kept throwing in our faces. What a laugh! As they uttered it, they were busy pocketing the bribes that ultimately brought down one of them and sent the other to jail. *Prestige*, indeed! It's a word they're probably still throwing at Yura Balovlenkov today!

We decided to stage a warning hunger strike from April 2 to April 12, 1982, simply to demonstrate to the authorities our determination and give them a chance to solve our problems without scandal. At the same time, we announced an exhibit of photographs of our families, which we had enlarged and hung as a show in my apartment. We issued a press release and invited both foreign journalists and friends, if they thought they could risk it.

At six o'clock in the morning of April 2, I heard strange noises just outside my door. Then there was the sound of trucks arriving outside our building, followed by two black Volgas.

From them emerged plainclothesmen, who surrounded the building. Three of them came up to my floor, the eighth, and did something to the elevator so that it stopped at the fifth floor. When my visitors emerged from the elevator, they had to walk up the last three flights, and when they reached the eighth floor, they were greeted by the three hulking plainclothesmen, who ordered them to turn back. "No one's allowed on this floor," they were told.

No point in insisting. When they got back outside, other policemen checked their papers. When pressed for the reason for all this, their answer was, "There's been a robbery in the building."

After the first day of fasting, we were allowed to leave the building. We drove through the chilly streets of Moscow, looking for a way to draw attention to ourselves. But a ten-day strike was of little interest. Not enough drama, since the outcome was certain. Symbolism is not hard news. Tragedy is more interesting.

Our strike ended just before Orthodox Easter. Our watchdogs had relaxed, so we could invite our friends in for *kulich*, the traditional Easter cake. Following custom, I wanted to have the cake blessed, which Yura and I proceeded to have done in a nearby church. It was a strange impression, that church, with its gold and incense and chants, a whole other era into which we had just stepped.

We observed Easter according to tradition. We served drinks. All of our group took a few sips, and were sick on the spot. After ten days of fasting, we should have known better.

Then back to writing letters—hundreds and hundreds more. Each morning I would check the mailbox, to find . . . nothing.

Iosif was summoned to OVIR, and for a moment we had a flash of hope. But no, he had been called to be informed officially that his request had once again been refused.

We issued a press statement, thanking all those who had supported us to date. It said, among other things:

It is to be regretted that in this vast country, not a soul could be found to take an interest in us, aside from a

handful of faithful friends and an impressive number of
plainclothesmen. Unless the Soviet authorities move to
rectify this situation, we intend to begin, one month from
now, on May 10, 1982, an unlimited hunger strike. We
are determined to fight to the end, whatever that end
may be. . . .

It was the crucial point of all our lives, the most important
step that any of us had ever taken. Behind us were years of
humiliation. Now we were determined to rise above our miserable lives—to choose, if necessary, between liberty and death.

"Think of how much we're going to save on food," we used
to say, laughing. But it was only half a joke.

Anyone who applied to OVIR had a good chance of losing
his job and often did. Then both OVIR and the KGB would
contact the prospective emigrant and suggest that he could get
his job back if only he would give up his "crazy ideas." A candidate for emigration was a social leper. If he cared about his
friends, he would break off relations, to keep them from getting
in trouble. Furthermore, such an applicant falls into a self-made
limbo, compounded by superstition. Why look for work if you're
leaving? Or: Don't make any plans, for fear they might come to
pass, and then you might change your mind.

We all lived on our savings, and on the rare food packages
that our spouses managed to send us. I also had a part-time job,
at 50 kopeks an hour, housecleaning and babysitting—not wonderful, but at least it kept me off the rolls of those accused of
parasitism.

The taxi took us back through the Moscow we had left five hours
earlier. I wondered where the Air France flight was at this
minute? Over Hungary? Maybe West Germany? We were driving along the Embankment, past Yura's house, past the Ministry
of Foreign Affairs—like Inna's a wedding-cake building—past
the Kremlin and the dreaded Lubyanka Prison, with its huge,
new addition under construction next door, where the KGB
would have its headquarters.

My mother opened the door in response to my insistent

knocking and almost fell over. She had waved good-by to the sound of the departing Air France plane as she left the airport. What had happened? Was it all right? We threw ourselves in each other's arms, laughing and crying at the same time, happy to have one more day together.

The hunger strike began. The first days are always the most difficult. Both body and mind weaken. Then the situation stabilizes and the suffering is easier to endure. The warm water, the only nourishment, becomes less nauseating. The important thing is to remain as alert as possible, both mentally and physically. Our plan was to not take to our beds until the final phase of our strike, when we would have no choice. As long as our legs would carry us, we planned to lead as "normal" a life as possible. I would get dressed, receive the press, write letters, do the cooking for Tania and any friends who might drop by to see us. On Sunday, when there were not too many of us in the apartment, we would go out together—sometimes to the cinema, other times to the country or to some special historic site that none of us had had the opportunity of visiting. The fresh air did us good.

As the days slipped by, our symptoms grew more acute. Pain in the chest at first, due no doubt to the weight of the thorax on a diminished body. Failing eyesight, which, in my case, was irreversible. I used to have 20/20 vision. Now I am hopelessly nearsighted.

Fear and anxiety became our constant companions, especially at night. We could barely hear the Voice of America, but amid the static we could sometimes catch the sounds of our names, which was a comfort. And there were other, unexpected comforts, too, from the most unlikely sources. One day, about halfway through our third week, one of the plainclothesmen stationed outside my apartment door said to me—under his breath, but still loud enough for me to hear, "I hope to hell they hurry up and let you go!"

Actually, I got along well with my "guards." I loaned them books and gave them chairs so they wouldn't have to stand all day or all night. I gave them food, too, which they accepted gratefully. Once in a while, I would stick my head out the door and ask, "You have a match?"

"Sure."

We exchanged smiles. He pitied me, and I pitied him.

"If I were you, I'd sneak out and buy some of those sausages they sell down at the corner. They're really good."

The same man who gave me that advice handed me a flower one day when I came home.

"One of your friends left it for you," he said. "Wouldn't want it to die."

I was on the verge of tears as I took it from him. So they were not all unfeeling brutes.

Unexpected comfort on the one hand, disappointment and deception on the other. On the day we began the strike, there was an international meeting of religious leaders from around the world in Moscow. One of them was Billy Graham, the American evangelist. We had written to ask that he spend a few minutes with our group during his stay in Moscow. We knew the letter had reached him, because Edward had delivered it personally, and one of Graham's aides had promised the evangelist's support. But Graham apparently had better things to do, since he neither showed up nor tried to contact us. I have since heard that we were not the only people who had been disappointed by the fiery preacher.

Our spouses were moving heaven and earth on our behalf. In Chicago, Frolov's wife Lois's suit against the Soviet government was reported on the Voice of America, which termed it a "smart move." Not that anyone really believed the American courts could ever collect the money from the Soviets, but Chicago was an important city to the Russians, a place where they bought a great deal of grain. Maybe the court could freeze Soviet assets, or use the Chicago mart in some way in this war of nerves. In any case, Frolov was older than the rest of us, and less robust, and his health was deteriorating visibly, so we hoped this simple, ingenious ploy might work to his advantage.

June 1 was International Children's Day, proclaimed as such by the United Nations. We decided to use it to draw attention to our strike and our cause by marching through the streets of

Moscow bearing posters of our spouses and children. As the law required, we duly wrote to the Central Committee to inform it of our plans and indicating the hour of our public demonstration: noon. Then, on the evening of May 31, Frolov received a telephone call from OVIR. "Your visa is ready. You can come and pick it up whenever you like."

All six of us were in his apartment (Vitaly Volobuyev fasted in Novosibirsk) when the call came. He was so stunned that he collapsed in his chair. The remaining five of us left and returned to my apartment, where we spent the night drawing up battle plans for the next day's events. At dawn, we saw that my building had been encircled by security forces. At eight, we realized that they were not going to let us march. They advised us to "stay put." At noon, they called Tanya Azure out onto the landing. "You'll have your exit visa in a month's time."

Two down and five to go. We embraced her fondly and sent her on her way, back home to Vladimir.

At five past twelve, they told the remaining hunger strikers—that we were free to do whatever we wished. Well done, comrades! It would take us a good half hour to reach the spot where we had informed the Central Committee we would be demonstrating, which meant we could only begin at twelve-thirty, a half hour after our appointed time—in other words, we would be breaking the law.

Andrei Frolov decided to go on fasting for another week, until he had concrete proof that the visa had been granted. During this week Maria Yurgutis had been dragged from my apartment and sent away, and Vitaly Volobuyev called from Novosibirsk with good news. He had received permission to leave. We did not see Tanya again for a month, when she stopped off to see us on her way to France.

Now we were three. Three skeletons. We could feel death approaching, day by day, hour by hour. We took to looking into the future we did not expect to see, sitting around a table "spinning a saucer," which is similar to a Ouija board. We clasped hands around the table and asked questions of the saucer. According to how it moved, it answered us, telling us all kinds of important things such as, "In autumn you'll be free. Don't worry."

Our combative stance gave way little by little to the lethargy
of approaching death. We were in our fourth week of the strike,
and I no longer even had the strength to walk to the door to let
in my friends. I took to my bed, where I read over and over my
last will and testament, which I kept on the night table. Behind
the front door, I could still hear the muffled sounds of my plainclothesmen. They would be with me till the end. Friends still
came, bringing me flowers as we had done for Inna.

On the thirtieth day, at the insistence of one of Edward's
friends, I gave out my father's classified phone number. I had
always refused to release it before then, because I did not want
Edward to harass my parents. Nor did I want to be accused of
high treason. Now I had nothing to lose, and somehow it didn't
seem to matter.

And then my father came to see me. My hunger strike was
in its thirtieth day—or thirty-first, I can't remember which. All
I know is that what happened that day is one of the most painful
memories of my life.

Reading what Edward has written, someone might be led
to believe that my parents did everything in their power during
all those years to keep me from leaving. Truth is never that
simple. I have said it before, and I say it again: I would not want
my worst enemy to be obliged to deal with the dilemma with
which my father was faced. The stress he had to live with would
have sapped the strength of the most indestructible person on
this earth. He had two solutions: to make his daughter hate him,
ruin the life of the child that he loved (and I am convinced that
he did love me, however bitter and obstreperous and impossible
I had become); or to let me leave the country and see his career
come to an end. *Career* is not the right word; his vocation, his
calling, his *raison d'être*, for he was a proud man, a Communist
firm in his convictions.

That proud man came into his daughter's apartment and saw
his child dying. That proud man's heart broke. That proud man
stood in the doorway and saw his child curled up in a ball, her
arms wrapped around her skeletal knees, staring fixedly at the
wall, trying to retain the last bit of warmth in her dying body.
And that proud man broke down and sobbed. That proud man,

ramrod straight, brought me for a moment out of my torpor. I turned and looked at him for a long time, trying to understand who he was, and then I, too, broke down and began to weep bitter tears. "Mama. Daddy. What have they done to us? What have we done to each other? O God, do forgive me!"

And then we were together again, father and child, in each other's arms, smiling, crying. I was filled with his warmth and his love.

It was finished.

My last night in Moscow—again. As day was breaking, we once again drove to the airport. It was only that morning that I realized that the authorization required from my parents was a pretense. The authorities had only one goal: to make the spouses and children of those who had left think twice before they asked for permission to leave. If the authorities had thought there might be an advantage to my leaving, they would have let me go long before this. If they had seen some advantage to keeping me in Moscow forever, I would never have been able to leave. They would have kept me for the rest of my days, as they were keeping thousands of other *refuseniks*.

It was freezing cold, and the wind was brisk and biting as we entered the airport once again. My mother was with me, furious about what had happened the day before and intent on giving the authorities a piece of her mind today. "They may not know whom they're dealing with," she said as we approached customs.

But she had no need to worry. From all appearances, harassment was not the order of the day. The amber beads posed no problem, nor did Faulkner. Body search? Whatever gave anyone that idea? Even the same "border guard" seemed well disposed toward us—assuming it was the same man, for in the gray light of December, they all looked alike.

"Air France flight to Paris is now boarding."

Customs. Passport control. No problem. Onto the aircraft. Seat belts fastened. Tania and I holding hands. The roar of the motors. Were we really leaving? Would someone come, at the last minute, and remove us from the plane? The doors were closed. We were heading down the runway. Airborne. *Good-by, Mother Russia, good-by.*

Three hours later, we were among the first passengers to leave the plane. Several French policemen, looking as though they had been outfitted by Yves Saint-Laurent, escorted us to a tiny, boxlike room, then disappeared, after having asked us for our baggage stubs. For a moment I had a sinking feeling that they were going to send us back to Moscow on the next Aeroflot flight. But no, the French were trying to protect us from the journalists, so that our initial contact with the West would not be traumatic. The intention was good, but as soon as we passed through French customs, the journalists arrived like locusts: microphones, flashbulbs, requests for on-the-spot statements and interviews.

We stayed only one day in Paris, before taking a TWA flight to Washington. Later Edward told me TWA gave us free tickets. I never thought something like that was possible. Tania was in a good mood, laughing and joking and contemplating the clouds above and the sea below, capturing the rays of sunlight that filtered through the cabin curtains. I leaned back in my seat and closed my eyes. I felt like a teenager on her way to her first date—except I was not a teenager but a woman of thirty on her way to meet her husband of forty. Mrs. Lozansky. Yes, that was who I was. It took six years to prove it, but I was, first and foremost, *Mrs.* Lozansky. I savored the title and possibilities: "How nice to see you, Mrs. Lozansky." "Thank you for stopping by, Mrs. Lozansky." "We're looking forward to seeing you for drinks at six, Mrs. Lozansky."

It was snowing in Washington, and the plane was late. We bumped down, the engines roared, and we ground to a halt. In our red fox overcoats, Tania and I appeared in the doorway and were blinded by what seemed to be hundreds of flashbulbs. There was a battery of microphones, and cameras were pointed at us. I felt tiny and foolish and unsure about what to do.

Then, out of the crowd, I saw Edward. He was carrying the biggest bouquet of red roses and carnations I had ever seen. No, he had not changed. All my worries about how we would find each other vanished in an instant.

It would be all right.

I was going to be a wife again, an ordinary wife. Sure, I would have to adapt to all sorts of new things—pizzas and hamburgers and blue jeans and hot dogs, and Lord knows what else.

And then I was in Edward's arms, and everything was all right. All those years of waiting and worry, of fighting and hoping, had been rewarded.

Not quite.

Yura was still held prisoner. As long as even one of our group was still held prisoner, our victory was not complete.

On the forty-second day of his hunger strike, OVIR had called him. He was helped into a taxi and driven to the OVIR offices. There, a female functionary helped him fill out the necessary forms. Yura was so weak he could hardly hold a pen. For the hundredth time, Yura swore and declared that he, aged thirty-three, had married in December 1979 Lena Balovlenkov, an American national, residing at Baltimore, Maryland, and respectfully requested permission to join his wife in the United States. He did not mention in the request that he had been filling out applications for the past three years, that his wife had made several trips to Moscow. Nor did he mention that the doctors he had asked to monitor the evolution of his fast had laughed at him and obliged him to submit to psychiatric examinations. "So your wife is American? How interesting. In that case, show us her passport? You can't? Then how do you expect us to believe what you're saying is true?" Nor did he mention in his request that he had a daughter, Masha, whom he had never seen. All he asked was that he be allowed to emigrate so that he could lead a normal life, with his wife and children.

He was told that his request would be answered "in the shortest possible delay."

As he climbed into a taxi, together with his mother and a friend, he allowed himself to be photographed brandishing a bottle of fruit juice, with which he was breaking his fast. After fifty days, he had lost a full third of his weight.

Ten days later, he was able to eat boiled vegetables.

On the eleventh day, the authorities held a press conference, the first of its kind. In the name of the Soviet government, the OVIR spokesman said, he formally protested the interference of the United States in the internal affairs of the Soviet Union.

"I am speaking specifically of the case of Yuri Balovlenkov," he said to the assembled journalists. "On this point, I have only one thing to say: We cannot and will not grant him permission to leave the country, it having been ascertained that it would be against the best interests of the State."

At that point, Yura began another hunger strike. If he is alive today, it is because the government has allowed his wife to enter the country and given them hope that the decision will one day be reversed. If it is a lie, so be it: I would much prefer to know that Yura is alive, even in Moscow, than six feet underground. Meanwhile, Lena is back in Baltimore, still waiting for that magic day, which may never come, when Yura will be granted permission to join her and their two children.

Edward, Tania, and I are blissfully happy. Tania has taken to America like a fish to water. She writes and speaks English perfectly. Her teachers pen margin notes on her homework congratulating her on her command of the language after such a short time in the country. She loves tennis, skiing, popular music, her American classmates. Her assimilation is, if not complete, nonetheless amazing.

But until Yura is safely here with us, until I see his reassuring smile and feel his comforting hand on my shoulder, this story, this struggle, will not be over.